"As a great believer in the potential of Collaboration, this book strengthens, spurs and enhances supportive reasons".

Major General Aviv Kochavi,
former IDF Chief of Staff.

"Inspiring book which places the value of collaboration as a fundamental principle of leadership and relevant corporate management in the new world. In a fluent and simple way Omri Gefen outlines the ways to create growth, to manage crises and to build a healthy culture of transformation and adapt new paradigms. I found the models, insights, personal stories and the emphasis on Collaborative Intelligence to be highly valuable, in my journey of innovation and digital transformation, in a world of rapid change".

Einat Uzent Ravid,
CEO Altman Health (A large medical firm)

"Complete partnership in the organization and with its surroundings is a crucial condition in any process of change, mainly in these concerning strategy, organizational structure and culture".

Ofer Bloch,
CEO Israel Electric Corporation

"*The Power of Collaboration* is a fascinating journey to the world of contemporary leadership and innovative management. For big organizations, in a world of storms and upheavals, organizational adaptation and adoption of new perceptions is essential. Throughout my personal experience of an organizational and managerial change, I found in this book breakthrough ideas for managing collaboration and empowering commitment and synergy".

Nir Levinger,
CEO Coca-Cola Israel

Out beyond ideas of wrongdoing and rightdoing,
There is a field. I'll meet you there.

Rumi

The Power of Collaboration

The future of human society depends on us. The only way to secure our children's future is by Collaboration and trust. This world can be a better place for us and for all, and this is the main challenge and mission of leaders from all sectors and nations.

This book is based on a new paradigm which can create the change we need. It reveals how to understand, analyze, create and improve all forms of Collaborations, with one central and powerful roadmap.

Demonstrated by many examples from organizations, and based on a unique and innovated model, Gefen defines the "Architecture of Collaboration". He attempts to create a shared language–simple, structured and efficient–for one of the most significant challenges of this era.

Gefen presents a warning mixed with a vision: the only chance for human society to deal successfully with the challenges of our time is by empowering Effective Collaboration, facilitated by the transformation from "Ego-System" to "Eco-System". Isn't it clear that the only way to manage climate crises, pandemics, poverty, terrorism and other global concerns is together?

Transformation is in the hands of and is the responsibility of leaders and managers. This book is for them, in all sectors and roles.

Omri Gefen is a senior consultant, leading processes in complex settings in and between organizations, mainly working with management and leadership in the fields of Collaboration, Trust, Negotiation, Mediation and Consensus Building. He is also the head of Negotiation training in the Leadership Executive Program at Tel-Aviv University, he teaches at Raichman University and is a founding partner of the Gome-Gevim Group. His personal journey creating impact in Israeli society is woven into this book, including thousands of hours and countless processes within and between organizations and communities; deep familiarity with the business, public, security and social sectors; and his insights as an entrepreneur, CEO and partner.

The Power of Collaboration
From Ego-System to Eco-System

Omri Gefen

Routledge
Taylor & Francis Group

A PRODUCTIVITY PRESS BOOK

Designed cover image: Shutterstock

First published 2025
by Routledge
605 Third Avenue, New York, NY 10158

and by Routledge
4 Park Square, Milton Park, Abingdon, Oxon, OX14 4RN

Routledge is an imprint of the Taylor & Francis Group, an informa business

ISBN: 9781032848013 (hbk)
ISBN: 9781032846026 (pbk)
ISBN: 9781003514992 (ebk)

DOI: 10.4324/9781003514992

Typeset in Garamond
by codeMantra

Contents

Introduction

As dawn was rising over the city of Salvador de Bahía, the beautiful Brazilian song "sadness has no ending, happiness does" ("Tristeza não tem fim, Felicidade sim") by Gal Costa was playing over and over in my head. My visit to northern Brazil was the last part of a yearlong journey through South America, which included an encounter with new cultures, fascinating human encounters and trekking through magnificent landscapes and challenging mountain ridges. Above all, it was also a meaningful deep personal journey for me. After a five-year period in the military, which included serving as an officer and commander, it took me some time and distance to develop humbleness, openness and intimacy with myself. It was during those moments that I had no idea if and how my journey would play out.

The month I spent in Salvador began with the Festival of Iemanjá, the goddess of the sea, and ended with the Carnaval. As part of the ceremony in honor of Iemanjá, citizens of northern Brazil gather together for hours of ecstatic praying, ending with the local fishermen heading out in their boats carrying gifts brought by thousands of participants. They form a circle of boats in the water and all at once toss over the flowers, fruit, jewelry and other gifts into the sea. All along the coastline, a silence takes over, broken only when the last gifts sink underwater. That is the sign that Iemanjá has accepted their gifts and prayers and that she would not take the lives of seamen in the coming year. The participants then break into spirited songs and dances, all through the night until the following morning. It was only six weeks later – following an unexpected adventure – that I first understood the profound meaning of religious faith when it comes to the sea.

The Carnaval in Salvador is considered the most vibrant and passionate in Brazil. It has clear African roots and is characterized by a sensuality with a hint of violence. Three consecutive days and nights of non-stop dance, motion and excitement. The month I spent there gave me a deep sense of connection to the place and the events, without which I would have most likely been standing and watching from the side as swarms of locals danced behind the Trio-Electrico trucks to manic Afro-beats, that made the familiar sounds of Samba seem delicate in comparison.

I, too, underwent a powerful experience there, having felt a deep connection to the place and the culture, as perfectly described in the song I mentioned earlier, the same song with which the carnival was closed. In stark contrast to the joy of music and dance, a sudden sense of emptiness and melancholy takes over you at the end of the last night of the carnival. The sky slowly cleared. After many hours in which it was almost impossible to move unless you were swaying at the right pace and direction of the dancing mass, the streets emptied. I went down to the little marina of Salvador, for no apparent reason, and sang to myself this song again and again, without the slightest idea of where I was headed the next day.

Years later, in a TEDx talk for teens, when asked to describe my trajectory as an entrepreneur and social influencer, I talked about the concept of serendipity, "accidental discovery" or "unplanned fortunate discovery", which is only made possible if we are open to chance and allow it to enter into our lives. In the words attributed to Louis Pasteur: "in the fields of observation, chance only favors the prepared minds." I shared with them the points along the course of my life where chance management was as important as the parts where I operated with a clear knowledge of my destiny and long-term plan. That morning at the Salvador Marina was one of those moments.

At the marina, a number of yachts were moored, and as I was sitting on one of them and exchanging carnival experiences with the skipper, a bearded and somewhat grumpy man passed us, rowing in a small dinghy boat toward the pier. Out of the blue, he asked me, in a deep Australian accent, if I was interested in coming to Africa. Without knowing why, I answered: Yes, of course. The next day, we set out on a journey that was, in retrospect, one of the most important milestones in my life.

It turned out that this guy, Steve, had been delivering yachts around the world all his life. A tough and unpleasant sailor. This time he was asked to transport an old yacht from Spain to Cape Town and invited an Australian friend named Brett to join him. The two arrived in Salvador with the eastern trade winds of the North Atlantic, and from there, they planned to take advantage of the western trade winds of the South Atlantic to reach Africa. The yacht had no means of navigation, and the voyage entailed challenges and dangers. They were required to take on a third crew member, so Steve suggested I join them. Growing in Jerusalem and having never sailed before in my life, I was completely oblivious of the challenge of the voyage and only inquired how long the journey would take so that I could inform my family back home. Steve told me that it would take a maximum of 25 days and that is what I told my family.

It was only after 46 days that we entered the marina in the Cape of Good Hope in South Africa. Swaying, I hurried to a phone booth, and in a collect call, I informed my worried parents that I had safely reached the shore. In that call, I found out that they had already worked to establish a team of experts from the Ministry of Foreign Affairs and the Hebrew University, in an attempt to locate a small yacht, nameless and with no means of communication, sailing through the great ocean.

Our journey was lengthened mainly due to a strong storm, with waves 10 m high, which lasted several days and diverted us away from our track. After the storm had subsided, no wind blew. We were unable to start or repair the old engine. We simply stood in the heart of the ocean for days on end, hoping for some wind, sewing up the torn sails. We were also deeply worried, because during the storm a large tank of drinking water had detached from the deck and plunged into the depths of the sea. Throughout the six weeks of our voyage, we took shifts at the helm, day and night. Three hours of shifts and six hours of rest, during which we also prepared our meals. Rice day and pasta day, alternating. We ran out of fresh food as early as the second week. The skipper navigated using maps and the old navigation device, sextant. At various points of our voyage, we were wet down to the bone from the rain and the waves.

But the greatest challenge actually lay in the interpersonal aspect of the journey. It didn't take more than three days of mutual attempts at making some sort of connection for us to realize that we had no common language. I found myself part of a team that performed superbly in extreme conditions, but feeling alone in the wilderness of the sea – a huge ocean that stretches in every direction, with no land on the horizon. My body easily adapted to the ongoing challenge, but the loneliness that I experienced during that time is a kind that I had not experienced before or since. I found myself adapting to it during the voyage as well, making the most of it and of myself, but it's highly unlikely that I would want to repeat such an experience again. Among the many things I learned, this voyage taught me about uncertainty and my ability to live in such a situation.

Loneliness and uncertainty, adaptability and resilience are probably intertwined. I have encountered this over the years in my work with senior executives – especially CEOs, those standing at the top of the pyramid. Personally, I have experienced this for over two decades as CEO of Gevim Group. As much as we surround ourselves with high-quality and committed people, and as much as we maintain warm and intimate relationships within our organization as well as with our customers, suppliers and partners, at the end of the day, we are alone on our journey. It is an empowering state of being, as much as it may be a weakening one.

Alongside the constant longing for cooperation, partnership and teamwork, and alongside the desire to share the burden, a profound apprehension of the meaning of personal responsibility for us as leaders is always present. The success of the voyage at sea depends on the crew, but first and foremost on its captain, and the captain is trained and is expected to be strong, brave and independent. Herein lies the first and deepest dissonance of managers and leaders when it comes to the sphere of collaboration. Even if we strongly believe in it and want it, deep within us we find it hard to let go of the tools of leadership and control, whose existence stems primarily from the fact that responsibility lies in our hands.

My next meaningful encounter with the sea took place years later, when I joined a skipper's course. The first time my instructor took us out on a sailing lesson on a yacht, he said: "When you throw the anchor into the water, make sure the other end is tied." It immediately struck me that this was a managerial event taking place, and so, we constructed a unique platform for managers.

Of the dozens of management groups we took out to sea, it was the one group that experienced a particularly high sea, leaving many of them seasick and even a little angry, that felt an improvement in the dynamics between the managers. It was that management team, which was task oriented and results oriented, that experienced a higher level of sharing and intimacy. This is what the head of the division shared with me about two months later. Another time, a senior manager

from a banking organization descended to the dock and said, at the beginning of the processing talk, that it was an experience that well illustrated the concept of "the ground underfoot is unstable, and this is precisely what we experience every day". The sense of uncertainty constituted the main challenge for managers in all types of organizations worldwide, in dealing with the Covid-19 crisis that began in the spring of 2020 and for Israeli managers during the war following the October 7 terrorist attack.

The most interesting thing we found among all the groups we took out to sea was the disparity between what happens inside the boats and what happens between the boats. Managers are given relatively complex tasks considering they lack any real experience at sea and operate as a team in performing those tasks. An interaction between disciplines occurs, raising issues of decision-making and team leadership, all under conditions of constant change (winds) and uncertainty (an environment unfamiliar to most of us). The team tasks, no matter how complicated, are carried out successfully. A difficulty arises as soon as the first task is given which requires cooperation between several boats.

In transitioning from a complicated event to a complex one, most managers simply get lost. Regardless of the type of organization, during post-activity processing, managers describe their sense of frustration, going around in circles at sea for a long time. They say this is exactly what happens in their organizations in interfaces between units as well as with other organizations: "The work within our teams is good, but in processes and events that require collaboration beyond the teams, disciplines and divisions, we go around in circles, linger, get stuck and lose resources."

The gap between teamwork and the more complex interface work and between the teams scattered across the sea clearly symbolizes the change and the novel challenge many managers and organizations face, across all arenas and sectors. The story of the new era has nothing to do with teamwork. Most managers today deal very well with team leadership. Those that fail for the most part will be ejected elsewhere and are the exception. The head of a training unit of a large security organization illustrated this to me during one of our conversations:

> We re-examined the role of mid-level managers. In contrast to the past, today they are not really troubled by the challenge of managing their teams. It works well for them. The difficulty and challenge for them exist in cooperations with parallel factors within the organization and other factors outside of it.

Is it possible that in such a short period of time such a big change has taken place? Apparently, it is exactly the case in some places, while in others the pace is somewhat slower. This mainly depends on how quickly change occurs in the external arena in which these organizations operate. In the business arena, the sense of urgency is stronger, and thus, changes are accelerated. In the security arena, certainly in the Middle East, which is not characterized by stability, changes are rapid and constant. In other arenas, change is slower to occur, so it is more challenging to harness managements into processes of change when it comes to issues of collaboration, although due to the Covid-19 pandemic, we are seeing an acceleration of transformation everywhere.

Indeed, in all organizations and in all domains, there is a growing recognition of the need to address the collaborative challenge. The evolving understanding is that we are dealing with a rapid revolution rather than a slow evolution. This recognition is based on the understanding that the new story is one of complexity. In the new era, it is not possible to create significant relevance and impact on our own. We need others. At times even for our survival. In some ways, this is not really good news, because for many reasons it is better to operate alone. But it is no longer possible to do so. The question today is not whether there is a need for collaboration but how to construct and execute it in the best and most accurate way. The good news is that it is definitely possible.

I established the Gevim Group following the assassination of Prime Minister Yitzhak Rabin, as a mediation center and the first social business in Israel, with the aim of creating a change in the discourse and in the way we handle disputes and live together in Israeli complex society. We implemented mediation in many systems, at a time when the tools of mediation were unfamiliar in the country. Later, we developed a model of negotiation DBN – Dialogue Based Negotiation, which is taught and implemented in many organizations. The needs that arose from the field, understanding the collaborative challenge of the new age and the belief that an appropriate response could be created, which includes profound perceptual change and practical tools, led us to develop a structured model for managing partnerships and cooperations.

At around 2010, we began by searching the academic and practical world for existing models. We were surprised to find that beyond the attempt to formulate principles of action, no uniform, coherent and simple model had been created that could be implemented by managers. We were also surprised by the scarcity of literature and research in the field, especially in light of the fact that awareness of it already existed. The very process of constructing our model, and its application in many systems over the last decade, has helped us gain an in-depth understanding of the challenges that exist in collaborative arenas.

The fundamental premise is that the world can and should be better, for us and our children, and the understanding that the only way to accomplish this is through collaboration has made me delve deeper into exploring and operating in this field. The desire to make an impact, to carry forth a new and relevant message and to accelerate the necessary change in human society has led me to write this book. The book, much like the way I perceive my life and professional practice over two and a half decades, and similar to the model presented in it, strives for simplicity.

In the process of writing the book, I was once again called to the sea. It was written in a number of pulses, in periods when I was disengaged and on isolated islands in Greece, in a state of being of total simplicity – while I was involved in rendering assistance to the most complex processes taking place in Israel and some overseas. In my view, simplicity is essential for navigating in a complex world. Accordingly, a simple model was constructed and is hereby presented as the central axis of the book. The model's simplicity is a necessary condition for managers to adopt and apply it in leading people and systems.

In addition to the model and its applications, and in recognition of the value of the vast academic knowledge accumulated in the field and in areas related to it, I have read over the years and in the process of writing this book hundreds of articles and books. I have brought here only the main points of the ideas I had been exposed to, in an attempt to make them accessible. My writing is mainly nurtured by my experience as a manager involved in many partnerships and as a consultant who, over the years, has accompanied many managers and systems. The most important lesson I learned from this journey is humbleness. I do not pretend to bring here an absolute truth but rather a perception and tools from which anyone can choose what is right and proper for their application and use.

In essence, the core value for the reader is in gaining a deep understanding of the arena of partnerships and an acquaintance with a relevant paradigm and the possibility of adopting a new language and an applied work model. The book is based on decades of practical experience and thousands of hours of processes and, at the same time, presents a unique summary of the vast knowledge accumulated in the world. The perspective presented in it is practical and based on the stories of managers and leaders in a changing and challenging world, on my experience as a manager and entrepreneur and on the accumulated field experience of many others that I have accompanied throughout the years. The insights, dilemmas and solutions are presented and processed in a manner accessible for managers and leaders – especially for those who want to be more relevant in their leadership in the new era.

This book is designed for leaders and managers in all types of sectors, organizations and communities. It is useful for consultants involved in organizational processes, strategy and innovation, as well as for community leaders and those sitting at the intersections of internal and external organizational interfaces. The model and tools presented are relevant in all phases of the life cycle of partnerships and collaborations – from the preliminary phase, through the construction process, to the long-term maintenance and continuity phases. Hence, the book may also serve as an applicable lever for entrepreneurs, self-employed individuals and small business owners. Since we are all partners in various circles, influencing and influenced by many relationships, the issues brought forth in the following chapters are important to all of us, in all circles of life, as an infrastructure for managing relationships in this complicated era.

The first and second chapters discuss the complexity that characterizes the world today and the changes related to the issue of collaboration, which has become extremely central in our time. The third describes the key barriers to cooperation, also defined as our "blind spots" as leaders. Most of the time, we do not correctly identify our failures and our responsibility for their formation, and therefore, we do not produce the appropriate responses to those failures. The book then continues to deal mainly with the architecture of collaborations, describing a structured and systematic model for the effective management of collaborations, with complementary aspects. Other chapters deepen our understanding of collaborative leadership, collaborative intelligence, the new role of CCO, coopetition and practical solutions for strengthening collaboration in and between organizations. Alongside these are references to different sectors and inter-sectoral partnerships, inviting readers to focus on what is close to their heart.

Let us imagine for a moment, as citizens of the world, that in dealing with the most challenging issues, a full and effective partnership would exist between all parties involved in each of the following areas: health, education, social leadership, productivity and employment, poverty, old age, violence among children and youth, young people at risk, environmental pollution, terrorism, immigration, international crises such as the Covid-19 pandemic and more. If that were the case, we would be living in a completely different reality. I have no doubt that it is possible – in every corner of the globe.

Chapter 1

The world is changing
Revolution. not evolution

It is not the strongest of the species that survive, nor the most intelligent, but the one more responsive to change.

Charles Darwin

"Once upon a time, when life was simple …" This is how the book I read to my children some years ago began. Indeed, things were once simpler. These days, both of them are making their first steps in their twenties, in a very complicated world. In order to survive, develop and live a happy life, they must be more responsive to change than all the generations that came before them, and the change is most intense than ever. This is the way things are now and will probably be even more challenging in the future. These kids, like many others, know that what they learned at school is not what they will need for their future. This evolving era in human evolution is about transformation and not information. It is about being relevant, adapting, moving quickly and collaborating.

As managers, most of us now wake up every morning into complexity, and this is also how we end our day. The Covid-19 crisis that erupted in 2020 and affected the entire population of the world is a good illustration of extreme complexity. As I write these lines, the medical challenge is still a central concern, with approximately six million fatalities worldwide, and alongside the fading of Covid, there is an eruption of a merciless war in Eastern Europe. After two years of instability, the sweeping understanding is that there can be no assurance of routine, stability or security in the complex era in which we live. As leaders and managers, we must examine our paradigms and perceptions. Organizations of

DOI: 10.4324/9781003514992-1

1

all kinds are required to reassess their situation and come up with new strategies and work plans.

In the last decades, a revolution has been taking place in human society – in all dimensions including technology, information and the expansion of networks, globalization, mobility, employment and more, in profound conceptual changes which characterize the young generations and in the diminution of authority and hierarchy. These are revolutionary and fast-paced processes rather than a gradual evolution. B.C. (Before Covid) and A.C. (After Covid) resemble an acceleration of these changes, some of which we cannot yet explain, like the "Great Resignation". The changes directly correspond with the revolution taking place in the collaboration arena, which is becoming a central player in the new era.

At the same time, we are witnessing trends of increased centralization and decreased collaboration. In his book *21 Lessons for the 21st Century* (2018), Yuval Noah Harari claims that the current technological revolutions may completely change our perception of cooperation. Technology has brought forth artificial intelligence into our world, which has the capacity to analyze a large scope of information simultaneously and most efficiently. By implementing the appropriate technologies, organizations will soon be able to analyze, research and process a lot of information on their own, without exhausting too much energy on cooperations and connections with other individuals and entities.

We are familiar with these trends from the business sector across the world, which is characterized by over-centralization, in large organizations such as Google or Facebook that apply this technology to penetrate our lives, and from governing institutions that increasingly control civilian life. Political elites and corporations are accumulating vast power and a new totalitarianism of knowledge, rendering collaboration redundant. Traditional democracy, acting under the assumption of the existence of balances and brakes, is no longer valid. The pulpy fusion of authorities, operating hand in hand with the mass media and tycoons, has brought about an indifference toward citizens, who are inevitably awakened to create alternative mechanisms for collaboration and influence in this era. It is safe to say that due to the economic and social changes following the Covid pandemic, a new generation will emerge, "the C-generation" which will act to change the political and social order. The frustration and despair of this generation, as they are forced to face an impossible economic reality, will most likely generate profound changes in the traditional power centers.

Complexity, complexity, complexity

Between the hierarchical and traditional structures that are disintegrating and changing the rules of the game toward increased collaboration, and the technologies and measures that increase control among organizations and governments, rendering collaboration redundant, stand leaders and managers. Some operate by trying to preserve the existing system and old world ways, while others are driving the wheels of the new era, promoting change in the existing system. Regardless of their position, they must all deal with the new era and be observant of the processes of change from a new perspective affecting issues of collaboration.

The processes of change, especially from the managers' point of view, relating to all aspects affecting collaboration, can be summarized by the acronym "VUCA". This term originated in the U.S. Army and is echoed today on every stage addressing issues of managers and organizations in the new era. It comprises the following terms:

- Volatility
- Uncertainty
- Complexity
- Ambiguity

This term corresponds to the definition of "a world in disrupt", which represents the change of familiar world orders, power centers and organizational structures, and Nisim Taleb's image of "black swans" (2009), which depicts chaotic randomness, characterizing unexpected events generating dramatic impact. In the old world, the assumption was that there were no black swans and, moreover, that this phenomenon was impossible. According to Taleb, some events are unpredictable since their occurrence is impossible to deduce or be prepared for on the basis of past experiences. Among such phenomena, he indicates World War I, the dissolution of the former Soviet Union, the rise of the internet and its application, the economic crisis of 2008 and the emergence of natural disasters of mass magnitude and influence.

In light of a reality that is characterized by uncertainty and randomness, we are not able to estimate the odds that extreme events will occur, nor can we anticipate what their impact will be. There is no doubt that "black swans" will continue to surprise us. In our current reality, surprise has become a permanent phenomenon. The year 2020, with the spread of the Covid pandemic, is a universal landmark on the path to a new reality, with a myriad of implications on all kinds of organizations.

Lately, there is a call for new terminology, and one of its interesting forms is known as BANI:

- What used to be volatile has ceased to be reliable.
- People do not feel uncertain anymore; they are anxious.

- Things are not complex anymore; instead, they obey non-linear logical systems.
- What used to be ambiguous appears incomprehensible to us today.

Regardless of the term used, it is imperative to grasp this profound notion regarding the nature of our world, as characterized by all these components. Thus, one must adopt a new perception and different manner of preparedness – both personal and systemic – regarding management, strategy, leadership and collaboration. Following is a brief outline of its most prominent features and implications for organizations and managers, which will serve as a conceptual basis for the issues brought forth in this book:

- Constant change is the most permanent feature – at the individual level, it refers to multiple shifting of different roles and physical locations, as well as a diverse and dynamic multitude of tasks. The fast rate of change grows exponentially. Change is a constant variable. It is customary to talk less about managing change and more about living with change and perpetual transformation.
- "The chaos threshold" – a dynamic situation characterized by stress between stability and change, between order and disorder, between predictability and unpredictability. In a complex system, relation between cause and effect is not necessarily a factor. Predictability and structure become difficult to identify.
- Uncertainty – we don't really know what a new day will bring, in any possible aspect. Strategic plans were once devised for a five-year period, while today it is customary to focus on a stretch of one to three years. Routine life usually entails an average of 80 percent certainty and 20 percent uncertainty. With the advent of a black swan, or a "Chinese bat" in the case of the Covid pandemic, the situation has overturned, exhibiting 20 percent certainty and 80 percent uncertainty. It seems the future is challenging us to live with 50 percent certainty and 50 percent uncertainty. It is advisable that we internalize and embrace this challenging state of affairs.
- There hardly exists a problem which has only one solution – many question marks always arise. Decision-making processes are not characterized by making a choice between various alternatives but by integrating their various components. As managers, we have to cope with paradoxes that necessitate a new and different way of thinking.
- Multiple components in reciprocal multidimensional relationships exist continuously – the managing experience in a complex world is manifested by multiple partners, customers, managers, suppliers and more. There are

factors with various agendas of their own that affect and are affected, and it is important to identify and take them into account.

- Contexture – everything is connected and dependent on everything and all is interwoven. It is impossible to relate one variable to a single one. Mutual dependence increases between people, units, organizations and sectors. If in the past any given unit was capable of performing a task from start to finish, today it depends on other factors for its performance.
- Internal organization – a complex system has its own logic and phases of development. For example, our brain, simulating a complex system, functions without any external control but rather controls itself. This is a self-organizing complex system. The internet is another example, at least in its early years, of a system that is not externally controlled but operates in constant motion and development.
- Obscuring the relationship between cause and effect – negligible causes, which are seemingly considered unrelated, may produce immense effects. The current presupposition is that any software, no matter how good, will not be materialized in the same accurate way as it was conceived. Small and unexpected changes produce significant effects, mostly such that are unpredictable. One example of many is the civil uprising in Syria which led to a large immigration movement, thus influencing trends and processes in Europe. The immeasurable impact of the war in Ukraine is another.
- Social and organizational flattening – traditional authorities are weakening throughout all aspects of life. The matrix structure assimilated in many organizations intends to provide a solution to complexities, while it simultaneously produces its own complexity. For instance, today a large portion of mid-level managers report to two different managers: a professional manager and a site or region manager.
- Technology and digital revolution – technological changes create different relational systems when it comes to information and its accessibility, as well as various kinds of networks and interactions which also affect organizations.

The term "complexity" is frequently associated with the term "complication". Needless to say, everything that is complex is also complicated, while not all that is complicated is complex. Complication characterizes situations and processes that require planning while affording the ability to clearly foresee the consequences deriving from various decisions. Complication occurs in coping with challenges and problems within familiar arenas and in recurring situations. Programming a missile that will hit a target at a certain point or construction of a high-rise building is a complicated task, while managing changes, leadership and raising children are complex tasks. And so is collaboration.

A simple problem has a solution, and the challenge therein lies in choosing the best and most effective one. A complicated problem includes a number of components – some are known and others are not, some are related to each other, and others are not. The challenge is to combine them into one causal chain, on the basis of which the most suitable solution can be solidified. A complex problem entails a high level of uncertainty, and it is often impossible to predict the probabilities and impacts of our intervention. The consequence of a certain course of action is unforeseen. There isn't necessarily a best solution that is also the most suitable one. The challenge is to harness all the relevant participants who may contribute to the comprehension of the problem and to its solution, in the hope that they will be willing to cooperate. For this purpose, it is necessary to rally a wide range of stakeholders and complementing perspectives. A "wicked" problem is characterized by paradoxes, dilemmas and internal contradictions, creating the sense that no solution can be found. The only chance of resolution lies in full and wholehearted cooperation of all the relevant players.

Complexity in all sectors is affected by the social arena, which in itself is ever changing. Social protests are characterized by being difficult to predict. They are not directed by one single factor and are not subject to orderly and linear processes. Tahrir Square in Cairo, Hong Kong, Teheran, Belarus, Balfour street and more – all signified the decline in value of the hierarchy stock. These protests influence the social and political reality and weaken the natural hierarchy prevailing in their respective countries.

The "millennial generation", also referred to as the Y generation, and the Z generation that follows are changing the social and organizational reality. As a rule, they tend to engage in action and contribute more in flat organizational structures rather than hierarchical ones. The internet, social networks and novel technologies have been absorbed into their being since infancy. Information sharing is in their nature. They are usually described as being unfocused, capable of multitasking and possessing a high capacity for teamwork. As a rule, they are endowed with a readiness to learn new things and the ability to cope with changes. They dislike hierarchical management, particularly of the rigid type. Despite the differences between these two generations, it should be borne in mind that millennials constitute the major mass of employees, as well as junior and middle management, in organizations. They prefer cooperation, networking and managers who recruit them as partners rather than being led.

The hierarchy stock is in constant decline due to work processes within organizations and not just because of the influence of external trends. As information disperses more broadly across all levels of an organization and beyond, rather than remaining concentrated at the top of the pyramid, senior executives become less informed and increasingly reliant on employees during decision-making processes. In an era where information is power, as it becomes more accessible to everyone, power in its previous configuration is weakened. The sources of power and authority of leaders and managers have changed.

All features of complexity as described here converge into an intensive day-to-day experience. It becomes apparent that these executives feel as if they are standing on a rocking boat surrounded by towering waves, from within and without.

Generally, the organizational arena is slow to adjust in relation to the external challenges deriving from changes taking place in the world and in human society. Hierarchy, monitoring, performance analysis, employees' engagement, control, planning and order, male dominance, delegation of authority – all are still prominent patterns and features. Organizations in the business arena are required to perform fast adjustments or perish; therefore, these traditional features are gradually weakening. The public sector and the third sector experience slower evolution, yet in all kinds of organizations and sectors, managers are required to deal with complexity.

Managers today must function simultaneously in a number of parallel worlds, operate under obscure conditions and incorporate many considerations, some of which may even be contradictory. They have to be able to simplify a complex issue and translate it into simple tasks and goals, be open to constant learning, be creative and take risks. In the current reality, they are required to conduct and manage a huge range of employee types, an extremely wide variety of interfaces and relationships, as well as develop inter-cultural intelligence and conduct wisely in a "Glocal" world (global and local simultaneously). They must identify and analyze complex situations and understand that what worked well yesterday may not necessarily work today and will surely be irrelevant tomorrow. They are forced to initiate and conduct partnerships as a necessity in a changing reality. As time goes by, it appears that this is the most important skill for future managers: they must be experts of collaboration.

Leadership, leadership, leadership

The key to the processes of change and adjustment to the new era lies in leadership. The four most important terms in the managerial and organizational arena today are as follows:

Accountability – an advanced combination of reliability, taking full responsibility for actions, constant investigation, decisions, policies, avoidance of removing one's own liability and laying blame on other people or circumstances and a commitment to report and provide explanations when necessary. Accountability also entails reference to joint and reciprocal action, related to managing relationships and work interfaces. Senior management involves wide systemic responsibility, not just about what is defined in the area of responsibility of the manager and unit. If a manager today acts as if he/she is responsible only for his/her task, missions and teams, he/she does not understand the new reality.

Agility – constant and rapid changes and the limited capacity to implement long-term planning make it necessary to maintain a high level of agility – a combination of speed and flexibility. It refers to quick adjustment to changing circumstances, in conjunction with leading structured and orderly processes. The method embedded in high-tech organizations and which expresses maximum agility is called Scrum. It is a project management methodology for software development, based on agility, transparency, constant learning, self-mentoring teams and rapid implementation. Its premise is based on complexity – on the understanding that it is impossible to fully predict and plan in advance a comprehensive development process. In other arenas too, agility has become a condition for development and sometimes even for survival.

This was the case of restaurants during the Covid lockdowns. Their very basic DNA is hosting and serving. In order to survive, they underwent a quick and deep adjustment to packaging and delivery. Those who did not change usually did not survive. Those who did still continue with this new business line, even though it is not necessary now. It sounds easy. It's actually not. Today one must possess high levels of adaptability quotient (AQ). Intelligence quotient (IQ) and emotional quotient (EQ) alone are not enough.

Relevance – As managers, we are used to asking ourselves and our surroundings one basic and significant question: How can we be more efficient? Our duty and intent are to perform in a manner that uses the least amount of inputs to achieve the highest amount of output. This is well embedded in organizations and managerial theories and practice, since it began more than 100 years ago, as the Scientific Management (Taylorism).

These days efficiency is not enough. I can be very efficient, but if I am not also relevant and effective, I will not exist. Big firms such as Kodak and Nokia nearly vanished, not due to issues of efficiency but mainly because they were not fast enough in grasping how the world is changing. Effectiveness is the ability and capability of producing desired results and outputs. Relevance is about our surroundings.

One of the amazing changes occurring in this era is the shift that organizations are making from the idea of stockholders to shareholders. We must be relevant not only to our stockholders and boards but also to our employees, clients, vendors, society and surroundings. Each of us as managers should ask questions about our effectiveness and relevance aside from questions about our efficiency.

Collaboration – Accountability, agility and relevance are dependent on collaboration. Collaboration and leadership are completely interwoven. This term will be explained throughout the book. Basically, it refers to two or more factors engaging in a process in which they are involved for the purpose of finding a solution to a challenge or problematic arena, in order to produce a higher value than each of them could produce on their own.

In light of changes in society, processes of flattening in organizations, weakening of hierarchy and the emergence of matrixial structures, managers find themselves ever more engaged in challenges of interfaces, mutual dependencies, motivation and influence without authority. These processes take place in managers' interfaces with their employees, with their colleagues and with higher ranks in the organization. "Managing up", or the effect of subordinate managers on those ranking above them, is perceived in many organizations, especially in the business sector, as legitimate and even necessary. Most managers today are involved in cross-organizational interface much more than in the past.

The perception of leadership has also developed in conjunction and according to these change processes. The direct connection between complexity and leadership is discussed in Thomas Friedman's book *The World Is Flat* (2005). Friedman describes, among other things, the transition from a doctrine of Command and Control to one of Connect and Collaborate. In recent years many new modes of leadership have emerged – all of them incorporate, in one way or another, four central components:

1. Senior managers are required to adopt an attitude of humbleness, constant learning and coping with diversity. The image of the charismatic and heroic manager, all-knowing and in full control of all occurrences in his system, is no longer valid.
2. Managers are required to demonstrate high capabilities of dialogue, communication and constructing relationships. Nowadays there is an understanding that these features are essential to materialize organizational objectives and do not only exist in the arena that was once defined as "soft skills". Nowadays, relationships are the foundation for everything, and it is important to distinguish between friendship, which is "nice to have", and relationships, which are a "must have".
3. The ability to lead people includes recognizing trends, creating a relevant "narrative" and new meaning, boldness, integration and improvisation. These qualities are more important than ever before.
4. The ability to recognize the unexpected and live in peace with ongoing uncertainty is a basic condition in all current prevailing perceptions.

One of the most significant models is defined as "Adaptive Leadership". This model was developed by Ron Hefetz and Martin Linski (2009) at the Harvard Kennedy School for public policy and deals with the capacity of leaders to direct organizations to substantial changes required in the face of changing reality and maintain relevance over time. Such policy is mainly intended to cope with complicated problems which require systemic thinking and actions of many people in order to promote change, a condition whereby it is no longer possible to settle for the personal charisma of a leader and formal authority.

Adaptive leadership refers to the action and not to the person and his qualities. Therefore, any person, from any position, will be able to promote change in the system, and anyone can implement leadership. However, only rarely do we work toward achieving adaptive change, mostly due to preserving norms and boundaries, power of authority and status quo, regulating internal conflicts and the tendency to provide technical responses to challenges. The approach of adaptive leadership always involves risk taking on the part of the process leader, since implementing such complex steps depends on recruiting other people and cooperating with them. Implementation of this perception of leadership is mostly dependent on the ability to generate and incorporate some levels of partnership.

Change processes related to collaboration may be technical, a type of gradual evolution characterized by the avoidance of revolutions and risks. The changes may be adaptive, summoning revolution and rapid paradigmatic in-depth changes. Either way, it is clear that in the new era change-invoking leadership will always choose collaboration as its central lever. This is a clear and tangible trend.

When we truly understand the reality of the new era, with all its characteristics and implications, we recognize that a paradigmatic change is also needed in perceptions regarding collaboration and cooperation. All the changes related to leadership, managerial practices, structures and organizational processes prevail in direct relation to the field of collaboration. The obligatory paradigm, in looking toward the future, is one based on relationships and cooperations rather than hierarchy, oversight and control. The basic unit for observations and impact is not the individual but rather the relationship – between individuals, units, organizations, sectors, cultures and values; between different variables; and between leaders and all the above factors. The main challenge for us as managers today is not so much the issue of "team work" as the issue of cross-units and cross-organizational collaboration. This is the new story of all managers and leaders.

Changes in the perception of collaboration in the last decade

Cooperation is not a new idea. Thousands of years of evolution have taught us to cooperate for the purpose of survival in small groups. People once lived in tribes, villages and towns and always maintained social relationships for their various needs. People know how to work together as teams. Collaboration is much more challenging.

The individual survival system, created millions of years ago, is not yet prepared for the collaboration challenges we encounter today. Therefore, in order to create effective collaboration in complex arenas and on a large scale, clear structures, consciousness and a new language are required.

One of the oldest documented examples of cooperation was revealed by pilots during the First World War. While flying over the deserts of the Middle East, the pilots identified an artificial V-shaped pattern which they coined "kite", a circle of stones from which two "arms" extended, forming an appearance similar to kite tails. Archaeologists who studied the structure on site concluded that it marked a hunting facility, dating back to the Chalcolithic period (about 6,000 years ago). The groups of hunters who lived in these areas built two low stone walls, spread over hundreds of meters. Some of the hunters chased after deer or other animals that lived in these areas during that period. As the walls converged into the shape of a funnel, the animals reached a point of a steep step, from where they fell down into a ring enclosed by a high stone wall. The other hunters would then ascend from their hiding place and hit the animals with flint arrows covered with poison.

What, then, has changed throughout history?

Everything. The world is changing at a crazy pace, and at the same time, everything related to spaces of collaborations is changing too. The emphasis we place on this issue in every aspect of our lives is new – from international business partnerships to community education and welfare services, from coping with complex issues of climate, pandemics and terrorism to how we treat issues of poverty, immigration and employment. Systems and organizations that used to operate separately and independently combine with other entities at various levels of partnerships. There are more and more initiatives emerging from the connection of individuals, groups, communities and organizations for the purpose of promoting issues together.

This is a revolution that is evident in many real-life applications, some more familiar than others:

Waze is an example of an Israeli application that was created to tackle the frustrating issue of traffic jams. The brilliance of this application lies in its simplicity and the lack of effort required in order to contribute to and benefit from the cooperation facilitated by this technological platform. All we need to do is connect to the network, and a set of algorithms and satellites will do the work for us. Only a small number of users are active in reporting hazards and police cars, while everyone else enjoys the simple, accessible and effortless collaboration.

The Israeli company Mobileye also acted in an inspiring way in terms of the collaborative aspect. In 2017, Intel acquired 84 percent of Mobileye's shares for a legendary sum of 15 billion dollars. Ostensibly, Intel seemed to have acquired a groundbreaking technology; however, it acquired a much higher value than that. The genius of Mobileye's people was reflected in aspects that go far beyond the use of technology. Over the years they have developed an extensive network of partnerships with most of the leading entities in the automotive industry. In fact, Intel acquired a very significant entry ticket into an important multi-million industry – "Intel in Car". Mobileye created relevance and value through a model based on cooperation. In the words of Brian Krzanich, Intel's CEO: "After the acquisition of Mobileye, we see ourselves as market leaders. When viewed in terms of performance, or performance to cost ratio, it becomes evident that we are now leading. And in this market we shall win."

Wikipedia is a prominent marker of a profound cultural revolution. Most of us grew up on the premise that "knowledge is power." Knowledge that I possess and no one else has becomes a relative advantage for me. The phrase I propose to adopt today is: "Knowledge is power. Sharing knowledge is strength." Easy to say and hard to implement, especially for those who grew up on the old paradigm. Millennials and their successors have been raised on a platform of sharing knowledge and information, which is an available and a reliable and convenient source for many topics. This platform is created every moment based on cooperation between countless people all around the world. People spend time and contribute their knowledge for various reasons; thus, in their way, they are part of a profound change in human society.

In addition to these ventures and countless others, a world of new and renewed concepts is also evolving. These represent significant processes that are increasingly gaining importance and volume. The most prominent in this new arena are as follows:

Co-creation

In the past, value creation and value chain were defined by the organization. The customer was defined as a consumer or, in the best-case scenario, as one who offers feedback along the way. Organizations are changing their traditional thinking from product orientation to customers' experience orientation, by means of co-creation. The new customer is no longer willing to remain passive and often wants to be involved and influential regarding a product or service. Customers are now interconnected, conscious and empowered, and some are partners in information-sharing communities.

This concept is not only attributed to co-creation of a product but also to a change in the configuration of service. A patient seeing a doctor expects to be a partner in the service products he receives by means of dialogue, to understand the benefits and risks of any possible treatment offered. When patients see a doctor today, they have much more knowledge and information than they had in the past pertaining to the relevant issues and therefore are afforded full transparency from a position of eye-level dialogue. Perhaps not all doctors like it, as it requires more time and energy on their part; however, they cannot rely on their professional authority without offering the patient the option to become involved and exercise choice (Topol, 2015).

An example of a completely different arena is that of John Deere Company, which manufactures agricultural machinery. A few years ago, the company pivoted from its traditional mode of operation and created an active network with its customers to share their experiences – a fact that has played a significant role in the Company's growth in recent years. Nike facilitates technological means for customers to participate in their shoe design in accordance with their personal taste. Similarly, the success of eBay is partly attributed to the buyer–seller dialogue. This kind of dialogue poses a challenge for many organizations since it requires transparency, accessibility to information, investment or resources in the dialogue as well as the ability to understand the pros and cons involved in that process.

The idea of co-creation, which characterizes this era, means neither transferring activities or outsourcing to customers nor adapting products and services. "We need to regard the market as a potential space of Co-Creation experiences, where considerations and choices of individuals define their willingness to pay for their experiences" (Prahalad, 2004). This idea represents a much more fundamental change and reflects the partnership of the customer with the company in the process of creating value through dialogue between him and the company, at his discretion. This demonstrates the focus on the relationship between the individual and the company.

This dialogue is developing in the arena of B2C (business to customer – between the service provider and the end customer) in conjunction with that of B2B (business to business – between organizations). The Boeing Company provides a fascinating example. At the time when the company was required to deal with challenging market trends, it chose to make a dramatic shift in its perception of innovation and collaboration. In the development of the 787 flag aircraft, the Dreamliner, in order to improve its performance in terms of speed and fuel consumption, Boeing decided to incorporate the entire supply chain involved in the aircraft's manufacture in the design process itself. As opposed to the usual and traditional method of first planning and then submitting a tender to suppliers, the suppliers were selected in advance and were considered partners throughout the entire process – from planning to execution. This was a preliminary and unique move both for Boeing and in relation to all corresponding companies. The result went beyond any expectations and led to the manufacture of a more technologically advanced aircraft, in a faster and more economical process, all the way to market entry (Time to Market).

Another term in this context is "collaborative networked organizations" (CNO), describing the development of collaborative business opportunities between different entities through digital interaction. In most cases, a certain degree of affinity exists between organizations participating in the collaborative network, and these generate cooperation for business and social purposes (Camarinha-Matos, 2008).

Collaborative economy

The year 2013 is marked as the year when collaborative economy began to take center stage, with its wide scope of terminology and field applications. At first, it was all about companies that specialized in this arena, such as Uber and WeWork. Gradually, companies from other sectors, including high-tech and finance, started to adopt these models. Eatwith, for example, is a platform that brings together those possessing culinary assets with those who have complementary needs. The Friends for Health organization assists in transferring medications from those who do not need them to those who do. Collaborative economy allows people to generate value for themselves by means of maximizing their assets for business activity.

Collaborative models have an economic footing and a socio-communal footing. The interest in these models derives from the wish to create economic savings and operational efficiency and provide new experiences for customers, employees and suppliers. Currently, all industries are beginning to adopt these models. For example, a high-tech company developed a program to encourage employee collaborative carpooling through prioritizing parking spaces. Their narrative focused on considerations of air pollution reduction and strengthening the connection between employees, but clearly an economic interest also exists for the company, reducing fuel and parking costs. This is a legitimate combination that motivates organizations into action.

Some define the collaborative economy as one of the strongest trends in society, one that will only grow stronger. Others define it as "Co-wash", similar to the definition of "Green-Wash", attributed to those who saw a business opportunity in the ecological trend and "embraced" it for economic reasons only. The Airbnb model is an alternative to the traditional hotel, wrapped in the veil of sharing economy, compared with the phenomenon of "Couchsurfing", which reflects the attitude of true collaboration. Another significant example, which is developing around the world as well as in Israel, is collaborative housing (Co-Living), which exhibits a very wide range of applications – from profound communal collaboration to its use as a marketing strategy. Needless to say that with every trend, there exists a tension between appearances and essence.

As the trend of collaborative economy develops and is also explored, a few things about it become apparent. First, it is clear that the main driving forces are the young generations who are accustomed to sharing and expect it in their workplaces, as consumers and as entrepreneurs; many of them seek to reinforce a sense of belonging and are not motivated by any need for control and ownership. Second, it turns out that organizations which truly adopt this direction are required to perform a cultural shift, and this is no small feat. Third, we find that entities which were greatly identified with the collaborative trend don't necessarily honor the values and morals they promote. For example, Uber and Airbnb are digital capitalist platforms circumventing regulation, without the slightest hint of collaboration. Being a kind of monopoly, much like Facebook, they gain unlimited power, which, in practice, is stronger than the direct power of the masses of consumers. The giant corporations of the collaborative economy are both part of the gospel and the danger.

Collaborative consumption

PUBLIC is a new search engine which was created by people and is not controlled by entities with economic interests. Initially, the platform was designed for the benefit of musicians interested in sharing their creations; however, it's evolving into other areas of interest, based on users' experiences and needs and not on organic promotion and advertising. It is a social, equalized and decentralized search engine, designed to produce a new internet economy through blockchain and artificial intelligence, as part of the network's eco-system. Another example is the online insurance company Lemonade which built a consumer model that converts insurance funds into social investments in accordance with the wishes of the insured rather than capitalizing the funds for shareholders.

These are only a few of the many examples in the consumer arena, which is being redefined in light of the declining demand for central systems, as consumers are getting tired of paying large sums of money for their services. As part of the alternatives, we are increasingly buying and selling through social networks and collaborative consumer sites, raising finances through crowdfunding (such as "Headstart"), and have access to a great deal of free information that allows us to save part of these expenses.

This is one channel within the collaborative economy, marking a new trend of P2P, "Person to Person". This new trajectory signifies the people's control rather than that of the traditional controlling stakeholders. Although the road is still long, there are more and more new and unprecedented processes, involving connections between people as a development that directly corresponds with networking and innovation. This is a complex trend in itself, characterizing many start-up companies, requiring more agile interactions and cooperations and less control and planning. The new entrepreneurs are establishing businesses whose narrative is the leading force.

Collaborative innovation

These days, it's impossible to talk about innovation without collaboration. We know that usually a few people thinking together produce better solutions than one person thinking on his own. The same refers to multicultural and multidisciplinary teams, provided communication among them is effective and progressive. That is one of the main reasons for more diversity in organizations. Most innovation experts today emphasize that the future of innovation will rise from connections and convergence between fields and disciplines rather than from diving deeper into each one of them.

Some organizations promote innovation by means of generating more connections outside the organization. In recent years, another fascinating trend has emerged: cooperation between entities and industries which are virtually unrelated. More and more organizations are testing potential partnerships outside their natural arena, in order to strengthen their relevance. Collaborative innovation occurs on four levels:

1. Adoption and transfer

    Technology from one field is transferred to another. For example, the camera pill, swallowed in order to detect cancerous tumors, applies a technology that was transferred from the field of guided missiles. Another example is the cooperation of the Lego company with NASA space agency, which together promote research in their areas of technology, engineering and mathematics to develop applications in the work process with science students. The project includes the use of Lego tools at NASA for the purpose of experiments - for example, testing the performance of small models under conditions of zero gravity. The experiments are filmed and used to teach the topics among school students. In return, NASA provides Lego with ideas and study materials for developing new products.

2. Novel creation

    Collaboration based on technologies and knowledge that any industry introduces to the creation of something new. For example, the development of Renault's spa vehicle together with L'Oreal's Biotherm company, where a climate control system nourishes the skin to avoid dryness. Another example is the production and marketing of soft drinks containing ingredients affecting beauty and health, as resulted from the cooperation between the Coca-Cola Company and the French pharmaceutical company Sanopi.

3. Inspiration

Inspiration occurs when one industry is inspired by another to produce an innovative solution. One such popular example is a bicycle company that repeatedly suffered damages caused to their packages during shipping. To tackle this problem, they began sticking television stickers on their packages, which caused the shipping companies to handle them with greater care, resulting in a miraculous decrease in return of broken bicycles.

4. Connection

Connection relates to combining capabilities of different industries to jointly create a product or service. Fiat's "Loft" model is a good example, as it simulates a comfortable living space. In order to complete its cozy feeling, Fiat and Lavazza cooperated in the design and manufacture of a unique coffee machine that was integrated into the car. Another example is the cooperation between Raspol – a large fuel company in Spain – with Burger King. In this framework, 150 shared points of sale were established at gas stations, which are operated by Raspol's employees under the guidance and professional responsibility of Burger King. For Burger King this move has led to the company's most significant growth in Europe to this day.

For Starbucks, the company's cooperative strategy is their most significant growth leverage. To enhance customer value and experience, Starbucks cooperates with PepsiCo in production and marketing of several products. Their ice cream is produced and distributed by Dreyr's, while their supermarket coffee is marketed and distributed by Kraft. The partnership with Jim Beam Brands introduced Starbucks into a new field: Cream Liqueur production sold in liquor stores and restaurants but not in the chain's coffee houses (Gulati, 2007).

In the past, inter-sectorial connections hardly existed, while today they are becoming a prevalent and natural part of the profound and rapid revolution in the field connecting innovation and collaboration.

Holacracy

The origin of the term "holacracy" is derived from the ancient Greek word "Holon", which means "everything", when referring to a part of something big, whole and perfect. This term indicates the nullification of hierarchy and flattening the entire organizational structure, with no definitions of managers and employees. The employee belongs to workgroups according to his skills and wishes. What makes this strategy a winner is the power of idea rather than the power of authority. A holacratic organization functions by division into functional circles. Each circle or group is in charge of a particular area, independently. There is no hierarchical management in the group, as it is part of a cluster of groups in the organization. Sometimes the circles work in parallel or as subordinates of other circles. The circles are defined by tasks, functions and roles. One circle may emerge from another circle following a task that has to be performed. Some circles include representatives from other circles, creating a broad scope of synergistic work.

This method makes more sense to the younger generation, and since everything is based on a clear outline of rules, it does not generate anarchy. Freedom of action, expression and thought produce a very high level of involvement, connectedness and commitment of all employees, hence creating faster and better solutions. There is no need to receive executives' approvals or get involved with corporate politics in order to make an impact.

The core values in the holacratic model are equality and collaboration. The rules and regulations in the organization are determined in a charter written by all employees. Subsequently, a goal is defined for each position holder, as well as areas of responsibility and assets. Each employee (or team) determines his own course of action and can use all relevant assets within areas of his responsibility – as long as he does not cause harm to the work of others.

The concept of self-management of employees is not suitable for everyone. Zappos, a giant American shoe and clothing online company, has adopted the organizational structure of holacracy in 2014. This move is described as a great success. On the other hand, Twitter is one of the companies that tried to work holacratically but along the way realized that there are also drawbacks. Thus, for example, components such as evaluation, feedback and control are difficult to create in a holacratic organization, even though they are extremely important to the generation of a healthy work environment. Moreover, not all employees possess the same capacity for self-management, and for them, holacracy does not provide a safety net.

The idea of abolishing traditional management is still hard to digest. However, the central ideas of holacracy, which consist of teams without official management, with more emphasis on teamwork and less on bureaucracy, are gaining momentum in many organizations in various forms. Experts estimate that in the upcoming years, more and more organizations will shift toward operating on the basis of this innovative framework or will be established from the get-go in accordance with this conception (Roberson, 2015).

Chapter 2

Paradigm shift
From efficiency to relevance

Contributing factors to collaboration in the new era

The trends of change described so far affect the formulation of a new conception, which holds widespread consent: collaboration is no longer a recommendation. It is a necessity. In a survey conducted in 2012 by IBM, 1,709 CEOs from various industries and countries were asked: "What is the most important condition for generating business growth?" In response, 69 percent pointed to collaboration within and outside the organization as the most important factors. Roles and responsibilities, organizational values and more were rated lower. In 2015, Dell EMC Company conducted a survey in which 3,600 senior managers were asked what would drive their business forward in the upcoming years. Forty six percent answered that expanding collaborations between units within the organization is the most important lever. This answer received the highest rating, preceding innovation, empowerment of employees, budgets and so on.

In fact, nowadays there is consensus that collaboration is a necessity – an element that is absolutely essential for effective functioning of systems and attaining goals in various aspects of life. "Collaboration is critical to business. If we fail to integrate systems, people, processes and products, we will not be able to produce value"; "We do not have the privilege of working in separate verticals. Customers are changing and require new solutions; systemic ones" – these are insights that managers are repeatedly and more emphatically articulating in business organizations.

DOI: 10.4324/9781003514992-2   **19**

Recognizing the importance of collaboration is mainly derived from the trends and challenges of change. The exponential rate of changes, in conjunction with growing uncertainty, makes it difficult to rely on linear and independent planning and increase the need for great flexibility within the systems and their interconnections. Professionalism, specialization, expertise and specification of knowledge and human capabilities, on the one hand, alongside complexity of problems and the need to provide interdisciplinary solutions, on the other, require collaboration among many diverse factors.

Authority, control and hierarchy have not yet lost their central place in many of the human, organizational and communal systems; at the same time, perceptions and practices based on equality, participation and sharing of knowledge, power and influence are also growing. With the reduction of resources and increase in competitiveness, many recognize the significant potential of "expanding the pie" by means of partnering.

In recent years there has been a shift toward developmental consciousness. In the past, large parts of human society operated within automatic patterns of survival consciousness – remnants of the time when humans actually lived under survival conditions. The transformation nowadays is also difficult, as the business world has deeply embedded within us a competitive consciousness resulting from living in a world marked by limited resources. "Survival of the fittest" is still the prevalent narrative; this is how we understand biology. For many years, mankind has conducted itself in this manner regarding human relations, politics and business. However, today we are witnessing the emergence of a new narrative. This narrative, according to which collaboration and partnering are beneficial for the achievement of goals, is starting to occupy an increasingly significant place.

Today's complex business environment, with its ever-intensifying competitiveness, dictates a new agenda. In order to generate innovative and effective cooperations, organizations must create an environment of cross-organizational collaborative work. This allows for sharing of information, breaking down existing thought patterns and developing groundbreaking new products and services. The need for cooperations frequently derives from the very conduct of units and organizations in a number of parallel arenas as a foundation for achieving goals. A common and meaningful source of motivation is a necessity for survival. Dealing with crises, the constant need for adjustment and creating relevance in a changing environment require the strengthening of internal and external collaborations.

Sense of urgency serves as a powerful catalyst in accelerating collaborations resulting from crises and survival. At the outbreak of the Covid-19 crisis in 2020, many cooperations were quickly formed, due to the sense of uncertainty and fear and the need to urgently find solutions to the situation, and thanks to technology and global networks. Experts estimate that during this period an important foundation was laid for sharing information from an eco-system perception, one that will outlive the pandemic. Many defined it as "the new normal" and "the next normal", and these terms are very common in the last years regarding many arenas.

One example that illustrates the depth of potential change is the fact that CELL Press, publisher of the most important magazines in the fields of biological and medical sciences, received in March 2020 an estimate of 20,000 articles dealing with the pandemic. As the Chinese shared with the global scientific community information about the unfamiliar virus from the very early days of the outbreak, hundreds and possibly thousands of laboratories abandoned their ongoing research and harnessed their expertise to study the topic. In an extraordinary move, CELL Press management decided to make these articles available directly to the scientific community without first reviewing them.

Prof. Hagai Ginsburg, former Dean of the Biological Chemistry faculty at the Hebrew University in Jerusalem, refers to this issue:

> What we are seeing is a revolution. Throughout many decades, access to knowledge in the scientific press was only facilitated after very careful screening and an in-depth scientific examination. What happened here reflects an understanding that sharing knowledge, even if uncontrolled and unmonitored, is much more relevant to what is required in this type of pandemic. Free flow of information is required to advance a solution to the coronavirus. This phenomenon may have an effect on creating a change in consciousness and movement forward, making science less traditional in its approach.

Virtual as well as geographically dispersed teams have quickly evolved in recent decades, especially among global organizations, as the foundation for cooperations between organizations around the world. Cooperations in this arena create various complex challenges relating to cultural gaps, language, modes of communication and more. Creating relationships established on trust and common understandings among these teams is an extremely essential condition for effective work interfaces. One of the important and interesting elements in their work is the reduction of traditional and centralized authoritative management, strengthening the aspect of self-management and flattening the structure – a feature called SMT – "Self-Management Teams" (Peters, 2007). This element has been found to promote effectiveness of multicultural and multidisciplinary teams, provided relationships are good. These teams cope more easily and quickly with complex and dynamic projects.

There are three key aspects that generate business growth: better innovation, better sales and better operations. In non-business organizations, three parallel aspects can be identified as development of new services, better customer satisfaction and improved organization performance. All these aspects require a high-quality level of collaboration:

1. Better innovation – when people from different fields gather and produce new ideas by establishing relationships and advancing the development of new products. The economic logic is to reconnect existing resources – products, expertise, technologies, branding, ideas – in order to create something new from something old. It is obvious to anyone involved in innovation that it is inseparable from collaboration, as part of a single coherent conception. But whereas in the past innovation mainly relied on one brilliant and creative person, today it primarily relies on teams – preferably heterogeneous.

2. Better sales – one of the benefits of collaboration is the principle of Cross Sales – that is, selling various products to existing customers, as well as an inner-organizational array, whereby one unit sells to customers of another unit. Economic logic dictates that it costs less to sell to an existing customer than to a new one. Large accounting firms are a good example of a business arena that has recently adopted change. These firms combine several disciplines, each working independently and functioning as a separate PNL (Profit & Loss): tax services, consulting services, auditing, accounting and transaction consulting services. At times, different people from various units will work with the same client, without maintaining any connection between them and unaware of the integration and the value to the client. That is exactly where the potential for relevance and growth of these companies lies. They are not differentiated in the market by professionalism and service, but if they deepen the potential of collaboration between the units, they will differentiate themselves from the existing organizational culture, characterized by clustering partners from different fields, separating various professions and competition within the organization. These are profound processes of change, whose importance for organizations has only recently been recognized.

3. Improving operations – streamlining work processes and qualitative decision-making, based on acquiring solutions and expertise developed within the organization, and concentrating services into central business units increasing efficiency of processes and reducing costs. Mr. Akiva Mozes, former CEO of Israel Chemicals Ltd., initiated the merging of land transport and storage systems, in a manner that required high-level cooperation between a number of subsidiaries.

The group's sales turnover soared from $1.8 billion in 1999 to $7.2 billion in 2011. A significant portion of this increase is associated with these organizational changes.

When these three axes exist simultaneously, the organization can potentially experience large-scale growth. Morten Hansen, one of the most prominent researchers in the field of collaboration, describes these elements in his outstanding book *Collaboration* (2009). In his book he examines the impact of these elements on the outcomes obtained by Procter & Gamble (P&G) – a company whose core organizational culture is based on collaborations and that made a strategic decision to base half of its innovation on external cooperations. These collaborations have supported P&G in developing new products and fields over the years. At first the company produced only soap, but then every expertise that was added served as a lever for the next step, to the point of producing oils and drugs. Between 2002 and 2005, their revenues increased by 41 percent and operating expenses decreased by 2.7 percent. According to Hansen's estimation, P&G's impressive growth lies in the strong cooperations that characterized the organization during those years (Hansen, 2009).

Collaborations in the business arena are designed to produce higher value for organizations in terms of profitability, successfully coping in a competitive market, long-term stability, growth, development and openness to change, agility, quality of internal organizational culture and other aspects of value. Sometimes the need for collaboration stems from a desire to generate business growth, which drives connections to other entities that complement the value to the customer, including providing services and responses. Collaboration is, at times, a necessity and a survival need as well as an opportunity to create higher value and relevance.

In the past, every manager and every organization regularly asked themselves how to produce higher efficiency and achieve more with fewer resources. Nowadays, an organization can be very efficient, but without relevance it will cease to exist, and even if it survives, it will not necessarily fulfill its designation in the best possible way. Massive organizations such as Kodak and Nokia were efficient; however, they failed to examine the question of relevance in time and therefore nearly vanished from their business arena. These two entities sought answers, solutions and innovation mainly within their inner arena while neglecting to sufficiently look into the possibility of collaborations and new partnerships outside the space of their familiar comfort zone.

The transition from efficiency to effectiveness and relevance is a prominent and central feature of organizations in the new era. Organizational strategy which examines and defines objectives based on creating value and relevance currently provides vital infrastructure in all sectors. Public and social entities alike aspire to demonstrate a stronger influence, understanding that it is currently almost impossible to produce a significant impact alone.

In May 2017, the National Headquarters for Children's Online Protection was launched in Israel, aimed at preventing cyber violence and crimes against minors and providing a professional response to crimes perpetrated online against children and youth. In order to produce significant value and impact in dealing with a new and very complex issue, decision makers defined in advance that despite its direct subordination to the police, the agency will operate under the joint auspices of the Ministries of Internal Security, Education, Welfare, Health and Justice. Alongside the great complexity created by the mere integration of these bodies, the professional consolidated activity bears great importance. There is no doubt that no single entity could ever have reached the same impact. This is an example of understanding the relevance of collaboration in the governmental sector.

The factors that motivate managers, organizations, communities and other systems to collaborate include the following points, in variable combinations:

- The desire to produce value and relevance.
- Acting under the assumption that collaboration will increase the effectiveness of processes and products.
- Understanding that joint work is the right way and often the only way for problem-solving and taking actions.
- Recognizing the effectiveness of pooling resources between entities, given that each individual entity has limited resources for realizing the goal.
- The need to avoid redundancy and wasted resources in providing parallel and overlapping services.
- Acknowledging that when commitment of different factors is required to materialize objectives, their integration in a shared task is beneficial.
- The benefit of collaboration in increasing access to information and resources, enhancing and distributing them.
- The ability to expand markets, enhance capabilities and develop products and services by means of integrated forces and at reduced costs, with higher value to partners and customers.
- The benefit of collaboration when multidisciplinary and/or matrixial work is required, with interdependence between the various factors.
- The ability to leverage handling a complex issue based on different perspectives of the partners, leading to a broad, creative and holistic vision.
- The advantage of collaborations in situations of survival and lack of choice.
- Applying the solution of collaboration from a leadership perspective, especially in dealing with complex challenges.
- The conceptual shift according to which collaboration is perceived as more logical and acceptable.

- Generational shift resulting from the fact that Generation Y and Generation Z managers were raised on values of sharing as a natural and conventional issue.
- The mindset that working together is more effective than working alone, especially when different disciplines and experts from diverse fields are required in order to cope with a complex challenge.
- Enhancing impact and influence through collaboration.

One should bear in mind that collaboration carries with it various costs and meanings that are not always beneficial. One of the risks is seeing collaboration as the end goal and thus naively romanticizing it. Collaboration should be seen as a means to an end and addressed in a professional, structured and critical manner. In the following chapters, we will meticulously explore and present an analysis of the various aspects and considerations pertaining to the implementation of collaboration and the ways of coping with the challenges it raises.

It is likely that at this point, questions and thoughts may arise regarding our own partnerships, for example in our personal life. One of these arenas is our couple and family relationships. In all my professional meetings with managers, this challenging, and sometimes painful, issue has come up: the complexity of the relationships in our lives. In response I smile and share with them the story about an experienced and esteemed couples' therapist, who after a long and successful career, and just before he passed away, was asked how he broke down the mystery of couples. His answer was that it was very simple:

> When the couple starts their journey together, the husband expects his wife not to change over the years. But she does. The wife, on the other hand, expects her husband to change over the years. But he doesn't... And that's the key to everything.

Compared with the collaborative processes characterizing human society in the systemic sense, trends in the couple and family context reflect an almost opposite direction: a reduction in interdependence, and thus, in collaborations. While in the past, a partnership between a couple was essential in order to bear and raise children, it is now possible to do so in many ways, completely independent of any partnership. Men and women bring children into the world as single parents or with same-sex partners or choose to relinquish their biological destiny altogether.

The story of collaboration as presented here, in its systemic contexts, corresponds to some extent with the story of a couple and family partnership – including the needs, fantasies, fears, norms, environmental influences, period of infatuation, building of a relationship, maturity, long-term maintenance and more.

In the systemic areas, there are also many good reasons why one should avoid entering into a cooperation or partnership or why leave it at some point. Here, too, there is often a period of falling in love and excitement, which can be radically different from the relationship further down the road. After the initial phase of infatuation, deep elements of friendship and caring will evolve, alongside a capacity to handle disappointment, anger, frustration and more, as an integral part of any long-term system.

Entering a partnership demands a personal, mental and emotional effort. We must invest resources and energies in merely creating and maintaining an interface. Difficulties emerge from an imbalance of power between the partners, conflicting and divergent interests, gaps in perceptions, interests, intentions and implementation and various difficulties in communication and personal relationships. Sometimes, after creating the connection, it is difficult to sever the ties even if the partner is no longer suitable or if the partnership is not functioning properly. This produces cumulative frustration. Our life experience is filled with the failures and sometimes traumas resulting from unsuccessful partnerships and poor relationships. What we conclude from these experiences will have strong implications on how we treat future cooperations. Alongside the wish to sustain partnerships, there are cynicism and apprehension of their inherent destructive potential.

Take a few moments to outline the partnerships and cooperations you have created throughout your life. Now honestly define how many of them were successful, partially successful or a complete failure. When I examined my own partnerships, I found that the number of failures exceeded the number of successes.

Collaboration requires adapting to a different way of thinking, both on a personal and a systemic level, which is not always familiar or accessible to us. Collaboration requires change, and as long as we stay in our comfort zone and do not pay any real price for its absence, there is no reason why we should act in that direction. In organizational processes we often see that strong managers who are deeply rooted in their territories, or who do not pay a price for the absence of collaboration, find it difficult to get involved in the organizational change processes that are required in the shift to organizational culture and a collaborative structure. On a personal level, self-awareness and in-depth work are required in managing one's ego.

Another risk in partnerships is the natural and human tendency to shed personal responsibility. Studies that examined the practice of rope-pulling demonstrated that a person pulling the rope alone will invest 100 percent of his power, whereas two people pulling together will each invest only 91 percent. When six people pull the rope together, each of them invests only 78 percent of his ability. A person feels greater responsibility for the outcome of a situation when he is operating on his own. This is called the Bystander Effect. It is very common that after divorce, some fathers become more involved in their children's lives and invest more in creating meaningful quality time with them. They are less likely to be bystanders. When a task is shared within an organization by several units, the need to come up with a solution and the responsibility for its implementation may diminish, when compared with setting individual goals for each unit.

When we wish to create or improve partnerships, we must seriously consider aspects that are perceived as negative. While we may enter the process with a positive attitude, with adequate experience and with true intentions to build an effective relationship, it is possible that in our environment there are others with a different and, at times, even opposite approach. One may find himself sitting in the same boat with people who have had different experiences with sailing, some of them amazing and others traumatic, and all possible degrees between the extremities. The basic frame of reference between people fluctuates. There is much value in how we state our intentions, but response lies in deeds, precise planning and systematic and structured perception for creating and managing collaboration. The concept of implementation presented below helps to maintain order on the boat and in the relationships between the boats, recognizing gaps and objections alongside motives and opportunities.

The new paradigm for collaboration management

The new era has created the need for a new paradigm in relation to partnerships and interfaces. It is no longer possible to continue treating it as a matter of "take it or leave it", as it becomes increasingly central and important. We tend to establish cooperations mainly on interpersonal connections. When connections exist, collaboration will materialize; however, when they do not exist, the level of collaboration will be mediocre at best. Sometimes, however, an interface between units or organizations is required, even in the absence of relationships, or when the relationship is impaired. It is no longer an option to base oneself merely on friendship, familiarity or a shared language in such complex arenas, with the inherent differences existing between organizations, disciplines and cultures.

There are many different factors identified as the "decisive element" in the success or failure of collaboration – each one based on personal perceptions and experience. Some speak of approach, a shared understanding of value, relationships, trust, definition of goals and more – without having objective parameters that help partners accurately understand the gaps, barriers and leverages of change. In addition, in light of the pace of change and the importance of fast response, it is no longer possible to operate on the basis of prolonged slow processes. Effective cooperations require adopting an organizing model and a shared language rather than relying on the personal capabilities and goodwill of leaders.

Researchers have still not reached a consensus regarding a definition of the term "collaboration"; in fact, there are many. Wood and Gray (1991) created a basis for a definition which integrates many different ones and was phrased by Thomson, Perry & Miller (2009: 3):

> Collaboration is a process in which autonomous or semi-autonomous actors interact through formal and informal negotiation, jointly creating rules and structures governing their relationships and ways to or decide on the issues that brought them together; it is a process involving shared norms and mutually beneficial interactions.

The outcome of the paradigm according to which we have conducted ourselves up to now, and from what we have learned in our accumulated experience, is that most cooperations and partnerships are characterized by a waste of resources, a tendency to cling to legal and rigid formal mechanisms, slow moving processes, an absence of shared language, conflicts and escalations, as well as imposing fast solutions without any systematic structuring and link to organizational culture – something that ultimately leads to frustration and despondency at a personal level too. When a relationship fails, we often blame the other. It is clear that in such cases, no process of inquiry, learning or improvement will occur; thus, we will find ourselves repeatedly making the same mistakes in the collaboration space.

The new paradigm hereby presented offers a structured and systematic conception of collaboration. The paradigm suggests that we study this phenomenon from a professional, systematic, methodological, disciplinary mode and not just as a random and interpersonal issue. Only through disciplinary thinking and a structured work model can precise, effective and rapid processes be produced to create and empower collaborations and cooperations. The new paradigm includes a number of key principles:

1. Collaboration management – taking full responsibility for collaboration management, under the assumption that success depends on us and not on any other factor. It is a common misconception to think that we are not in control. When a relationship fails, the culprit is the other, not us. In cases of mediocre collaboration, we accustom ourselves rather than make an effort to change. Most of us are managed in collaboration but do not manage it. However, the new paradigm entails full accountability in all aspects.
2. High velocity value – cooperations and collaborations shouldn't and mustn't be built and managed in a complex, long and "heavy" manner.

We are compelled to create focused, accurate and fast processes. It is necessary to maintain an agile approach in the frame of these processes and connections. The more methodological and regulated the processes are, the more time, resources, misunderstandings, escalations and conflicts will be saved, allowing us to deal with unexpected changes and challenges. The key is simplicity.

3. Shared and unified, measurable and clear language – anything that can be measured becomes clearer and more tangible. A shared language enables a higher level of understanding and collaboration. When the path is linked to the organizational goals and products, collaboration is characterized by clarity and explicit value. When the collaboration language and its practical applications are well rooted among managers and in shared spaces, more accurate and effective processes are realized.

4. Transition from ego-system to eco-system – an integrated systemic perception, inseparable and differentiated, managed on the basis of interests and needs, creating value and relevance, disconnected from a personal and organizational ego. This principle is directly related to accountability and also directly pertains to collaborative leadership and organizational culture. Easier said than done.

Chapter 3

Collaboration blockades
Managers' blind spots

We build too many walls and not enough bridges.

Isaac Newton

The world is advancing at a rapid pace in understanding the need for partnerships, and managers today recognize its importance and define it as a necessity. Why, then, are we still surrounded by so many mediocre partnerships that dissolve into nothing, as well as situations of conflict and destruction of interfaces? Studies and fieldwork on this issue have identified ten central factors. They are defined as barriers, hurdles, challenges and blind spots for managers and leaders.

Morten Hansen (2009) explains that in most cases, when cooperations are not sufficiently realized, managers take up different directions and solutions which are usually not very helpful. According to his perception and based on his studies, they do not accurately identify the barriers and failures; therefore, their responses and solutions are far from being accurate and effective. For example, an organization will invest in a more sophisticated and expensive information technology array when there is no information transfer between units, whereas the problem is not in the information but rather in prioritizing transfer of information and the willingness of the units to share it from the outset. Hence, the solution provided is often irrelevant and ineffective.

Good effective collaboration does not happen by itself. There are too many risks and obstacles that will almost certainly prevent full realization of its potential. Our action matrices, basic instincts, codes and social patterns, prevailing competitiveness, frequent interpersonal failures and more, will lurk at us and

DOI: 10.4324/9781003514992-3

our partners around every corner. Senior managers fall into collaboration traps because they are often covert, below the surface and misunderstood. Managers stumble there not for a lack of experience or wisdom but because they do not have a professional and structured framework for diagnosing barriers and failures. A precise analysis of the challenges and actual factors disrupting cooperations is a necessary condition for selecting the right solutions.

As we are often unaware of our part and responsibility for failures in partnerships, we cannot know how to accurately identify the barriers and challenges. This is the reason why the barriers presented here are also defined as the "blind spots" of managers. The importance of understanding barriers and challenges is critical for improving and building effective interfaces. Most challenges are related, directly or indirectly, to leadership and organizational culture. There are definitely similar and overlapping areas among them. Distinction between them is mainly intended to develop awareness and establish a shared language and accurate identification.

The accountability challenge

Two leading Israeli organizations, operating in an area of utmost public importance, have been engaged for many years in conflict and mutual hostilities, including our-right clashes, exacerbated by the media. After one of the more severe crises, the CEOs decided to take pause and examine the situation, in an attempt to lead it in the desired direction. In a preliminary process, which included personal meetings with about a dozen senior managers from both organizations, it was repeatedly said: "We are in favor of partnerships! The problem lies with them! Look at what this person did, and how that man is operating. Just look how well we cooperate with this third party. Ask them." Unsurprisingly, the same argument was made by both managements: the other party is responsible for the situation. On the eve of entering the joint process, I decided to take the initiative and made a call to the third party's CEO. He answered my question about his organization's cooperation with each of the two organizations in a very simple way, after making sure things would remain between us: "Neither of them know how to cooperate. Don't let them fool you."

This phenomenon is repeated in almost every organization. Frequently we do not really take responsibility for the relationships in our lives and are hardly aware of our part when they fail. Therefore, it is worthwhile to examine ourselves in our relationships, within various contexts. Can divorced men and women admit to their responsibility for the failure of their marriage, or do they tend to accuse their spouse? Do claimants and defendants admit that they chose the conflict, or will they remain convinced that the other party dragged them into legal action? Take a moment to ask yourself: in your last failed partnership, in whatever field it may have been, was it you who was mainly responsible, or was it the other party?

Most of the time we tell ourselves a story. In social psychology this story is explained and defined as "attribution bias". Behavior is the result of connection between two general basic variables: our personality (culture, age, gender, background, perceptions and behavioral patterns etc.) and the situation (place, time, constraints, environmental factors, tasks, participants present etc.). Personality + situation = behavior. This equation is not only very simplistic and general but also very accurate.

When we seek to examine a situation in which we have acted in a way that is perceived as negative, our explanation will usually be situation focused rather than personality focused: "I was late because of unexpected traffic"; "I had to raise my voice at you during the meeting, because there was very little time left and we had to reach a decision." However, when we examine a negatively perceived behavior by the other, our explanation will usually be personality focused rather than situation focused: "You're late because you don't really care"; "You are aggressive towards me, regardless of what's happening in the meetings." Note that we constantly do this to others, just as they constantly do this to us.

Our judgments do not allow us to see reality as it is and, at the same time, block our ability to conduct an effective dialogue and create understanding and consent. This is one of the most devastating factors impacting relationships, even with those closest to us. This is how we justify almost every aspect of our behavior, while we fail to see the other side, unable to take the required responsibility for relationships and even for inter-organizational systemic cooperations. We pass judgments on organizations, cultures and disciplines that are different from ours. It is very common to hear claims adversely affecting collaboration between units from the same organization, including offensive statements about certain people and about the nature of the unit ("unprofessional", "detached from the field", "driven by their ego" etc.). This behavior has other roots, naturally, which are firmly planted in the cultural characteristics instilled in us, as well as in our upbringing. Have we been taught to address this issue in our educational system or in our undergraduate and graduate business administration studies? "Attribution bias" can certainly be learned, managed and reduced.

The way we act in our lives, as free human beings, does not always align with our roles as managers and our responsibilities as leaders, where it is essential that we become aware of the consequences of our "attribution bias" within broken relationships. A few years ago, two VPs working in a company in the defense industry revealed to me that their CEO was tired of the conflicts and lack of cooperation between them. During the meetings I held with them separately, the two expressed their belief that they did not have to maintain a good relationship, or any relationship at all, and that their personal relations do not adversely affect the work processes and interfaces of the divisions under their supervision. Obviously this statement is false and detached from reality, as illustrated by the African proverb: "When the elephants fight, the grass suffers." In fact, relationships between managers have a far-reaching impact on processes within the organization and its relations with its surroundings; leadership has a direct impact on collaboration within the system and outside it. The fact that some managers fall under the accountability barrier and choose not to recognize or acknowledge it does not mean that it does not exist.

"Consciousness of mediocrity" is another frequent phenomenon within the framework of the accountability barrier. Many managers make statements such as: "cooperation with them doesn't work; however, we have learned to live with it." Sometimes such a statement is accompanied by familiar expressions, such as: "The enemy of the good is the very good" or "If it's not broken, don't fix it." We accept partnerships and relationships of mediocre quality that produce value which is lower than the potential inherent in them and reconcile with multiplicity of escalations as if decreed from heaven, saying that "it is what it is".

The myriad of phenomena and patterns described above reflect a lack of full responsibility and accountability by managers and leaders. It is amazing to see how commonplace, legitimate and familiar they are to us, recurring on a daily basis.

The bureaucracy and organizational structure challenge – separate silos

In the split structure of organizations, in our perceptions of objectives and work plans, as well as in our bureaucratic systems, there is hardly anything that truly attracts collaboration. The most suitable illustration of the concept of modern management is a series of silos. None of us has ever been in one, but in the organizational arena, most of us have grown up and may still be inside such silos. Employees are bunched together into teams, which are gathered into departments, departments into wings and wings into organizations, which are assembled into sectors. It is only natural, then, that a conception of differentiation and separation is established.

The top inlet of each silo represents objectives and means available to managers, while the bottom outlet, the products. This is how organizations have been operating ever since the Industrial Revolution and firmly backed up by the concept of functionalism emerging at the turn of the twentieth century. The silo represents features such as professionalism, uniqueness, order and the clarity of knowledge held by employees and managers regarding questions of definition and belonging. This is human nature. The silo simultaneously enables and blocks thought and action.

There are no windows or passages between silos. During a process carried out in an organization dealing with the shaky cooperations that existed there, a VP commented: "Everyone performs his role within his own kingdom, handling things just fine, so there is no reason to work together. If we all do our best in our own roles, nothing more is required." When considering the common perception, that every manager handles his tasks and resources with no interest, time or availability to deal with whatever takes place in other units, he is absolutely right. He prefers that no one intervene in his affairs. His words can be construed in light of the manner in which organizations have always operated, assuming that "what was, will be".

However, that manager is obviously wrong when it comes to changes taking place in the present and the forthcoming future. The complexity characterizing the new era requires cooperations. Organizations are changing in form, their interdependence increases and some are gradually shifting toward network or flat structures. Many projects and processes require matrices and high connectivity between the various units. Senior managers are required to maintain cross-organizational accountability, beyond the sole and separate responsibility for their silo. It doesn't matter if we define it as a "traditional", "classic" or "modern" management concept – it is important to realize that it is no longer relevant.

We must remember that the changes are relatively new and that the familiar organizational model is deeply ingrained. In the early twentieth century, Max Weber defined this structure as a premedial and bureaucratic structure, characterized by centralization and definitions of powers and procedures. The characteristics described below still exist in many organizations to this day, making it difficult for systems to implement effective collaboration:

A. The splitting phenomenon – duplication and splitting of authorities between multiple entities. This is highly prevalent in the public sector but is not limited to it. A clear example of this phenomenon is the two programs aimed at prevention of violence and crime that were operating simultaneously for years – "City without Crime" and "Community and Crime Prevention Division". Both began at about the same time, in 1999 and 2000, and both operated under the Ministry of Public Security. In order to minimize duplications, local authorities divided the two programs between themselves. It took about twenty years for these two entities to be merged into one. That is two decades of wasted resources and sub-optimal effectiveness.

B. Organizational closure phenomenon – the organization maintains boundaries and structure, thus ensuring identity and stability. This is done by means of rigid procedures, standardization and bureaucracy, in order to minimize external influences, among other things. Subsequently, walls are created, making it difficult for the organization to adapt to the changing reality.

In a major organization in the Israeli Intelligence Community, upon taking office the new CEO instructed his managers to "raise the walls". The direct and operative meaning was to avoid, as much as possible, transferring information to other parallel organizations with which cooperation was necessary. As a result, this organization itself was largely excluded from information and processes that might have enhanced its relevance. Many of the managers shared their relief when a new CEO was brought in and completely overturned the directive, sending a clear statement to lower the walls and strengthen mutual transfer of information with other organizations. The former CEO sincerely believed that the delineation of knowledge would serve the organization, and up until his last day in office, he failed to comprehend that the world around him is rapidly changing and that his actions are causing harm to the organization and to its relevance.

C. Conflict of interests – these are caused when each entity operates to achieve its own goals without systemic vision. In most organizations, this phenomenon lies in setting completely different goals for each unit and, on this basis, generating separate work plans, thus consequently creating different interests.

A global industrial conglomerate, comprising dozens of different organizations, operated ten separate research and development units for years. Each unit was located in a different area and engaged in different activities, completely disconnected from the other R&D units. A new CEO who took over the position defined R&D as the organization's main growth lever for the upcoming years. He instructed the array to cooperate on six key developments that would serve the entire organization. Six integrated teams were created according to defined issues; however, for over a year, the teams made no progress in their work processes. Beyond barriers of trust and intercultural encounters, it was an organizational culture of separate territories that was detrimental to the process. For many years, every R&D unit had worked as a separate "island", and a managerial decision or new strategy, enlightened as it may have been, was unsuccessful in generating the desired change in work processes.

Even if people have a tendency to cooperate, they do not do so in a vacuum. When faced with modern management styles, which today can already be defined as traditional and outdated, they meet many managers who consciously and unconsciously place barriers preventing people from cooperating resulting from the same old organizational perceptions. These managers tend to sanctify precise definitions of separate responsibilities while maintaining strong, even if covert, control mechanisms. They strongly believe that clearly defined responsibilities are beneficial for the organization. Defined goals and indices are submitted to each manager every quarter. They are responsible for the outcomes of their work and are given incentives to encourage them to meet their goals: bonuses, pay raises, options and promotions. All of these are given to whoever successfully performs what is set out for him in his own territory.

This is the all-too-familiar organizational essence: a decentralized system with clear definitions of responsibility, authority and reward for performances. An effective system as such produces great value up to a certain point. The problem is that according to his job description, each manager becomes independent and strives to maximize his unit. Realizing his own goals is important to him, whereas his interest in helping others to achieve their goals is minimal at best. This is how the separate silos are strengthened, with scarcely any connection between them. The barrier lies in the old managerial perception and the organizational culture that supports it and is parallelly affected by it.

The phenomenon defined in sociology as "Ingroup – Outgroup" is very common in organizations. It means that organizational units tend to perceive themselves in a relatively more positive light than others and parallelly develop more negative attitudes toward other groups. It exists both within and between organizations, as well as within and between communities, empowering competitiveness and sometimes even struggles and aggressiveness. It is difficult to expect employees and managers, operating within a competitive arena, to work well with whoever is outside their unit, without clear directives and supportive work processes. Organizations that encourage internal competition between units, believing that it will lead to the best products and motivation for success, will not allow proper internal cooperations; it is a mistake to expect and direct toward this goal as long as no substantial change in perception is made.

Organizational hierarchy is a feature of this barrier too. Researchers in the organizational field recognize that hierarchy does not encourage collaboration. In a hierarchical structure, competition between units leads to greater suspicion of managerial decisions – especially those decisions that are perceived as beneficial to other units. This strengthens the element of competitiveness (Grant, 1996).

A strong hierarchy, especially in global organizations with dominant central headquarters, creates opposition to cooperations, primarily because the units themselves perceive it as a guideline that does not meet their needs but rather those of headquarters' only. Resistance stems from the fact it was imposed from above and was not carried out in a cooperative way.

Nevertheless, hierarchy can also promote collaboration when the person positioned at the head of the pyramid makes it clear that collaborations constitute his central directive and that he expects his managers to act accordingly. In strong hierarchical organizations, the CEO dictates the direction and the organization complies and acts in accordance. Often, the direction is to strengthen the work of interfaces and collaboration.

The competitiveness challenge

"Never play cat and mouse when you are the mouse." This quote was uttered by a manager during a discussion about work interfaces between his organization and other organizations. He mentioned it while explaining how he perceives the concept of "Win–Win". What does this statement actually mean? "When I need you or when I am weaker than you, let's cooperate, but when I am stronger than you, I have no use for you." This perception reflects short-term vision of relationships and understanding their sphere through a prism of power relations and competitiveness.

For many, there exists a deep and tangible gap between the slogans and statements of win–win and the capacity to fully comprehend the meaning of the concept and assimilate it in personal conduct and organizational culture. We tend to operate in the format of win–lose, even if it seems that theoretically we believe otherwise. One will maximize his profit and achievement by means of stopping or reducing the profit and achievement of the other. This is the concept of "either you or I".

Being conscious of our basic patterns and modes of operation is a prerequisite if we wish to put a stop to the commonplace automaton and opt for a real win–win solution. The best definition is "Act. Don't React".

Why do we act this way? In his book *The Power of Positive No* written by William Ury and published in 2007, he defines humans as "Reaction Machines". He describes the reaction trap, which causes us to react subconsciously within the range of fight-flight-freeze. This is our instinctive reaction, activated by the amygdala gland, which is responsible for our physical survival.

This ancient survival response appears in interpersonal situations too, which our system recognizes as situations characterized by a certain level of threat. When I receive an email containing an unpleasant remark, it is quite possible that I will respond instinctively, without applying my discretion. When I sit down with someone and during our conversation he accuses me of something, it is very likely that I will have a hard time listening to him. I will most likely interrupt him and return the blame, having no real control of the situation. If one of my partners performs an action that I consider to be unfair, it is very possible that I will react in a similar or perhaps even more extreme manner.

When we are reactive, we lose control, even if we feel otherwise. There are many examples, but if we are being honest with ourselves, we can see that we all experience both sides of the situation on a daily basis. It is then that we tell ourselves, an hour or perhaps a day later, that we should have and could have reacted differently, that we should have checked, asked and considered.

When faced with the reactive responses of others, we can usually see how they do not necessarily correspond with reality and are not the result of being in complete control. It is relatively easy for us to recognize this in others. In his book, Ury writes that as long as we are caught in the reaction trap, we are unable to cooperate, conduct intelligent negotiations or respond with a "Yes" or "No" in a conscious, accurate and proactive way.

We often justify the automatic operation mode by legitimizing a particular type of conduct, worldview or even managerial perception. The Hebrew proverb "Jealousy of writers breeds wisdom" is one of countless sayings meant to justify a competitive worldview. "We must maintain constant supremacy, and I want my people to hold a knife between their teeth. If we start talking and cooperating too much, our jaw muscles will weaken and the knife may fall," said the manager of a very mission-oriented organization. "Competition is healthy, it keeps us sharper and more precise" – these words were spoken by a manager from an organization that is competitive in its essence. This is a legitimate approach, but the key is in balances, in the ability to choose by understanding the changes that are taking place in human society and in the spheres in which we operate.

We live in a culture that advocates a competitive perception, in every aspect of our lives, beginning in early childhood. Our dichotomous outlook separates winners from losers. Israeli culture brings these perceptions to particularly impressive levels. There are those who would say that this has to do with our history, a nation formed out of a division into 12 tribes, and others would say that it derives from our struggle to survive, which has been our lot for thousands of years. It may also be explained in our indoctrination to the ethos of "don't be a sucker" and the influence of Israeli politics.

Ran Saar, CEO of Maccabi Health Services, one of the leading Israeli Health Maintenance Organizations (HMOs), speaks about the impact of the competitive culture and perception characterizing Israeli organizations:

> Collaboration begins with culture. As someone who has experienced Israeli culture, whether in the military or in civilian systems, we are not a nation that knows how to cooperate. We do not have a culture of cooperation. Between the tension of cooperation and competition, it is clear that we are much more competitive. We have fully adopted the culture of capitalism and achievement, foreshadowing our founding fathers. We compete with our neighbors,

ever-examining each other's grass to see who's is greener. It is deep and ingrained in Israeli culture. Competition is a positive thing. You can reach extraordinary achievements with the help of competition. I'm not speaking out against competition. It's easier to create a competitive corporate culture when you sit on the platform of a society driven by achievement. You hardly find cooperative organizational structures in Israel. Personally, I am a very competitive person. Even golf is a world war … I also managed to maximize the competition at very high levels in the organization. We reached an extreme place, and realized that change needed to be made.

To illustrate the competitive Israeli culture, let us consider the following question: what happens when a denim store is opened? In other parts of the world, it is most likely that a store selling matching belts, boots and hats will open on one side and a store selling plaid flannel shirts will be opened on the other. In Israel, it is more likely that two more denim stores will be opened on both sides. On the contrary, the only ball game in the world not played for the sake of winning was invented in Israel: the game of Kadima (matkot). So there is still a good chance to also produce a "matkot mentality" here.

It is important to clarify a key point: there is definitely room in our world for competitiveness and the concept of win–lose with all its applications. This is especially true when all other possibilities have been explored, and we conclude that this is the most appropriate approach in particular situations or interfaces, as well as in emergencies and situations devoid of choice. The central question is whether the move is done by volition or by course of action into which we are drawn without choice. This is a question of conscious awareness. The corresponding question is related to understanding the consequences of action in this context: Do we feel comfortable with the potential price of the competitive perception when it involves long-term relationships? Finally, we have to face the question of application: Do we have a range of capabilities that enable us to operate on any channel we select? When everyone starts asking these questions, our world will change.

It is also important to fully understand the concept of win–win, which means that in order to maximize my profits and achievements I will allow the other to maximize his own. This is not a form of submission. It does not necessarily encourage compromise but calls for other solutions, based on processes different from those familiar to us. It is connected to creativity and innovation, which emerge from an in-depth dialogue and mutual recognition of needs and interests.

As part of the rapid and profound change generated in human society, all these features that drive us to empower cooperations – networking, growing interdependence, frequent change and more – no longer allow us to cling to perceptions of competitiveness as we did in the past and act in these patterns, consciously or unconsciously. Even if we have a task-oriented DNA, and need to continue cultivating the "fighting spirit" outwardly, it does not contradict creating a collaborative organizational culture internally, as well as with other organizations. Leaders who are stuck in the competitive paradigm as a leading narrative remain in the old world and thus diminish the relevance of their organization.

Leaders in the contemporary age are required to choose consciously and wisely. They must examine the potential value of each choice considering short-, medium- and long-term effects, in conjunction with costs and possible risks. They need to be aware of their biases, patterns and habits – personal, cultural and organizational – and repeatedly examine them as factors affecting decision-making processes. They must deeply examine what is the value of every choice they make – not only for themselves but also for their customers, employees, partners, shareholders as well as the public, the organization and the company.

It should be borne in mind that the competitiveness barrier exists alongside other barriers, in particular the modern management barrier. Yet, it stands on its own – both in matrixial and flat organizations, as well as in innovative organizational structures. Even when other barriers are almost non-existent, this barrier is still present in all its glory, carrying a decisive effect on the organizational culture.

The ego family challenge: arrogance, pride and "Not Invented Here"

When managers are asked what they think is the main barrier to cooperations, their immediate response is "ego". When asked if they are led by their egos, the answer is no.

We all have an ego – certainly anyone who chooses to manage and lead. We wish to lead and influence, and without our egos we would never have reached this position. It is therefore important to recognize the legitimacy of the ego. The key question is if we manage our ego or it manages us. The difference is subtle. Some managers are addicted to the sense of power and control, ever aspiring to increase them. We must ask ourselves, what sustains our ego and pride. In their "classic" form, ego and pride are sustained by one's success. They are founded on proof of strength, respect and power, on profits at the expense of others and on establishing status – sometimes by weakening others.

The term "post-pride" is gradually taking hold. The need for recognition and reputation in organizational life is well known, the "struggle for a logo" and the question "who gets credit for success?". Pride in its traditional sense seemingly has no legitimate place in Western cultures. However, in practice it is a disguised form of pride, affecting decision making and weakening collaboration.

The former President of the United States, Harry Truman, made a statement that is easy to identify with but hard to implement: "It is amazing what you can accomplish, if you do not care who gets the credit." People who concern themselves with receiving credit and respect often behave in an arrogant and obtuse manner. We should remember what it feels like to interact with people who are full of themselves, act arrogantly and have answers to everything. In general, these people are less attentive; thus, maintaining a dialogue with them is difficult. It is legitimate to have an ego; however, when it controls us, we must be aware that it is highly probable that it will harm our relationships and partnerships.

This barrier also includes an element that can be called the "sin of arrogance", also defined as "hubris" and the "sin of pride". In Greek mythology it was Antigone who thought she knew the will of the gods, Creon who decided on his own what was good for the gods and Icarus who did not listen to his father and flew too close to the sun with his wax-adhered wings, only to have them melt away. For all three, pride, arrogance and lack of humility brought on an unfortunate ending.

In the physical world, we are all "sinners" and not only due to explicit arrogance. We simply "know" things. A manager holds his position based on capabilities, experience, professionalism and mostly success. Managers are required to come up with answers to various issues and problems many times throughout the day. This habit affects the formation of the perception that a manager, or his organization, can provide answers and responses independently; therefore, it is unnecessary to exhaust energy in sharing and learning beyond the boundaries of the organization or unit. We assume that we alone can do the best, while collaboration is perceived as "weakness" and the "inability" of a person or organization to cope and perform things by themselves.

While in the mythology the arrogant is punished and must pay for his hubris, in reality he is often rewarded for it. Based on his success and the reinforcements he has received along his path, he will choose to continue operating with maximum self-sufficiency and minimum dependence. It makes sense, but it comes with a price tag. The assumption that we "know" generates mistakes, and beyond that, it makes us feel less comfortable in our interpersonal relationships.

The "knowledge bias" has a decisive effect on the obstacle defined as NIH ("Not Invented Here") – a term describing an organizational culture that clearly prefers not to make use of research or knowledge created outside the organization's boundaries. Such conduct often entails a heavy price. A significant portion of the report analyzing the 9/11 terrorist attack focuses on this issue. In retrospect, it was found that all the information was in the hands of the intelligence agencies which operated in the United States during those years and that the attack could have been prevented if the information had been shared between the agencies. The Commission of Inquiry described the interface between the agencies in a pictorial way: "The agencies are similar to a group of hospital specialists, where each of them orders tests, looks for symptoms, prescribes medications. What is missing here is a doctor who verifies that the specialists work as a team." In-depth analysis shows that organizational culture in the intelligence community was characterized by an overall sense, apparent in every individual entity, that it was good enough to perform its tasks by itself and that cooperating with other entities was, therefore, unnecessary.

The 9/11 Commission report reveals an interesting comparison between the Cold War period, when each intelligence and security entity operated separately and independently on different goals and objectives, and the complex situation that emerged in 2001, certainly with regard to dealing with the threats of Islamic terrorism:

> The agencies' culture, living by the notion that information collected by them is their sole property, must be replaced by a culture where agencies will have a sense of commitment and a duty to make this information accessible to others.

The NIH organizational culture was defined as a key factor that facilitated the execution of the 9/11 attacks. The organizations and people involved had no interest or desire to step outside the boundaries of their units, share, learn and receive assistance from others. This affects not only information transfer but also the willingness to see others and make any effort on their behalf.

Studies conducted over the years have conclusively shown that managers, more than their employees, are reluctant to learn from others or help them. They see their problems as unique and different. They usually prefer not to be involved in learning from others, transferring technologies, cooperating on a new product or a proposal to a customer, even when the situation is favorable.

The NIH barrier is directly linked to the ego family, as well as to other barriers previously mentioned, including competitive culture and the traditional silo structure. Understanding the NIH barrier is extremely essential for generating changes in the desired direction. This is an elusive phenomenon, precisely because it is perceived as natural, and therefore, we will delve a little deeper into the causes of its creation:

1. The island culture – communication takes place mainly within the unit and the relevant group and less so in wider circles. People who work together easily develop a culture of an island, isolated from others.

They promote their perceptions and beliefs while rejecting other perceptions. The more cohesive the group, the more closed it is to external influences. There is a tendency to look for solutions from within – rather than learn and share.

2. Status gap – many people feel uncomfortable crossing status lines. Those who perceive themselves as more veteran, knowledgeable, successful and more will not be inclined to consult or cooperate with others who they consider to be less worthy. People of lower status will also prefer not to enable sharing and learning, for fear of feeling unease by the gap. For example, in high-tech companies a difficulty frequently arises in the interface between development units and quality assurance units, since the former is considered to be higher in status than the latter. Operational units are considered to be of higher status than supporting units, and medical personnel hold a higher status than nursing staff, to name just a few.

3. Self-reliance – as managers, most of us prefer to rely on ourselves more than on others. The fundamental and natural concept is that everyone must settle their own affairs, and therefore, some are less inclined to share with and learn from others, even within the same organization. Some of us also instill the concept of self-reliance in our employees, making statements such as "you have to fix your problems by yourself." If this is the norm, people will prefer to avoid being helped by others, thinking: "I'm not sure that I'm better than others, but I have to cope by myself and refrain from asking for help." Some say that this approach is more prevalent among male managers.

4. Exposure – a sense of apprehension and reluctance to reveal problems, difficulties and limitations. Turning to someone from a different unit and confessing that "we cannot really manage and we need help in this matter" may be perceived as a failure. People are apprehensive to expose their weaknesses, especially to experts from other units. When asking for help, people are more vulnerable and susceptible to the judgments of others. As a result, many prefer to avoid seeking help or will only turn to those who they truly trust, even if that person is not an expert on that matter.

The "Keep It Here" (KIH) barrier is similar to NIH, with emphasis on non-sharing of information. The total opposition to information sharing is clearly evident in a message conveyed by the former Federal Bureau of Investigation's (FBI) Assistant Director, Thomas Pickard, to the organization managers at the time preceding the 9/11 attack: "Too much sharing of information with the outside world may result in career obstacles." The norm at that time was that each entity had to fend for itself, and therefore, no approach was made to other intelligence agencies for assistance.

Some people deliberately refrain from cooperating with others. They do not offer help, do not share any information they may have and will not invest any time or effort in it. Sometimes they will refrain from giving anything, although they will not declare as such. Sometimes they may give a little and hold back a little. Some may agree to cooperate regarding a given matter but in practice drag their feet. They can offer significant help to others but choose not to do so. Beyond criticizing the KIH barrier, it is important that we understand its causes, which are all very natural:

1. Priorities – we are too busy and burdened. At any given moment, we are required to prioritize between tasks. The prevailing feeling is that there is no time to help others. Every request for help seems like a burden that pulls us away from meeting our own goals. Sometimes a simple trade-off takes place: should I perform my tasks, or help others and delay mine?
2. Loss of power – people fear that sharing their knowledge, information and wisdom with others will render them less powerful. It is therefore clear that in such situations, they will refrain from helping, choosing to hoard the relevant knowledge at their disposal.
3. Narrow motives – when people are rewarded only for their best performance, they will focus only on that. We tend to focus more on our goals and less on assisting others. Most organizations still operate by focusing on goals and rewards for their achievements.

The emotional challenge

Every manager, at one time or another, experienced the fear of losing control and becoming dependent on others; having to rely on employees and customers is quite enough. This barrier must be addressed in its full gravity, because it is directly related to a phenomenon known as "loss aversion". Sometimes people avoid entering partnerships for fear of what will subsequently happen and of what they might lose versus what they may possibly gain. The agony in losing 1,000 dollars far supersedes the pleasure derived from gaining 1,000 dollars.

The fear barrier is a key issue, especially in organizations or among position holders who feel "they have something to lose". They prefer to remain in their existing position rather than enter partnerships that may adversely affect them in the future, even if there is a chance of gaining more from this course of action. The mere thought that someone else is now in charge and their actions might cause me harm scares us a lot, keeping us in a seemingly "safe" state, a status quo whereby we know our situation and avoid any possible loss.

Most managers successfully cope with their sphere of responsibility. But there is fear – tangible and conscious or covert – related to people and entities that are not under our direct control or influence as managers. This is especially intensified in the modern organizational culture of the silos, where each unit is expected to deliver predetermined products. Those who experience a dependency on others, especially in matrixial structures, often feel great frustration resulting from the difficulty to complete their tasks while relying on others who they cannot manage.

Cooperation with any person or entity generates a full set of commitments and constraints, of which we are exempt when we act alone as individuals, as units and as organizations. In such situations we must be considerate, accountable, exposed to harm, relinquish control and develop dependency. Given the opportunity, we would not choose any element from this list. There has to be a very good reason for anyone to get into it.

Another fear that arises in these situations is the fear of change inherent in leaving our comfort zone. The possibility of change occurring in our status and power of influence, once we share it with others, will most likely cause distress. There is also a natural fear of losing assets and relevance. Sharing knowledge and abilities with another entity may render the one sharing redundant, if the other entity learns to operate independently. Fear of an unprofitable investment carries great weight for those pressed for time. Every collaborative effort involves risk, and no assurances are given that any investment of resources, time, money and people shall be recovered. When negative experiences accumulate, the belief that partnerships are mostly time-consuming and unjustified becomes all the more justified.

Fear is intensified in organizations where the organizational culture itself is unforgiving to errors and mistakes. In such places, in order to avoid mistakes and their consequences, managers will conduct themselves in the safest and most secure manner. One way is to trust only ourselves and perform whatever is required of us on our own. This is one of the factors that curb cooperations even within organizations. The wish to avoid exposing problems and difficulties creates a situation, whereby turning to another person in the organization for the purpose of learning, following lack of success, may in itself be perceived as failure.

Another phenomenon amplifying the barriers of fear and competitiveness, which has become increasingly prevalent in recent years, is that of "judicialization". Legal language is, by nature, competitive and belligerent. Lawyers are educated and calibrated for defense and victory and instill confidence in people operating in spaces where they may be harmed. Legal contracts are drafted in a negative form: indicating points of no liability, what will happen if so and so, which court will discuss the matter and more. Jurists perceive themselves as defenders, formulating matters so that they may be resolved when the relationship encounters disagreement. There is a place for legal agreements in building partnerships and cooperations, but it cannot be the core.

For the head of the construction division of a large high-tech company, "the penny dropped", as he defined it.

> All the construction projects we performed over the years ended up in court. Some of them involved very long trials. Whether we won or lost in court, we always lost. I analyzed the processes, and suddenly realized that it was because of our use of legal language, and because those who led the way in the field were the legal advisers of both parties. I decided to roll back the role of our legal adviser to a consultant rather than a leader, and in the future I will be the one making decisions. In our next project we will plan an integrated work team with the construction company, creating a partnership and mutual trust.

The path the head of the construction division aimed toward began with combining the teams from his company and the performing contractor into a joint team on the foundations of in-depth discussions of fears. A built-in model of non-judicial mediation was assimilated into the work process, alongside personal guidance for certain managers who were identified as more challenged in the collaborative aspect. About a year after the project had ended successfully and without any conflict requiring legal action, the head of the construction division said he hoped that the same contracting company would win the next tender. His choice to lead a process in which only a limited space was given to the legal aspect, comprehending the impact of the legal perception on decision making and cooperations, is a brave decision. This move reflects his willingness to take responsibility, manage risks arising in the process differently and deal with his natural fears in a novel way – without the stewardship of legal gatekeepers.

Successful cooperation depends, to a large extent, on the degree of strength, confidence and maturity of each of the partners. The more such elements are present, the greater the chances of achieving long-term success. Another stipulation is the ability to address things as they are, being fully aware of fears and other emotional aspects and a willingness to cooperate with the other party. This builds mutual understanding and trust, precisely because it produces potential vulnerability. It will refine the process and release tensions and interpretations; when left unspoken, their presence only intensifies.

Cross-cultural challenge

When cultural gaps emerge, everything becomes more complex: language, perception, manner of expression and listening, thought, comprehension, interpretations and patterns. This barrier addresses both disparities between different ethnic cultures and the differences between various organizational cultures. David Bohm (2018) defines organizational culture as an ensemble of symbols, values, norms, beliefs or ideologies, creating common meaning and understanding among members in the organization.

Statistics show that the success rates of international business mergers are quite grim. The main explanation for this phenomenon is the difficulty in merging cultures. Everyone operating in the global arena is well aware of this, and much energy is directed at addressing these gaps. International companies strive to create an effective multicultural dialogue. When a meeting is held with a person who speaks a different language, representing another culture or country, we are well aware of the cultural gap and are attentive to these disparities and to the need for accurate and clear communication. This is tangible and obvious. When are we less aware?

The difficulty lies in the phenomenon defined as the "proximity trap". When people belong to the same organization or community and share a certain degree of homogeneity in their background, they become insensitive to deeper differences. Once we are unaware of differences, whether due to lack of consciousness or because of the "proximity trap", we tend to assume the existence of a common understanding, a similar perception and a shared view of reality. In practice, however, this is not the case. Within the organizations themselves there are essential differences in the worldviews of people from various units: marketing, sales, manufacturing, supply, quality control, finances, human resources and more. People operating in each field view the world from a completely different angle, creating a point of potential clash between professional values and cultures. Variability can be found between units operating in the same professional arena resulting from different organizational cultures created over the years. The most painful conflicts take place inhouse. It surprises us that others perceive matters in a manner different from us.

Geert Hofstede, a leading name in cultural studies, defined culture as a collection of qualities distinguishing members of one human group from another. Following a survey he conducted among workers, he formulated four dimensions distinguishing between cultures: power distance index – PDI; uncertainty avoidance; individualism and collectivism; masculinity versus femininity. Each bears a great influence on intercultural diversity within and between organizations. For example, in the individual versus the collective axis, we may find one department that emphasizes achievements of the individual versus a department that emphasizes its teamwork. Due to the fact that collaborative organizational culture is affected mostly by the significance given to hierarchy and authority, focus will be placed on this dimension.

"To what extent will you be willing to express an opinion that is different from that of your direct manager, during a meeting with other people in attendance?" Hofstede's study posed this simple and brilliant question to employees and managers in 84 IBM organizations around the world, creating the "Power Distance Index" PDI (Hofstede, 1984).

In cultures characterized by low PDI, hierarchy and authority take up less space. Similarly, dialogue between different ranks in the organization is more simple and accessible. However, in cultures characterized by high PDI, behaviors emphasizing power and hierarchy gaps are to be expected, to an extent that often no room is left for direct interpersonal communication between various class members. This phenomenon is called "Mitigation" – a softened message. This term refers to an attempt to reduce the importance of a message or sweeten its delivery. It is the kind of tone we use when we try to be polite or when we are ashamed or embarrassed. This occurs while interacting with authority figures within a cultural framework in which authority is highly valued. In such cases, softened speech is natural and appropriate, though it may entail a dangerous impact on decision-making processes.

In Russian culture, as well as in Arab and Eastern cultures, the PDI is very high. In the United States, it is moderate, mostly depending on location: city versus small town, north versus south. In the Scandinavian countries, this index is very low, and in the rest of Europe it fluctuates but is mainly moderate in its degree. Israeli culture is characterized by a very low PDI.

The most tangible examples of the impact of high PDI and mitigation can be found in the field of air-traffic accidents. For nearly a decade, an increasing number of accidents occurred at "Korean Air". Hundreds of people lost their lives due to high PDI, as part of the mentality deeply ingrained in Korean tradition and their organizational culture. The aircraft's condition and the pilots' skills did not cause the accidents; it was miscommunication within the cockpit that was the cause. In some situations, soft speech is more appropriate and adequate, whereas in others, such as on a stormy night in the cockpit, it may become problematic. The first officer did not tell the captain directly that they made an error in altitude and direction and that swift action must be taken but rather used implicit speech: "I hope we are at the right altitude and direction." In this case, the consequences of the high PDI were fatal. The situation was so catastrophic that the company was boycotted in 1999 by many entities worldwide. However, since that year, following a profound change in the organizational culture, Korean Air has been considered one of the safest companies in the world (Gladwell, 2008).

The worst plane crash in history occurred on March 27, 1977, in the island of Tenerife. A cluster of circumstances and a sequence of errors caused the accident; however, the high PDI, which characterized the crew in KLM's cockpit, was the most significant and crucial culprit of all. Various factors, especially heavy fog, caused an hour's delay in takeoff. The captain, Waldhausen van Zanten, was one of the most experienced and valued pilots of the company, with 11,700 hours of flight experience, as well as serving as a pilots' trainer for the company's 474 aircrafts. Anyone familiar with relationships between people of unequal status within a hierarchy can easily imagine the situation created in those moments in the KLM cockpit.

The prolonged delay made the captain impatient. He knew that it would not take long before passengers would have to get off the plane and take a break in the terminal. Regulations limiting staff working hours added to his tension too. The Captain was very familiar with the small field, now completely shrouded in fog. Since he had already lost his patience with waiting, he decided to take off. When the first officer made it clear to him that permission to take off had not been authorized by the tower inspector, the captain replied, "Nee dat week ik, vraag maar" ("No, I know, ask for it"). In other words, the captain said he knew what he was doing and steered the Jumbo Jet plane on the runway – until he suddenly saw in front of him the Pan American plane crossing the track. That is what caused the deadliest air-traffic disaster of the twentieth century, killing 583 people. The crew sitting with the captain in the cockpit knew it was a critical mistake of discretion but did not stop him. Such an event could not have occurred in a situation where authority held less impact.

This phenomenon was also a major factor in the Columbia space shuttle disaster and the nuclear reactor catastrophe in Chernobyl. To what extent does it take place in everyday life in organizations? All the time. This is important in our case for two main reasons – the ability to influence and manage up and understanding the importance of the gap between various organizational cultures as a factor greatly impacting interfaces and partnerships. The authority curve is highly significant in decision-making processes and cooperations within and between organizations, both with regard to different national–ethnic cultures and relating to organizational culture. The relationship will be fundamentally affected by the difference between units or organizations. Mitigation has an impact on many aspects: expressing different perceptions and opinions, personal courage, tolerance for mistakes, capability of investigating and learning, discipline, relationships and more. It is interesting that many employees and managers are not aware at all that they are acting under any influence. It is important to identify these patterns in meetings between organizational cultures to narrow the cross-cultural barrier.

One of the most prominent phenomena in the collaborative space is that the higher the levels of authority and hierarchy, the lower the tendency to cooperate. In most cases field workers, middle managers and junior managers find it much easier to maintain cooperations with entities outside their unit and organization than with their supervising managers. This phenomenon may arise due to proximity to the task and realizing the value derived from joint work or being distanced from territorial political considerations taking place at the top. The higher the PDI is in these organizations, so will it seep downward too.

Profitability challenge – ROI

"Return on Investment (ROI)" is a very significant term for any organization. It is the core of existence in the business sector, since investment is supposed to create value or at least return itself. A business manager will do everything possible to evaluate the profitability of his investment in terms of manpower, equipment, training, marketing and advertising, transportation and more. This is the way collaboration spaces should operate. A manager is obliged to submit a report of unsuccessful investments. This is usually not the case in the third sector and certainly not in the public sector.

The meaning of this barrier is a possible failure to assess deficiency or excess in interfaces between organizations. For some reason we act in a relatively random manner in this arena, with no structured models, and thus, we may easily miscalculate assessments and make wrong decisions. We may forgo a particular connection, failing to correctly identify the bigger picture and future potential, or we may create a connection that is inadequate and may result in a waste of resources and even damage. In business, financiers know how to create accurate estimates of possible value in interfaces between organizations. Yet they, and others too, find it difficult to examine chances and risks associated with bringing people together. Risk specification of large projects does not include conflict costs between units and organizations, should the partnership fail to materialize to its maximum potential. Since this frequently occurs, we should bear in mind that such struggles involve high costs for the project and the organization.

Researcher Morten Hansen (Hansen, 2009) describes the trap of "over collaboration". Organizations invest a great deal of resources in creating connectivity between units and people in the organization, in internal networks, in meetings, on digital platforms, at joint events and more. This may be of great value but may also cause great harm. If the invested resources do not entail changes in outcomes, then they are futile. In a number of studies that Hansen conducted, it emerged that inner-organization interfaces sometimes impair outcomes in relation to separate work while requiring more resources and time. Excess does not necessarily help, and in this context, managers and leaders are also required to know how to say "no" to cooperations and partnerships in some situations.

Sometimes we invest in collaboration, possibly even creating a momentary elation in shared activity, but do not invest in assimilation and maintenance. The ongoing and the urgent eliminate the efforts, and people in the organization develop cynicism and opposition toward collaboration: "We have already tried everything, we went on a tractor trip together, we cooked together, we even talked about our problems. But nothing has happened since. A waste of time."

Managements do not always see tangible value in collaboration, as described by the Vice President of an Israeli large bank:

> Banks do not change. Only through technology. There is no real incentive for change. Management is interested in one thing only – the business outcomes. Only now do bankers begin to see and understand the connection between outcomes and the organizational culture of collaboration.

It is important to recognize that cooperations and collaborations, of all kinds, are not an end in itself but only a means to achieve goals. In this context, one can mention an atypical example in the Israeli cyber community sector. After a decade of struggles between various organizations working in the field, a deep perception began to emerge within the organizations, realizing that for the benefit of the country, organizational ego should be set aside, and competitiveness and struggles should be converted into collaborative work. Leaders of the cyber arena currently describe collaboration as a leading value and essential strategy and not just as a tactical means.

The communication and relationship challenge

> When you speak, you only repeat what you already know, when you listen, you may learn something new.
>
> **The Dalai Lama**

We are all challenged by relationships and interpersonal communication. We live in an intense and stressful reality, not in a monastery in the mountains of Tibet, and yet at the same time, we lack education in this sphere. A muscular system shaped for decision making, exercising authority, persuading others and being goal oriented is strongly manifested in whoever is attracted to management and has grown within it. When adding to the above habits the instinctive activity managed by the amygdala, our natural attribution bias and judgments, the aforementioned barriers, especially that of ego, accountability, competitiveness and a perception of the modern organization that glorifies hierarchy and fragmented organizational structures, we end up with an extremely formidable challenge. The dialogic, attentive and empathetic muscle system is weaker among most managers although extremely essential in building and empowering relationships. It is not taught in Business Administration schools despite the fact that an increasing number of organizations are investing in training focused on relationship management. This is a barrier that constitutes a challenge in all interfaces and partnerships, wherever they may occur.

In general, it can be said that managers are calibrated more toward knowledge and providing answers and less toward asking questions and listening. This generalization is validated in studies and in the life experience of many. Partnerships are led by managers, and when they are impatient toward the process and toward others, it will directly be reflected in the interfaces between units, between organizations and in the end products of the processes.

The key to synergy is acceptance and inclusion of diversity, understanding that there are other ways to view the world besides my way. Recognizing different perceptions and their legitimacy, free of judgment, facilitates the creation of a psychological and emotional space between partners. This is an essential space for performing work with full commitment and willingness to cope with shared and separate challenges.

The communication and relationships barrier poses a major challenge, which lies in the premise that "everything is personal." Managers tend to say: "When interpersonal relations work well, then everything is fine. When they do not work, then the interface squeaks and is often totally disrupted." Namely, unless managers keep proper relationships between them, cooperation is doomed to failure. That is why the model presented below defines the relationship element as responsible for a quarter of the totality necessary for creating and promoting effective cooperations. No matter how important, partnerships cannot be established on good relations alone.

In Martin Buber's teachings, and later in the Arbinger Institute books (Arbinger, 2016) as well as other publications, a distinction is made between the two basic conceptions also apparent in the discussion about collaborations – to what extent does a person think only of himself, and to what extent does he think of others including himself? The first concept refers to behavior driven by a perception that views others as a means to achieving my goals. Others may be meaningless or may interfere with my goals and thus must be removed. This concept, which produces an inward mindset, affects how we manage relationships. At the organizational level, this concept will create separations, a narrow viewpoint and defensive action.

The second concept, which is usually focused on an outward mindset, generates empathy toward others and consideration of what is important to them. I do not act only to materialize my own interests; on the contrary, I act in this manner because this concept motivates me. At the organizational level, this perception produces a wider view, openness and reciprocity that generates collaboration.

Most of us believe that we see others, but the problem is that in practice, we only see ourselves. This is caused by a lack of awareness and the story that we tell ourselves, which Arbinger refers to as "self-deception". The main question is which perception does the organization encourage and what characterizes its leaders and the organizational culture. This is the basis for many behaviors which affect the degree of competitiveness or collaboration. Another question is how much we invest in relationships versus organizational goals. Our resource quota is limited, our capacity for attentiveness beyond our tasks decreases and we tend to neglect issues that seem "irrelevant" to the task – like the subject of relationships. However, it is now increasingly obvious that the success of the organization depends on relationships within it and with its environment.

The "no worries" challenge

One of our most painful problems has a name, surname and family name – and that is the combination of the words 'It'll be okay'.

Yitzhak Rabin

Some time ago, a CEO of a large high-tech company called me for an urgent crisis intervention, and this is what he told me:

This is a mega-project, led by two excellent development teams. We are a year and a half into the project, and another such period is expected ahead. We are advancing towards a critical milestone in about a month and a half. As the current situation stands, there is no chance that we will meet the target date, and consequently, the project will be shut down by the U.S. management, and hundreds of workers in Israel will be out of a job.

At his request, I met with the top ten managers in a closed space for a continuous session that began early in the morning and ended late at night. All the standing issues were opened and closed. Finally, the managers met their planned task and continued to advance the project.

I bring this story here because of a statement made by one of the managers during the session. At an advanced stage of the process, he stopped the discussion, looked at his teammates and the other team's managers and said:

Tell me, are we insane? We entered into a mega-project, a challenge that neither we nor anyone in the world had coped with before, and we did not devote even one moment to this thing that we are now doing. We did not build trust and a relationship. We assumed that because we are all professional and committed to the task, it'll be okay. Only now, when we are already hemorrhaging, we are finally getting around to doing this.

The "It'll be okay" assumption is a space of blind spots and salient danger for any interface and cooperation. We assume that everyone is professional and committed and that almost everything will be solved on the move. Sometimes we are apprehensive to expose conflicting issues and reveal them during the early stages, preferring to maintain vagueness. Sometimes we are captivated by enthusiasm and novelty, skipping over what seems less relevant. Sometimes we know and trust the other party and do not feel the need to invest in the relationship or delve into issues, in the interface aspect. Sometimes we are focused on tasks and solutions, clearly defining the "what" and "how" but not the "why". In the absence of a professional point of view at the whole set of barriers, we are missing the map that may help us deal with them appropriately.

Here, too, an interesting analogy with relationships can be made. Should we ask a couple moments before their wedding if they see any risk in their shared future, their response will most likely be decisive: of course not. However, the rate of divorces and the percentage of unhappily married couples does not exactly validate this assumption. But still they assume "it'll be okay."

In psychology, this phenomenon is defined as the optimism bias – people tend to think that statistics are mistaken when it comes to them. Some examples are car accidents, death caused by smoking, unprotected sex, wars and more. Among many people this bias is associated with hubris. Thus, for example, former U.S. President Donald Trump said on February 27, 2020, referring to the danger of the Covid-19 spread: "We are absolutely prepared for it, for everything ... even if it involves a large-scale outbreak, our risk level is very low." Later, on May 20, he said that "Covid-19 is worse than the Pearl Harbor attack and the twin tower disaster."

The defense and denial mechanisms, which help us deal with uncertainty, a lack of control or the reluctance to perform a certain act, are the basis for the optimism bias. In a relationship, we are required to be aware and active, to take responsibility and do what is necessary. When that doesn't happen, the story we tell ourselves, and sometimes others, is "it'll be okay."

A new organization was recently set up to address a complex national issue. In order to render it effective, six different entities were called upon to form a partnership. For several months during the preliminary stages of establishing the partnership, the unit managers in the organization invested at least two-thirds of their time on conflicts between themselves and their organizations, at the expense of the work itself. As the personal and organizational prices exceeded the endurance limits of the organization and its people, I was called upon to help them in the reconstructing their relationships, organizational settings and work processes.

After the completion of the process, I happened to meet the senior manager who was the initiator of the organization at a different occasion, after he had already moved on to another company. I asked him: "Why did you choose to invest resources in the physical structure, in technology, in recruiting professionals from the organizations, but not in clear definitions of building relationships and organizational processes?" And this is how he replied:

> This process generated so many objections and issues, and if I had lingered on them the whole business would have simply collapsed. I preferred to set up the business, and have these issues resolved at a later time. I assumed the process involved serious people and everything would be OK.

This is an understandable answer; however, it is possible that had this manager known what was about to happen, he might have chosen an entirely different process.

Barriers are often directly linked to priorities: "We are too busy to stop our routine and urgent work"; "We have no time to sit and talk"; "We are not available to construct and manage the partnership." Statements of this kind are common among most types of organizations. It would seem, however, that our priorities would be different if we understood to what extent the assumption "it'll be okay" tends to weaken the foundations of collaborations.

The trust challenge

Trust no one unless you have eaten much salt with him.

Cicero

Cicero, a Roman philosopher and statesman, who lived in the first century BC, had good reason to formulate this statement. He was murdered by his political opponents. Even today, the most common answer to the question how trust is formed lies in the premise that building trust requires extensive time shared.

But what if we don't really have the time for this in the new era? Today, we are required to build trust in haste with many different types of people and cultures, without the time required and the familiar infrastructure. We can no longer rely on the fact that we grew up in the same village.

The best predictor of cooperation between two parties is the degree of trust existing between them. It is the catalyst and foundation of any relationship – with ourselves, with others and with organizations. Where there is trust, a simple flow exists. Like a dance. When trust is weak or lacking, every step becomes heavy and cumbersome. Research and practice demonstrates that trust has a significant economic value in cooperations, as it reduces complexity and costs.

There is no other concept in our lives with so many different definitions yet still so elusive and incomprehensible, as "trust". The reasons for this paradox are clarified as one delves deeper into studies of trust. The concept of trust and the way we go about establishing it is very personal. The esteemed psychologist, Eric Erickson, theorized that there are eight development stages throughout life. During the first stage, which is shaped in the first year of our lives, trust or distrust are established in our psyche. This is the foundation for the normal development of our personality in the following stages. If we think about the true and practical meaning of this theory, we understand how far it extends. Events I experienced during the first years of my life affect the way I conduct trust relations and cooperations with my surroundings as an adult, even as an accomplished and experienced CEO. People around me are also affected by experiences they had undergone during a lifetime inaccessible to us. There is not much we can do to amend what was created in the crib – neither for us nor for the others.

The huge complexity of the "trust" issue may also derive from the challenge inherent in formulating a unified acceptable definition. When there are so many definitions, it is a sign that its complexity has not been cracked. For each discipline, trust receives a different definition and interpretation. A psychologist will attribute emotional or psychological conditions to trust, whereas an economist will refer to calculated considerations and risks.

Many try to refer to "trust" from one point of view only, because it is easier for us to grasp, but this approach is doomed to failure. Cracking this complexity begins by acknowledging that it involves two different aspects that are completely intertwined: the rational and the emotional. Dichotomous thinking of "either/or" does not enable us to fully grasp the concept of trust and how to work with it. Complex thinking of "both/and" is required.

This truth generates another challenge. In order to manage trust in an accurate way, I must possess high IQ (intelligence quotient) abilities: intelligence, analytical potential, clear and rational thinking. At the same time, I must also possess high EQ (emotional intelligence) abilities: intuition, empathy, self-awareness and emotional accuracy. In addition to the above, I also need to be motivated to build trust and be prepared to make an effort at the behavioral level in order to realize it.

Despite multiple definitions, the generally accepted definition of "trust" is a positive expectation concerning conduct of the other. Distrust means a negative expectation concerning conduct of the other. Lack of trust is a lack of expectations concerning conduct of the other. There is usually a dichotomy between the two situations we are familiar with – trust and distrust. It is important to realize that a third situation also exists, lack of trust, especially in relation to the initial stages of cooperations and collaborations.

The classic definitions which are relevant to trust in contexts related to collaborations are: "A situation that reflects positive expectations about the other person's motives, with respect to being prepared to take a risk in certain situations" (Boon, 1991: 194) and "Being prepared to act on the basis of words, actions and decisions of the other" (McAlister, 1995: 25).

Rational considerations regarding trusting the other and his intentions may explain why we trust a person or entity with whom we had previous experience or whoever has a reputation that provides us with a rational reason. This does not explain situations whereby trust is given at the initial stages. Such behavior is based on other elements, such as one's basic attitude toward trust – defined as personality-based trust (Driscoll, 1978).

Another element is defined as organization-based trust, referring to the norms and rules of the organization which allow the individual to place trust, whether as part of the organization regarding other people within it, or toward a person representing another organization. The organizational culture and the manner in which they operate affect the degree of trust placed in them and in their representatives.

A third element in our trust assumptions is based on categorical and stereotypical generalizations we make when relating to others. Our hypothesis is that we can trust a particular person according to the positive or negative behaviors of the culture and groups he is associated with. This type of trust is defined as "swift trust" (Meyerson, 1996).

"Potential-based trust" means that trust will increase the more we rely on the potential of a person or other entity to perform the work designated to him – related to his professionalism, experience or reputation.

"Intention-based trust" is another significant element when dealing with cooperations. I trust someone whose intentions are serious and genuine, who neither wishes to harm me nor wastes my time in vain. This element may also be perceived as rational, based on words and deeds, but above all it is based on feelings and emotions.

A final element, which is not commonly mentioned in research and literature but in my perception and based on my experience is of great importance, is "relationship-based trust". It is made up of our ability to conduct an open and sincere conversation with another person and our willingness to put things on the table and experience vulnerability. In such a relationship, it is important to maintain continuity and avoid surprises that undermine stability.

At the end of the day, trust is a very personal matter. Therefore, we must make an effort to understand how our partners interpret the concept of trust. We cannot make assumptions based on the way we regard the concept of trust. It should be borne in mind that trust primarily relies on the little things and on gestures that express empathy, curiosity, attentiveness, humility and authentic communication. This, more than anything else, is what builds trust in relationships.

Trust is commonly defined as a complex mental structure, which includes four layers: emotional, cognitive, motivational and behavioral.

> Emotional: "He hurt me, so now I am angry with him and feel rejection and contempt for him."
> Cognitive: "He will hurt me like he always does. I don't want to cooperate with him."
> Motivational: "I don't feel motivated enough to trust him because of past experience."
> Behavioral: "I have no intention of sharing my personal information with him, and will not trust him until he complies with my wishes."

Another interesting model, presented by Brené Brown at her TED talk in 2015, relates to the anatomy of trust. In her talk Brown said: "when we trust, we are braving connection with someone." The word "braving" is an acronym of the model elements:

- Boundaries – when we are absolutely clear about our boundaries and those of the other and respect them.
- Reliability – when we do what we said we would do.
- Accountability – I can trust you only if you are willing to take responsibility, apologize and try to make amends where you are wrong. You can trust me only if when I am wrong I take responsibility and apologize to you and make amends.
- Vault – hold your tongue. Information you share with me stays with me forever. What I share with you should be kept to yourself.
- Integrity – both of us will act with integrity, honesty, clean intentions and the courage to practice our values and not just profess them.
- Non judgment – the mutual ability to ask for help without judgment from the other. When there is trust, we can offer help without thinking less of the other, and make sure that they feel the same about me.
- Generosity – trust between us is based on assuming that we are generous to each other in words, intentions and behaviors.

Stephen Covey, in his excellent book from 2006, *The Speed of Trust*, offers a model based on five "waves" of trust. The image is based on a stone thrown into the water that produces ripples, with distant waves affected by close ones.

The first wave: self-trust – the confidence we have in ourselves, in our ability to set and realize goals, to keep commitments, "walk our talk" – and also the ability to inspire trust in others. To become a person worthy of trust in the eyes of ourselves and others. The guiding principle is credibility – from the Latin word *credere*, which means to believe.

The second wave: relationship trust – how to establish and increase "trust accounts" we hold with others. The guiding principle is consistent and stable behavior.

The third wave: organizational trust – this wave deals with the ability of leaders to generate trust in different organizations and systems. If a person works with people he trusts but is operating in an organizational culture where trust is lacking, it will greatly affect him. Hence, the importance of organizational trust is understandable. The guiding principle is alignment.

The fourth wave: market trust – the principle is reputation, branding and name among customers and investors. Receiving market trust is the power of the brand.

The fifth wave: social trust – creating value for others and for society at large. The key principle is contribution. By creating social trust we deal with distrust and cynicism and influence others to generate value and contribute.

James Davis conducted studies in which he found three reasons for trust development, based on the premise that when I trust somebody, it means that I am willing to take a risk and be vulnerable.

1. Ability – can the person do what he says he can do (in the relevant field)?
2. Generosity – does the person care about me? Will he act in my favor?
3. Integrity – does the person act according to his values, according to his system of beliefs? Does he stand behind his words?

When these three criteria are met, we will trust that person.

In situations where there is lack of trust or no trust at all, we are required to move forward in the process and simultaneously work toward building trust. Building trust in a relationship relies on two particularly important factors. The first, creating expectations about the partnership's future, specifically based on positive past behavior, reputation or formal agreements. It is a difficult but possible starting point. The second significant factor is an inclination to take a risk. The parties must agree that they trust each other sufficiently to take the risks involved at the beginning of the partnership. If these two presuppositions are realized, trust in the process itself can be strengthened.

Naturally, at first, these factors will exist in a modestly calculated and realistic manner. As things progress, attitudes that promote trust, as well as trust itself, will strengthen – leading to empowerment of the partnership.

According to this approach, trust is built gradually, based on small successes, accumulation of shared experience and materializing cooperations that maintain a low risk level. With time, trust intensifies, and so does the willingness to take more risks. The issue of mutual risks should be part of a shared discourse throughout the process, with the goal of building trust.

There are many more definitions of trust, too many to mention them all. In my opinion, when discussing the issue of collaboration, the most interesting definition is the one claiming that trust is based on our individual relationship with the unknown.

The key questions are: are we interested in trust? Are we ready to invest in whatever is required to purposefully build our partners' trust in us? Is this the mindset with which we approach partnerships, and is it the way things are conducted in hard times as well?

It is important to understand, especially in the context of partnerships and cooperations, that the more trust I put in others, the more vulnerable I am, especially if I have no direct influence and control over their behaviors. In fact, trust replaces control. The less control I hold, the more trust is required of me. Thus, the more human society and organizational space are evolving to flatter and less hierarchical dimensions, and the more the mechanisms become collaborative and egalitarian with less central control, so are we required to a greater degree of trust. This change is more essential and paradigmatic than what we actually comprehend. One can define the period into which we enter as the "era of trust and collaboration". There is really no other choice except to trust in order to create and leverage effective partnerships, at all levels and systems.

***

All ten challenges and spaces of blind spots, as described above, are features of our organizational culture. They affect the way partnerships are conducted within and between organizations of different organizational cultures. Peter Drucker, the father of modern management, said that "organizational culture eats strategy for breakfast." The challenge lies in a fact that most managers and leaders will testify to: there is a great difficulty in changing an organizational culture, and even if successful, it takes quite a few years.

One of the most powerful ways to transform organizational culture and empower partnerships is the use of an organizing and structured model. The following chapters will deal with this model, as well as in various ways for creating, designing and improving collaborations.

Chapter 4

The ECA model for managing effective collaboration

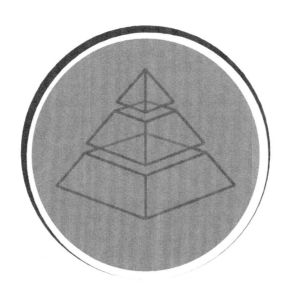

DOI: 10.4324/9781003514992-4

The Effective Collaboration Analysis (ECA®) model was born of the necessity to define, analyze and manage partnerships in a structured and systematic way, as a practical translation to the new paradigm, and in order to effectively cope with barriers and blind spaces. The model is used as a perceptual framework, as a shared language for entities creating and maintaining cooperation at any level and as a diagnostic tool. It allows us to focus, make rational decisions and create operative processes and steps in order to improve and leverage cooperations. The model is both systematic and practical, offering a relatively simple connectivity between the diagnostic and the performance level. The operative derivative of ECA is the intervention process used for building collaborations and empowering them. It is named Effective Collaboration Process– ECP ®.

The model is named ECA model, since it is based on the premise that collaborations and cooperations are measures for the realization of other purposes. Cooperation is not the end by itself; therefore, it needs to be effective for implementing goals. The model-based paradigm can be summarized by the following:

1. Collaboration management – accountability with all its implications, not just "managing" in collaboration. It refers to a situation involving elements of high-levels of control in processes, planning, perception, the ability to cope with challenges as well as taking responsibility rather than shifting blame for failure to the other party's court. This is a state of action rather than reaction.
2. Collaboration language – a uniform, shared, clear, simple and measurable language. The objective is to integrate all parties in the goals, indices, assessments, controls, incentives, shared processes and more.
3. High velocity value – a high and rapidly achieved value. When your tool is sharp and precise, long and cumbersome processes are no longer needed. And in the present age, there is no time for such processes.
4. From "ego-system" to "eco-system" – refers to a very deep transformation, whereby the model constitutes a significant catalyst as a practical tool for applying this principle.

The ECA model is constructed as a pyramid, symbolizing stability and simplicity. It consists of three levels of partnerships: Coordination, Cooperation and Collaboration. Alongside these levels, the pyramid has four sides which are the main elements of any cooperation and interface – Value, Structure, Relationships and Commitment. Aided by these elements, we can recognize and comprehend the areas of strength and weakness in any given situation, as well as the discrepancies in partners' perceptions regarding the situation. The three levels, combined with the four elements, provide us with intelligent and systematic planning when building a new partnership or trying to improve an existing one. The power of the model is in its simplicity; it is easy to understand and apply, and it also directs us to tangible and practical solutions. There are some who easily remember the two axes of the model using the definition of 3C + 4E – three levels defined in terms of CO and four elements.

Why was the ECA model developed?

Development of this model was based on the assumption that a systematic and structured approach is necessary in order to diagnose, assess, analyze and ultimately improve partnerships and interfaces. Just as in any other field where an orderly discipline and work methodology is utilized – project management, knowledge management, planning, acquisition, budget and more – in this field too, it was time to create an inclusive definition and a professional language.

The need for an organized and a systematic approach in this field has already been identified for several years. Managers and position holders have been looking for a practical lever to change the corporate culture and create a more orderly and less randomized response for conceptualization, evaluation, planning and operational measures of better quality and accuracy in internal and external interfaces in which they are involved. The vast experience accumulated by us in processes carried out within organizations and between them, in all sectors, has created an infrastructure of insights and knowledge, in conjunction with precision in presenting the central key question marks in the field. Since my team and I did not find a systematic and orderly model for designing and managing collaborations, we were required to construct one ourselves, and so, in 2010, the pyramid was designed and its applications were formulated.

Another significant motivation for developing the model and its diagnostic application – the ECA questionnaire – emerged from the need to quantify the quality of what is sometimes perceived as obscure and abstract. In the past, many managers perceived the field of collaboration as nice to have, no more, a feature that originates in "soft" worlds. The ability to translate this complex space into accurate numbers and data helps to produce accurate and significant clarity and impact. Part of the effect is due to the fact that a structured discipline and model help to create affinity to the core business of the organization and is not only related to the HR's agenda. It is a breakthrough of innovation in the field, which is also gradually translated to supporting technological tools. The day will soon come when a CEO will be able to watch a dashboard presenting an up-to-date illustration of cooperations between organization units on a regular basis.

In developing the model, we have consciously chosen to concentrate on the generic core of cooperation, at all levels and fields. Therefore, we thrived for the model not to function as a theoretical platform but rather to be applied as a daily work tool as well as an infrastructure for a shared language, thus promoting the conversion of the new paradigm into action, creating the required change in this field.

The model and its applications are already assimilated in various systems, at the conceptual as well as the practical level. At both levels, leaders adopt the concepts and develop awareness toward the importance of cooperations they lead and in conjunction adopt patterns of cooperative action. This benefits them at the strategic as well as the tactical level. Effects occur at both levels – of "being" and "doing" – on the day-to-day reality and in the organizational and inter-organizational culture, the culture of cooperations.

What are the main model applications?

These are the main possible benefits gained by applying the model, both in structured processes and in day-to-day cooperation management:

1. Creating one generic map, shared by all partners; a uniform compass for sailors all around the world, regardless of culture, location, role or type of vessel they lead.
2. Creating awareness, formulating knowledge and increasing attention to the field of collaborations in various organizations.
3. Making a clear and simple work model accessible for managers, enabling them to manage collaboration with awareness and accountability.
4. Assimilation of a new language and terminology, designed to gradually change the organizational culture and perhaps even change human culture in the future.
5. There is more than one way to create cooperations and collaborations; however, each way and every step must take into account the four elements of the model – from a strategic as well as a tactical aspect.

Why a pyramid?

The four elements of the model are represented by the four sides of the pyramid, yet there are additional reasons for choosing the pyramid as the ECA model format.

1. Layers

   Designing the structure as a pyramid facilitates the conceptualization and comprehension of the significance of the model's three layers. Each layer functions as a substrate for the layer above it. We can choose to climb to the top of the pyramid or aim for each step along the way, according to our goals and values. The model does not suggest that reaching the top of the pyramid is the best or desired option. The main intention is to create a shared language and a clear definition of the level of partnership and the step towards which one is aiming.

2. Interdependence

   The strength of the pyramid as a geometrical structure is based on interdependence between all its sides. Imagine that one side of the pyramid is weakened and stones begin falling to the ground. This will directly affect the strength and durability of the other sides. At one point or another, stones will start falling from them too, as they are no longer supported by the other sides. No element in the model can exist on its own over time. They all require a stable holistic structure, just like a pyramid.

3. Stability

   In this era of constant and rapid change, in an environment of uncertainty, chaos and complexity, we need an anchor of stability. The Egyptian pyramids, just like those created by other cultures, symbolize long-lasting human creations, those that persist even when the human environment that had created them had changed beyond recognition over thousands of years. According to the model concepts, the elements of ECA will serve us forever (for now), since they form a uniform and generic framework for all types of cooperations. These are fixed prisms through which one can examine complex and changing systems. Although they are permanent and stable, their contexts and applications are dynamic and require adjustments.

4. Simplicity

   The pyramid model is easy to grasp and memorize. It turns out that the human brain absorbs and maintains triangular and pyramidal structures with less effort than other shapes. The ECA model is simple, giving managers dealing with great complexity no reason to reject it. The shape in itself promotes the model's purpose, not only as a work tool and a shared language but also in the actual use of commonly shared visual perception.

Three partnership levels of the model

The first key aspect of the model marks the way in which the level of collaboration is understood and defined. Often, and especially in cases of cultural or

Collaboration

Cooperation

Coordination

perceptual gaps, we say the same things but mean differently, or say different things but mean the same. Sometimes, disappointment may emanate between interface partners, with one party holding expectations for a high level of partnership while the other party is aiming for a lower one. Hence, precise definition is of great importance. It produces a shared language, trust and accuracy in communication and work processes. Defining the levels also produces conceptualization and language, required for the purpose of creating awareness and systematicity in the work processes and in the corporate culture.

Coordination

Shared information, synchronization and information transfer. The essence is knowledge and information, control and synchronization in an organized manner that will allow organizations to better work together. Accumulation of knowledge and information helps to create power and affects decision-making processes; hence, this level of partnership, which is the most basic level, is highly relevant in many situations. This may also include standardization of processes and coordination of actions and tasks but not their shared performance.

One level lower than coordination is defined as co-existence – this interface reflects the awareness of an organization to the actions of other organizations, without working relations or interfaces. There is mutual awareness of the existence and activity of the other but nothing beyond that. The level of coordination also includes networking, which by definition involves knowledge exchange and sometimes shared thinking. There are those who define networking as a level of cooperation of its own merit; however, the ECA model perceives networks and networking as tools and means for creating and driving all levels of partnerships.

We refer to the term "coordination" as quite basic and simple to implement, but in practice it involves a great deal of complexity, which correspond with some of the barriers we have dealt with. In order to acquire knowledge and information, we are willing to share knowledge and information, and therefore gradual openness prevails in this channel, consciously and practically. However, performance will often be limited due to our desire to maintain our power and consolidate it, based on our knowledge and information, thus creating a competitive advantage over others. It is natural to declare transparency and sharing but, in practice, to do so in a limited way. It is sufficient to be positively perceived by others but not necessarily beyond that.

Synchronization of activities often allows each side in the interface to maintain more control over the activities in its territory. Thus, it will result in fewer incidents in the independent activity of the unit and organization and often even save resources. In order to pinpoint the term "coordination", we will use a number of concrete examples:

Training managers from two different organizations aiming for coordination will hold meetings and participate in training programs, share information about new speakers and models in their field and may also tackle various dilemmas together. If both organizations make use of the same training facility, they may try to coordinate their annual training programs and their use of the facility in advance, thus minimizing possible collisions.

The second example – work plans – is familiar to managers in all types of organizations. During December, all unit managers in the organization convene for a day or two in a cozy hotel and dive into long and boring sessions of presentations, in which each participant describes his annual work plan. These meetings are about sharing information only. Understanding the comprehensive picture for managers is important enough to hold this annual meeting; however, is it enough to produce the highest value for the organization and its managers?

Coordination is the foundation for the higher levels of cooperation and collaboration, with an intrinsic value. It does not require the allocation of too many resources or too much investment, nor does it produce high risk or dependence between partners. However, the central problem lies in the fact that this level of partnership only facilitates handling familiar problems and challenges, whose level of complexity is low, if at all. It allows the parties to focus on tactical and technical spheres rather than areas of strategic and adaptive challenges. Inter-organizational coordination, which is inherently complex, is ultimately defined as a technical activity, mostly at a tactical level. It mainly refers to pre-defined activities in a clear environment and is less relevant and effective when dealing with a complex and dynamic environment.

Cooperation

Cooperation will often be created as a response to a particular situation, challenge or goal or to tackle a focused task. Successful and effective coping, supported by expanding resources and capabilities, may be the factor that brings partners to cooperate in order to realize their objectives. These objectives can be completely different or shared. For example, one organization may strive to reach a new market share, while the other organization may seek to meet its customers' needs by offering a product which it cannot develop or deliver. The essence is effectiveness: maximization and expansion of capabilities, skills, resources and opportunities. The focus is tactic: project, operation, joint action and a demarcated move in terms of scope and time.

Cooperation requires an investment of energy and resources by the partners, which is higher than that required by coordination. Accordingly, the levels of interdependence between partners and the degrees of risk they take are higher. Organizations that define strict rules of isolation, with a limited number of interactions, focusing on procedures, instructions, control and planning, do not really know how to maintain cooperation. Coordination is primarily intended for achieving organizational efficiency, while cooperation is designed to achieve effectiveness. Coordination is essentially bureaucratic, while cooperation allows creativity and innovation. In short, coordination mainly involves shared knowledge and cooperation mainly involves shared action.

An example of significant and efficient cooperation between entities can be demonstrated by the events that took place in Israel during the summer of 2005 – the uprooting of Jewish settlements in the Gaza Strip, an operation that was both sensitive and complex. It was a campaign of unprecedented scope in Israeli history. It was impossible to predict the degree and manner of opposition that would be expressed by the residents of the settlements. Cooperation between the police and the military was extremely precise, in the aim of realizing the path they defined: "determination and sensitivity". The two entities created a system of shared planning, fully integrated their respective means and capabilities, defined a methodology and performed integrated training to ensure the precision of the mission performance. This is a rare and comprehensive inter-organizational cooperation, which had broad effects on the performance of the operation.

Let us revisit previous examples to refine the definitions:

The training directors of the two organizations, aiming toward cooperation, will invest in joint actions according to their interests and goals. For example, initiating a joint managers' conference that will allow both mutually beneficial interactions and a joint investment in a high-quality and more costly event than would have been possible for any single entity alone.

In the example relating to annual work plans, a unit manager or anyone on his behalf will sit down with the other units prior and during devising the work plan, and will jointly search for mutual interface points in these plans. They will locate the points of effects on the other units that can be adjusted to improve the effectiveness of all units and work processes and interfaces. In addition, they may consider whether initiating joint ventures and projects in the course of the year may be valuable as part of budget and operation planning and how to bring it into fruition.

Collaboration

Collaboration relies on the previous levels while expanding and intensifying them. The essence is relevancy. This phase occurs when two or more autonomous entities are involved in a shared process, for the benefit of solving a challenge or problematic sphere. Their involvement in the process includes frameworks and rules, norms and actions. The organization strives for relevance, and in order to achieve that goal, it chooses to make a significant and binding effort, which sometimes requires stepping out of familiar boundaries and comfort zones. The ability to work in collaboration with other entities dramatically improves the level of relevance. Collaboration allows us to deal with complex and adaptive problems that cannot be handled by one factor, as well as with strategic issues.

Collaboration aims to create a higher value than any entity can create by itself, mostly in the long term. Sometimes the process is perceived as long and cumbersome; however, even at this level focused processes can be designed, resulting in relatively quick performance (high velocity value). Leaders who choose to assimilate and drive collaboration among their organizations and with other organizations are also willing to create a change in their organizational culture. They are prepared to remove walls and partitions and create long-term commitments and joint operations, even in their core domains. The interdependence that results from collaboration requires each partner to be considerate of the other partners, aspiring toward maximal benefit and the realization of objectives and interests by all parties. The partners work together for a longer period of time, usually on a number of topics and issues. They are willing to invest more energy and resources and adapt work patterns and regulations.

Collaboration relies on the other levels, but first and foremost, it is a strategy that is translated into tactics and actions. In some ways, collaboration is a state of being, perception and culture, which requires a certain level of collaborative intelligence. Collaboration significantly depends – certainly more than the other levels – on the perceptions of managers and leadership. In conjunction, the required investment is higher than in the other levels; thus, the risk increases significantly. To minimize risk and maintain agility, built-in mechanisms for shared solution of problems and conflicts are required, alongside a relationship based on trust and effective communication. In many cases, collaboration is not the level we need to aim at, as one of the other two levels may suffice without the need for the investment and inter-dependence that is inherent at this level.

The difference between the collaboration level and the coordination level is clearly illustrated in the report of the Commission of Inquiry into the events of 9/11:

> The agencies cooperated, some of the time [prior to the attack]. But even such cooperation as there was is not the same thing like joint

action. When agencies cooperate, one defines the problem and seeks help with it. When they act jointly, the problem and options for action are defined differently from the start. Individuals from different backgrounds come together in analyzing a case and planning how to manage it.

Co-ownership – a concept defined as a situation in which the partners see themselves committed to achieving a shared vision with joint ownership of the lead and with a sense of responsibility for realizing the vision. According to the ECA concept, this definition is clearly included in the level of collaboration, and there is no benefit in differentiating it.

The term "multidimensionality", which will be introduced in the chapter dealing with the defense system, as well as the terms "fusion" and "merger", are located in the ECA model as a form of collaboration in its highest degree. Few organizations can be found in this sphere, as it requires relinquishing identity and capabilities in order to create a new entity. They may be under the assumption that they are beyond the model and have no need for a built-in and unified conception. In practice, however, since it deals with people, cultures, barriers and areas of blindness, it is likely that for them, too, the conceptions and practices derived from the model are definitely relevant.

The previous examples will assist us again in illustrating the practical differences between the levels:

In collaboration, the training managers of the two organizations will carry out a more in-depth process of understanding and sharing challenges, difficulties and interests. Through the process of significant sharing, they will strive to identify areas for creating a greater value. They may, for example, recognize that all procurement and finance staff in both organizations have similar characteristics and that each party has developed some capabilities that may complement those of the other party. On this basis, the various training systems may join to create a shared course for their procurement and finance staff. In the first stage, investment in building the course will be significant, and maintaining the interface will require allocation of time and attention in the future as well, but assuming it is a long-term valuable solution, it is likely to yield profitable results. In the example of annual work plans, alongside the different objectives of each unit, shared goals for two units or more will also arise.

If we take, for example, the interface between the organization units involving the customers, at the coordination level, the goal will be to produce information and operation synchronization; at the cooperation level, solutions will be offered to customers in joint actions; and at the collaboration level, a shared concept of value chain for the customer will be created. Each level relies on a different perception, requires a different level of investment and yields different products.

Summary of the definitions

Term	Definition	Essence	Realization
Coordination	Coordinātiō based on ordo – Order. Organization, arrangement, adaptation, synchronization.	Shared information, knowledge transfer and synchronization. Central motivations: power (knowledge and information) and harmony (synchronization and adaptation). Solution to simple challenges.	Sharing and learning between units and bodies, coordination of operations, standardization of processes.
Cooperation	Cooperatus, working together; a joint operation or task.	Shared action, and operation. Tactic. Maximizing potentials, options and resources. Central motivation: effectiveness.	Shared work on a task, project or a focused topic. Limited in scope, time, investment and risk.
Collaboration	Collabōrātus together + labōrāre – working together in order to create something bigger than possibly done alone.	Shared spheres. Strategic. Synergetic being and perception, adopting organizational culture, structure, language and work processes. Central motivation: relevance, solution to complex and adaptive challenges.	Shared work integrated in core issues, for a long period of time, with considerable investment and high risk.

A clear and amusing (or not) illustration, familiar to most of us, can be drawn from married life. A couple that functions at the level of coordination will synchronize and make arrangements during the day, frequently by taking advantage of text messages: "Fetch the kid from his class at six", "Remember that the air conditioner technician will be coming today" and so forth. We are all familiar with such a discourse. A couple who also chooses to operate at the level of cooperation will ensure that beyond the ongoing coordination and family operations, there will also be joint tasks and projects: Friday dinner together, an annual couple or family vacation and more. A couple who does more than that and creates collaboration will strive to end the evening with a glass of wine on the balcony, will go out once a week to a romantic couple's pastime and will enjoy the experience of partnership and friendship. Through a quick review of couples we know, we can ask ourselves: where do most of the couples stand in terms of the level of partnership?

We should remember that despite the many advantages inherent in clear and distinct definitions and coordination of expectations, in reality, the distinction between the three levels is not always so obvious. We must maintain flexibility in this aspect too so that the model will produce real value in work processes.

The four elements of the model

The model is based on four elements which are the basic ingredients of any level of partnership:

1. Value – the reason for connection, the potential revenue for each partner (person, unit, organization).
2. Structure – the formal and structural aspects, definitions, responsibilities and authority.
3. Relationships – "the partnership language", interaction, trust and communication.
4. Commitment + execution – translating into actions, assimilation, implementation and maintenance along the way.

These elements help us understand the quality and effectiveness of every interface and partnership at any given moment. Moreover, they accurately guide us in planning and constructing cooperations, as well as improving the existing situation. The hypothesis at the basis of the model is that strong and effective collaboration, in each of the three levels, relies on these four elements. It should create a significant value that each partner gains from co-working with others and establish a high and precise level of mutual understanding regarding the value which each party strives to achieve and receive. This collaboration must be supported by formal mechanisms, organizational structures, definitions, work routine, accountability and authority. It also relies on the spirit of the language and relationships based on trust and dialogue. Ultimately, it requires a high level of ongoing commitment of each partner to his fellow partners and to the partnership itself, as reflected in the day-to-day work.

Why? How? What? – the four elements as a Golden Circle

The manner of defining the four elements beautifully connects with the "Golden Circle" developed by Simon Sinek (Sinek, 2011), and although the ECA model was created before, the process is similar. The value element in the model directs us and our partners to examine the "Why?" questions: objectives, goals, needs, interests, motives and beliefs. What are the benefits of creating partnerships for us/for the organization/for the others?

The "How?" questions at the formal and informal level address the elements of structure and relationships. How do we drive better cooperation in order to realize what we have defined in the question of value – achievement of our goals and those of the other partners, maximizing potential profits and realizing the needs and interests of all partners?

The "What?" questions are resolved in the element of commitment. Once we understand "Why" we are in the interface and "How" we can support it, the question arises: "what" should we do in practice? What are the defined actions we are required to take as partners, and what is the commitment we and the others take upon ourselves?

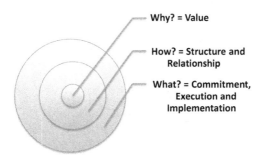

Why? = Value

How? = Structure and Relationship

What? = Commitment, Execution and Implementation

The value element

> Very few people or companies can clearly articulate WHY they do what they do. By WHY, I mean what is your purpose, cause or belief.

Simon Sinek

Sinek's words are very relevant regarding the topic of collaboration. The basic question in the value element, which constitutes a basis for the entire model, is "Why?". Partnership, at any level, is a means of serving the creation of value. It does not refer to behavioral values or social or organizational values. These are our goals, needs, interests, challenges, motivations, dreams and constraints and anything else that makes us do what we do. Without the element of a clear, stable and accurate value, it is not possible to build and promote the other three elements. The whole structure is weakened when parts of the value are not clear to the partners. This sounds obvious, but in practice, this infrastructure is seldom strong enough.

When discussing value, we are referring to the following elements, both in collaboration built up from scratch as well as in the existing sphere:

- Potential – the option of realizing a mutual value. In the process of construction and creation it is advisable to explore this option in a creative and unlimited manner, even if its realization will only be partial or gradual. This is the place for innovation and long-term vision, even if it isn't practically realistic at this moment. The other elements will balance out anything that emerges at this point later on.
- Objectives of each entity – what are the preliminary objectives of each entity, in the framework of the existing or potential alliance with another entity? It is totally legitimate that each entity aspires to realize different objectives.
- Vision and values – the more the issues around which cooperation exists, or will exist, are closer to the core of the vision and values of

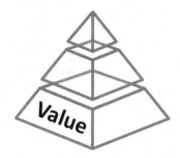

each entity, the more the interface becomes significant. If it concerns a secondary and marginal issue for one of the organizations, it will probably be reflected in the other elements, and eventually – in a weakened implementation.

- Interests and needs – organizational interests, as well as the personal needs of leaders, are the most important component in the value element. This is the key to maintaining any effective cooperation. In today's world, in which managerial guidelines and hierarchy are frequently observed in a limited way, there is little chance that any individual will really cooperate unless it provides a solution for him personally (needs) or for the organization he represents (interests).

The issues of interests and needs embody the most significant challenge. Managers often demonstrate a fundamental deficiency in aspects of precise understanding, awareness and tools to conduct a discourse of needs and interests. In many cases of new or existing interfaces, we make assumptions about the other party's motives, without taking time to stop and examine them. Often, we are unaware of the range of our own needs and the way in which we prioritize them; hence, mistakes and inaccurate decisions emerge (Chapter 9 is totally dedicated to this issue and its great importance as the basis of the model).

Discussion of the value element depends on the level of partnership we are aiming at. When referring to coordination, we will direct the discussion to information and knowledge, as well as to synchronization and compatibility of actions taken. When dealing with cooperation, we will focus on the expected results of the joint work. When collaboration is involved, we will direct the discourse to value and focus on deep understanding of interests and needs and on defining separate and joint long-term objectives.

The structure element

> Without chaos – nothing can evolve. Without order – nothing can exist.
>
> **Oscar Wilde**

When dealing with structure the basic question is "How?" – the manner in which a partnership should be executed in all formal and structural aspects, realizing that each level of collaboration requires structurality, clear definitions, orderly work, systematicity and a certain level of discipline. In the absence of this element, ambiguity in work processes will be too high, and dependency in interpersonal relationships will become exaggerated and illogical.

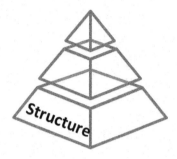

As part of the structure element, we deal with the following components:

- Organizational structure – to what extent does the organizational structure of each entity promote or inhibit internal partnerships as well as those existing with other entities? To what extent do hierarchy and bureaucracy make it difficult for the organizational synergy and inhibit it?
- Information systems – the existence of information technology systems shared by elements in the interface.
- Communication structures – formal communication mechanisms including physical and online meetings, email, sharing platforms and clear settings of communication patterns between entities.
- Roles and responsibilities – clear definitions of roles, responsibilities and authorities by each organization, unit and position holders, regarding everything that involves joint work processes. Excessive ambiguity in gray areas, which sometimes serves a small group of people, might damage the work process. Excessive definition and rigidity may entail losing agility. Therefore, it is important to examine to what extent definitions contribute to an effective interface.
- Work processes and regulations – here, too, the range between ambiguity and rigidity is broad and elusive alike. Alongside the need for definitions, it should be ensured that their implementation allows the relevant operational space and does not create bureaucratic encumbrances.

Discussion of the structure element depends on the level of collaboration we are aiming at. When coordination is involved, we will direct the discussion to a mode of formal communication and the existence of suitable information systems. When aiming at cooperation, the focus will be on defining accountability and authority in orderly and effective work processes. And when we direct the discussion to collaboration, the focus will be on defining organizational structures which support long-term vision and value.

The relationship element

> Work on developing a collaborative relationship so that when conflict arises, you will believe that you are allies.
>
> **Dean Tioswold**

The basic question related to the relationship element is "How?" – the way in which a partnership is supposed to exist in all informal and interpersonal aspects. This element is based on understanding the importance of relationships in every aspect and level of collaboration and awareness of the full accountability each partner holds for relationships with the other partners. Many things have been said about the relationship element: "Everything is personal", "Partnership depends on people and the alliance between them", "Trust is the foundation of everything", "Excess ego", "Speaking in different languages" and more. Despite being defined as "soft", and in some sense also "emotional", this is a space that needs to be managed through awareness and responsibility rather than by means of reactivity and avoidance.

As part of the relationship element, we deal with the following factors:

- Sense of partnership – is expressed in the answer to the question to what extent does every person in an interface feel that he is a partner to his co-workers or that they are his. It depends on the alliance built between people and in the way they assess the seriousness of the others regarding the joint process, even if collaboration was forced on them.
- Trust – the degree of trust between partners is a crucial factor of accelerating or hindering collaboration. The presupposition is that trust is not decided by a higher power or by the other's actions but can be managed in a deliberate and intelligent manner. This is the most significant lever in the relationship element.
- Interpersonal communication and the quality of dialogue – the level of openness, authenticity, sincerity and attention prevailing in the interaction between partners. High quality of dialogue also includes patience and effort to understand the other even in the absence of agreement and

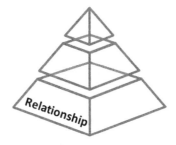

the willingness to examine the point of view of each side in the discourse. These elements are by no means trivial or commonplace in the environment in which we operate.

- Conflict management – the ability to understand that the occurrence of conflicts is natural and legitimate, alongside the ability to manage them effectively, while minimizing damages and escalating situations.
- Tolerance and inclusion – the level of empathy and sensitivity toward those who are different from me personally, professionally, class-wise or culture-wise. A mutual willingness to get to know the other with his various qualities and to learn his needs.
- Organizational culture – understanding the culture of the other organization; recognizing the dissimilarity between organizational cultures and the willingness to cope with the challenges created by the gaps; curiosity and interest in the other organization and its properties. One of the most important elements in dissimilarity between organizational cultures is the level of hierarchy, Power Distance Index (PDI).

Discussion of the relationship element, similar to the other elements, largely depends on the level of the desired partnership. When dealing with coordination, this element is mostly insignificant in most situations, apart from the trust element, which is necessary in every case. In cooperation, the focus will be on creating trust, effective dialogue, conflict management and teamwork between everyone directly involved in leading the process. When the aim is to create collaboration, large investment in construction and management of deep and stable trust with an open dialogue will be required in creating a sense of partnership and qualitative dialogue – both among the work teams and among the stakeholders and decision makers.

The element of commitment and implementation

Coming together is the beginning. Staying together is progress. Working together is success.

Henry Ford

The leading fundamental question in reference to the issue of commitment is "What?" – the most tangible and concrete aspects for the purpose of realizing the value and other elements. This is a practical element that is present in our everyday life, in the ECA model and within every partnership. It both structuralizes performance in practice and expresses it.

The reason this element is included in the model (with equal shares of 25 percent as any of the other elements in the pyramid) is to assert the importance of implementation, application, assimilation, performance and maintenance. The most dangerous thing is the disparity between statements and actions. Shimoni (2017) explains that the frequent strategy in symbolic partnerships is the use of partnership rituals and rhetoric, creating a distorted impression of cooperation. Under the guise of the ceremonial and symbolic "partnership" alone, mutual submission is practically taking place, with each side trying to promote its own goals and interests, which are not necessarily related and may even be contrary to those of the other party. Within organizations, the organizational vision frequently defines "synergy", "one life cycle" and "one company"; however, in practice nothing is manifested. This reality causes frustration, cynicism and lack of trust among managers and employees regarding statements and intentions.

This gap occurs on a daily basis between partners in work interfaces. They may emphasize the importance of cooperation and declare their serious intentions but in practice do not cash in the checks they have signed. Sometimes even when signing on they clearly know that they are doing so in words only, having no intention of following through. This is often obvious even in the initial stages to the other side too, making it into a game of declaration of intent. At times, the declarant does indeed intend to keep his word, yet multiple tasks and different priorities, or just lack of awareness, result in failure to realize it. Therefore, emphasis is placed on the familiar saying: "Walk the talk".

As part of the commitment element, we deal with the following components:

- Transparency – the level of transparency and information sharing in practice as well as its compatibility to the value and structure as defined.
- Priorities – is cooperation adequately prioritized by each of the involved factors? Both in accordance with the defined agreement and in terms of a sense of reciprocity.
- Availability – are the partners available for each other when needed?
- Resources – investment of resources by all of the partners according to changing definitions and needs.
- Application, implementation and assimilation – the degree to which statements and operative actions in the field correspond.
- Dealing with conflicts of interest – assuming that conflicts are a natural phenomenon, how do the partners actually manage to cope with these conflicts and disputes and the challenges that arise along the way?

Examining the commitment element corresponds with the level of partnership we are trying to achieve: for coordination to take place, the emphasis is on applying transfer of information and on the level of transparency. When we are in the state of cooperation, emphasis will be placed on performance of defined tasks and investment of required resources. When dealing with collaboration, the partners will be required to construct orderly systems of decision making, work plans and mutual objectives, dialogue and negotiation, conflict management, joint calculation, agreement regarding shared results, clear definition of transparency and cooperation, learning processes and studies for improving the interfaces and the implementations, raising resources and their allocation and ensuring systemic support (board of directors, political rank, public).

The matrix – 3C +4E

A basic understanding of the ECA model is sufficient for its day-to-day use. As mentioned, it is feasible to make use of the concepts and definition of the partnership levels that exist on top of each other in a vertical axis and make separate use of the four elements that constitute the pyramid sides. The model is simple; however, in order to understand it accurately and profoundly, and for the purpose of more sophisticated use and as the basis for work processes, it can be construed as a matrix connecting the sides and the levels. Every such intersection produces unique meaning:

	Value	Structure	Relationship	Commitment
Coordination	A Knowledge and information	B System synchronization	C Questions and sharing	D Transparency
Cooperation	E Effectiveness	F Accountability and authority work processes	G Effective communication Conflict management	H Investing resources in implementing defined objectives
Collaboration	I Relevance	J Shared platforms of work processes and communication	K Trust, sense of partnership, ongoing intimate communication	L Investing resources in processes and collaboration itself

Following is a clarification of the matrix components, according to the letter key used:

Coordination

A – The value at this level is knowledge and information. The focus is on defining the partners' interests pertaining to information, knowledge and data. In conjunction, and when relevant, a joint identification of another potential value may emerge through synchronization of actions and operations between parties.

B – At this level the structure is focused on system synchronization, relating to information defined as relevant and the way it is shared. It is important to define measures and work processes and, if necessary, to coordinate operations and timetables.

C – Relationship at this level is relatively basic and focuses on creating a comfortable ambiance for transferring information and synchronization. If it concerns sensitive topics and/or actions, a process of trust building is also required.

D – Commitment at this level is focused on transparency and anything related to defined information and maintaining the agreed upon work processes.

Cooperation

E – The value at this level is effectiveness through maximization and complementing capabilities and resources. For this, maximal cooperation is required among stakeholders regarding the relevant interests on the agenda. Furthermore, mutual objectives should be defined, especially short- and middle-term ones, regarding the process or the project.

F – At this level the structure focuses on clear definitions of roles, responsibilities and authority regarding work processes and regulations, so as to produce maximum effectiveness.

G – Relationship at this level requires creating ties and interpersonal connections, teamwork, shared language, mutual understanding and trust between the key players – in relation to the shared task.

H – Commitment at this level is based on creating an agreed upon and clear framework, with tasks to be executed, milestones, acceptable assessment parameters and mechanisms for follow-up and improvement.

Collaboration

I – The value at this level is relevancy, and it is imperative to understand how cooperation can intensify it for all partners. A deep understanding of organizational interests and personal needs is required. It is important to define joint objectives in conjunction with separate goals and analyze the long-term potential of the collaboration objectives.

J – At this level, the structure usually requires building shared platforms, arenas and spheres defining position holders in charge of the interfaces and the processes and, if needed, constructing organizational changes aimed at supporting collaboration and enhancing synergy between the parties.

K – Relationships in collaboration are highly significant and require close interactions, intimacy, high trust levels and long-term vision. It is important to invest in creating a sense of partnership and assimilating a culture of collaboration among the units involved and to construct mechanisms for dialogue and conflict management.

L – Commitment, at this level requires – beyond all that is defined in this element in its lower levels – work plans and mutual objectives, accurate definitions of shared maintenance mechanisms, agreed-upon value indexes, continuous improvement measures and clear decision-making processes.

Chapter 5

The ECA model as an analyzing tool

One of the most practical and useful applications of the model is its diagnostic tool. There are countless diagnostic tools available in the field of organizational study, including position and satisfaction surveys and various analyses. Most of them are excellent; however, they do not enable accurate identification of the relevant components at the interface nodes and knots. Using only a small number of questions, the ECA (Effective Collaboration Analysis) model serves as a diagnostic tool that aids during the preparation phase of processes aimed at improving partnerships and interfaces. It is advisable to apply the diagnosis before making decisions regarding the structure of intervention and change processes, as well as after. The model reflects the quality of partnerships using quantitative data, by means of a purely subjective view of those involved, and based on the model's four elements. The outcomes create a tangible image that aids in its understanding and in engaging managers in the processes.

The diagnostic tool is mostly applied in order to identify the current state of a specific interface between units or organizations, or to clarify the general state of the organization, with regard to the level of cooperation between the units or among members of management. For both applications it is possible to conduct cross-section analysis later in the process, to identify changes that occurred and gaps that must be addressed in order to further the process. The

DOI: 10.4324/9781003514992-5

following examples are designated to illustrate the diagnostic outcomes in various aspects. In principle, any result below a rating of five indicates a gap that must be addressed. A rating of four and below signifies a grave situation. There are hardly any cases with a rating of three or less.

Between organizations/units, when two factors are involved, the diagnosis provides a very accurate response to the manner in which each party perceives the interface. A comparative picture emerges, pointing to the different perceptions of the two parties in relation to each element and the factors included within it:

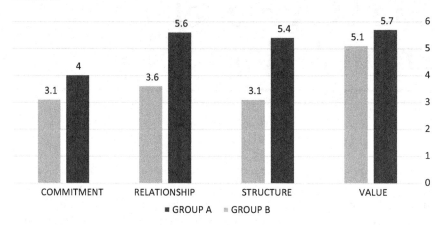

The above figure illustrates the state of cooperation between two large units in an international hi-tech organization. This figure clearly reflects a gap, whereby group B experiences low satisfaction in all the elements compared with group A. Should this condition persist, it will certainly generate a sense of frustration and disappointment. A gap also exists between the value element, which reflects that both parties acknowledge the importance of the interface, and the commitment element, indicating low-level execution.

The following example is of two companies – one from England and the other from the United States – that were required to work closely together. However, the interface was plagued by ongoing and escalating conflicts. The managers could not define the source of the problem, and to make it more difficult, each blamed the other. Using the model helped them to clearly focus on the gap: the managers of the British organization (marked in light color) gave low rating to the question relating the needs and interests of their US colleagues (marked in dark color) and even lower rating when asked whether they feel that their American counterparts understand their own needs and interests. This reflects a significant failure in the value element. There seemed to be a lack of clarity regarding what was of importance to each party. Based on the diagnosis, by working together with all

30 managers from both organizations, we were able to create a clear infrastructure of interests and needs that had been lacking during several years of joint work. Resolving the gap in the value element also created a solution in other elements, generating great improvement in work processes and mutual trust.

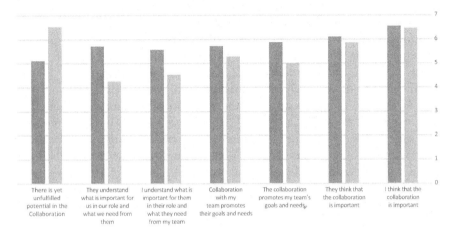

Naturally, most processes are focused on gaps that emerge in the diagnosis results. It is highly important to understand the various perspectives of the parties regarding elements of the interface. This example illustrates the state of the structure element, at the interface between manufacturing units and supporting units in a global pharmaceutical company. The mere fact that everyone involved can identify gaps and challenges in a similar way greatly facilitates the introduction and application of a focused process.

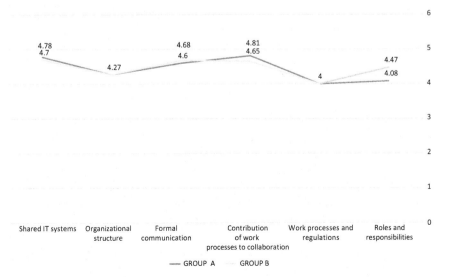

The next example illustrates an interface between senior management and middle management relating to the structure element. This properly expresses the issue of cross-system cooperations in every possible axis and is not merely reflected at the interface between units and organizations. The situation, as presented, once characterized the interface between presidents of courts, who are the senior level, but have very little managerial experience, and between the senior administration managers, who are the intermediate level, but possess a great deal of background and experience in managing the courts. Difficulties arose between the two levels, and as part of the change process, the ECA diagnostic tool was applied.

The model outcomes helped label the problem: where does the authority of middle managers end, and where does the senior managers' authority begin? This issue was part of the ambiguity principle for years. One could even say that senior managers deliberately exercised ambiguity, since it created an advantage for them in decision-making processes. Following the findings, they too realized that this situation was unhealthy, and thus they resorted to change, in order to create clarity on the issue of authority and in order to improve the dialogue between the levels.

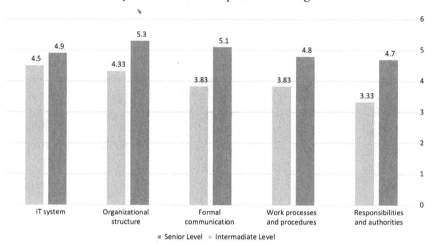

Assessing collaborations between three units or three organizations is more challenging. The numbers will always be less accurate than in an interface between two parties; however, identifying gaps and characterizing phenomena are still possible.

The following diagnosis presents responses provided by 220 intermediate-level managers from 3 organizations, who share many interfaces. The salient and emergent result indicated deficient relationships between the heads of the organizations ("senior managers"). Indeed, for many years, they were involved in power struggles and lack of communication. Laying the diagnosis outcome directly before them served as a significant catalyst in their ability to understand the severity of the situation and take responsibility for changing the nature of their relationships.

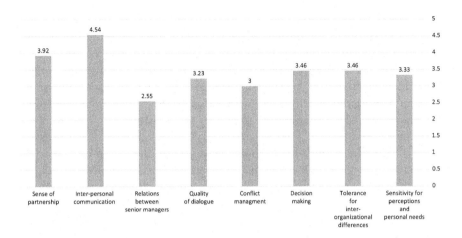

The ECA diagnosis can also be applied for the purpose of presenting an overview of the organization, as well as examining relations between specific units. The image generated carries great value for the organization leaders, creating the necessary conditions for open and deep discourse to take place. It can also help in recruiting those opposed to the change processes in a way that may result in greater collaboration and allow for a qualitative examination of process outcomes that are difficult to quantify. For example, as part of a focused strategic process in an annual work plan of one of the government ministries in Israel, diagnosis was conducted among 120 top managers. The VP of Strategy understood that strategic planning with significant impact depends on cooperation between the ministry's departments. The results presented to them created an excellent infrastructure for generating a number of possible solutions and cross-organizational workflows. Following are these products and their analysis, as presented to the managers:

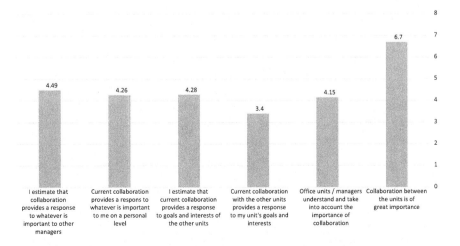

1. Value

   Clearly, office managers regard the partnership as extremely important. The current situation does not address the interests of office units and the needs of managers. They believe that their colleagues do not see the value and need for cooperations. This reflects, among other things, an organizational culture and managerial directive that, up to this point, have not assigned importance or priority to the matter.

2. Structure

   This element was found to be the weakest in the current situation. In fact, the organization is lacking in structured mechanisms necessary for effective work between units. It is very possible that this result reflects excessive bureaucracy and organizational hierarchy that often impair organizational cooperations. It is also clear that shared goals and integrated work plans are missing.

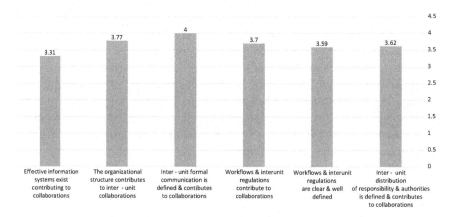

3. Relationships

   The sense of partnership as well as qualitative and effective dialogue is rated low. However, there are additional components in this element that require work. They can be significantly changed by means of increasing interactions and making them more precise, as well as by assimilating tools for effective dialogue management.

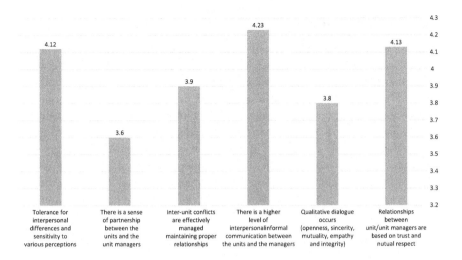

4. Application and commitment

In this context a fairly common image emerges: every party sees itself as the one aiming towards the creation of cooperation, while regarding the others as less involved. This corresponds with the concept of accountability, which is undoubtedly lacking in this organization.

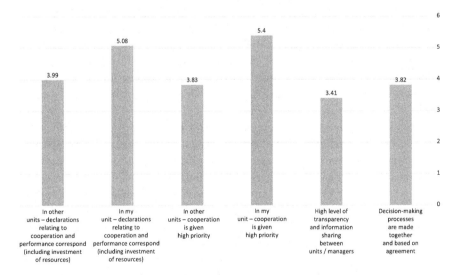

Relations between elements

A significant and fascinating part of the ECA's diagnostic application lies in the connections and balances between the four elements. An imbalance between the elements of structure and relations signifies a challenge to collaboration. The elements must support and be supported by one another. High structure rating and low relations rating reflect collaborations supported by procedures, definitions, bureaucracy and hierarchy. High relations rating and low structure rating reflect trust and flow in the interpersonal space, alongside high degrees of vagueness, disorder and difficulties in work processes. Low commitment rating usually emerges from low ratings in other elements. Low value and specifically a low perception of cooperation potential, lack of matching goals or misunderstanding of interests – all of these will result in direct weakening of the commitment element.

When all the elements are rated high and only the commitment element is rated low, we find that each party sees the other as uncommitted, not particularly invested in the partnership. This is a very common gap associated with the leadership and responsibility barriers. In almost every partnership, one party assumes it prioritizes and invests more than the other. Responsibility for mediocre collaboration is laid on the other party. At times this image reflects an organizational culture characterized by lack of accountability and collaboration, clearly illustrating the relation between leadership and collaboration. A state whereby the various elements are rated high while commitment is rated low can be the result of the "It'll be OK" barrier and the working assumption that things will work themselves out – whether due to a reluctance or inability to solve complex problems and a preference to postpone dealing with them or in order to allow for vagueness, for one reason or another. Organizational culture and leadership carry an important weight in these contexts, too.

Even if the value element rating is high, low rating of structure and/or relations will have a direct effect on the commitment rating. Structural or interpersonal barriers will naturally be expressed, both in the level of investment and prioritizations made by the partners. When commitment, structure or relations are rated low, while the value element is rated high, a discrepancy will appear between intentions or statements and actual application. If this is the case, one could expect a low level of trust in the intentions of the senior managers and leading factors by all those involved. This is expressed in statements such as: "There is no connection between what the CEO says and what actually happens" or "It's all talk, while in practice he does not really share or promote cooperations in the organization."

Sometimes low commitment rating can also be explained by a lack of awareness. In a process carried out with a global company in the internet arena, issues were brought up against the director of one of the European units, relating to the gap between her statements and her actions. The manager claimed that her unit was completely committed to collaboration with headquarters and the corresponding units; therefore, she could not understand the diagnostic outcomes, which presented her unit as low on commitment rating. When the discussion between the managers related to their perception of the gap reached an impasse, I intervened by opening a direct discourse with her:

"How many employees and managers are there in your unit?"

"About a hundred."

"Out of those hundred, how many are actively interfacing with headquarters and the other units?"

"Excluding me, perhaps three."

"And of those three, according to your rough estimate, how much of their daily activities do they directly invest in cooperations with other factors?"

"There is hardly any daily activity in this context."

"Can you estimate the scope of their activity on a weekly or monthly basis?"

"Maybe one percent of their activity per month is devoted to the other interfaces …"

Only when articulating the last sentence did she understand why her colleagues defined her level of commitment as low, and from that moment on, she began to strengthen and anchor her unit's commitment to cooperate with the other units. It was a pivotal point in the process.

It is rare to find a case where commitment is rated high while the other elements are rated low. This indicates either forced collaboration or a unique culture. In FIFCO, a Costa Rica–based company employing 6,000 people, the ECA diagnosis reflected such a picture. The reason commitment was found to be rated higher than all the other elements probably stemmed from a completely unique source. The key element in Costa Rica's culture is *Pura Vida* (pure life, in Spanish): simplicity, goodwill, empathy for others and positive energy. It turns out that this is what created a high level of commitment in the work interfaces between the units of the organization despite the fact that the other three elements were rated lower.

Applying ECA as a diagnostic tool – summary of advantages

- Simplifying complexity.
- The ability to examine cooperations over time at different points along the way and to generate a comparative and processive picture.
- Harnessing diagnosis to processes.
- Accurate and simple identification of points of strength and weaknesses and of gaps in the way the situation is perceived by the participating parties, as well as a clear focus on the issues that must be addressed within the work process.
- Creating a shared platform for change processes, by assimilating language and comprehending the situation as is.
- Call for action – decision makers are presented with a vivid picture, one that is hard to overlook. It is presented in clear data rather than psychological general descriptions, giving rise to action and taking responsibility for the improvement process.
- Calibration of awareness – experience has taught us that merely engaging with the ECA questionnaire creates a link to systematic and in-depth thinking of collaboration.

Network diagnosis

A good image of collaboration can be achieved by cross-referencing the ECA mapping with network mapping. This field was developed by Dr. Yuval Kalish, Academic Director of the executive program in the School of Management at Tel Aviv University and the Chief Scientist of StepAhead (a company that specializes in network mapping). Using the respondents' assessment of their relations with others, an image of the intra-organizational and inter-organizational network is obtained.

According to Dr. Kalish,

> At the core of network theory stands the realization that in order to understand complex organizational phenomena, observing each of the organization elements (people, staff, units) individually is insufficient; one must consider the ties between the elements and their quality. This is the only way to identify bottlenecks, detached elements, imbalance in relations and more. Thus we achieve an

understanding of the way the organizational environment supports interfaces and cooperations, and of the gaps in this context.

The figure introduced here presents a network image of collaboration among 60 senior managers of a large retail company. This image was based on the responses given regarding the strength of their connections with the other managers. An Effective Collaboration Process was initiated six months earlier, ensuing an intensive change process.

The mapping hereby presented is a good representation of a company, in which individual units were once completely separated. This is a condensed and beautiful network, with three players appearing in the center of all cross sections. What does this mean? It means they understand collaboration. They are the agents of natural change and know how to work, even at the informal level. We recognized and empowered them later in the process.

The trust network was also tested. We wanted to review the lower levels, which indicated lack of trust. The picture highlighted one manager in particular, with most of the arrows pointing out from him towards others. He was the company's best sales manager. The meaning of the arrows is that he trusted no one, respected no one, and as already known to us – belittled the change process and the idea that inter-unit interfaces may improve. These kinds of managers are great for the organization as junior task-oriented managers but definitely

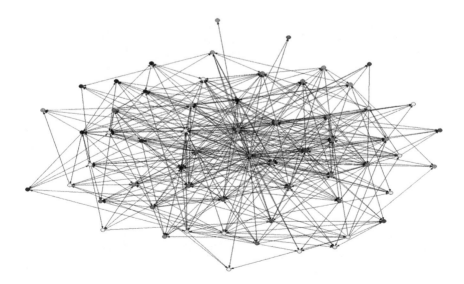

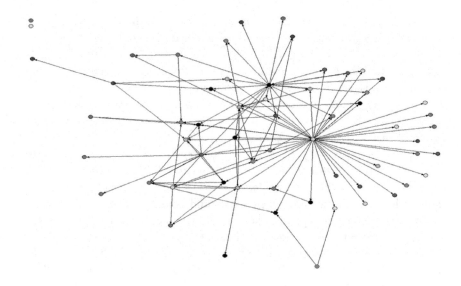

not as senior managers with influence on their surroundings. The company's CEO made a decision to fire this manager; he took a short-term risk of adversely affecting sales but removed a long-term significant barrier.

The simple and quick diagnosis performed by ECA questionnaires provides an extremely important infrastructure for implementation of the model in work processes. However, it should be borne in mind that the model is merely a tool and should not be glorified at all costs. Ultimately, what matters most are the outcomes and the effects of the processes carried out.

Chapter 6

Implementations of the model – ECP – Effective Collaboration Processes

The following words were written by a prominent leader from an organization engaged in a business partnership, shortly after it had been launched. His words reflect a prevalent picture of a partnership initiated without a structured process and consolidated guidelines:

> Over the last year, many difficulties have emerged in implementing the agreement, resulting, in my opinion, from a number of factors: the other party isn't really cooperating with us. They still wish to be the ones making the decisions, calling the shots, so no real equality exists; no full transparency between both parties; the agreement merely addresses principles, leaving many gray areas; it is not written unequivocally, thus leaving room for interpretation; some of the players still carry remnants from the past; one of the key players from the second party has a highly problematic personality, unreliable and aggressive; the joint decision-making process is flawed; a competition for resources is taking place below the surface.

Similar statements are often articulated in all varieties of partnerships and cooperations. It is difficult and challenging to bring together individuals and groups into a meaningful co-creation without having it dissolve or disintegrate.

DOI: 10.4324/9781003514992-6

Collaboration is an unnatural phenomenon; therefore, it is crucial to have good reasons to engage in such an endeavor. Collaborative leadership is essential for charting the path toward an accurate process and structure.

This chapter describes methods for implementing and performing collaboration, in order to support those who choose to lead change, strengthen the collaborative culture within their organizations and improve cooperations and partnerships with other parties. Creating and empowering the process of collaborations can be applied in a defined and exclusive manner, or it can adhere to other processes and nodes, which are already part of every organization. These are as follows:

- Broad organizational change processes. Naturally, collaboration is currently a central issue and goal as part of most change processes, in particular in those organizations that examine the questions of their relevance and strategy.
- Local change processes. When new interfaces are created following organizational change, in work processes or in setting up a new unit.
- Following an interface survey or organizational satisfaction survey. Sometimes the picture is overwhelming and generates high motivation to enter the process. Some organizations regularly require that units receiving low scores undergo an improvement process.
- Any project, new venture, acquisition or merger. In these contexts, it is advisable to perform the process as early as possible, to establish interfaces and create a potential stable infrastructure.
- Strategic thinking and planning processes and designing annual work plans.
- External or internal crises that disrupt the organization and require a rethinking of the current path. For example, many managers described how the Covid-19 crisis created a sense of urgent necessity to make a change and strengthen collaboration and thus helped to remove barriers.

The overarching definition for such processes is Effective Collaboration Process, or in short, ECP. These processes have recommended steps and comprehensible guidelines; thus, the architecture is clear, but the interior design varies, depending on associated contexts and factors. The Effective Collaboration Analysis (ECA) diagnosis promotes precision in intervention processes. ECP integrates tools from the fields of Mediation, Collective Impact and Consensus Building, intended to create win–win outcomes for the factors involved. These tools are assimilated as a shared language and presented in their advisory rather than their legal affinity – in order to create and strengthen deep mutual understanding of needs, promoting trust, relationships and effective communication.

What are the process objectives and outcomes?

The main objective of the process is to create and strengthen partnerships at all levels, to improve the quality of collaboration between organizations and the systems within them. This objective is a means to achieve the goals of the units and organizations involved in business, professional, social or organizational contexts. Qualitative collaboration is based on the strength and quality of the four elements. Following are the process outcomes:

   1. Value outcomes

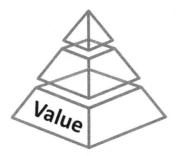

- Learning and creating mutual understanding regarding the partners' needs, interests and objectives.
- Consensus regarding objectives, interests and shared needs and understanding that they may be different and even contrastive.
- Creating shared understanding about the potential value of the partnership.
- Defining the level of intended partnerships, in order to realize the value – coordination, cooperation or collaboration. It is also possible to define different levels for different instances.

   2. Structure outcomes

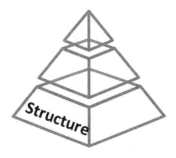

- Structuring a clear work mechanism, which includes processes, definitions, responsibility and authority, regulations, decision making and work frames.
- Systematic structuring of interfaces using set tools, as the basis for similar work configuration in the shared future.

3. Relationship outcomes

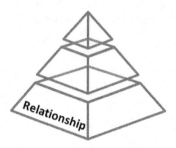

- Creating familiarity and closeness and intensifying them by means of a sincere and direct dialogue.
- Structuring, empowering and, at times, healing relationships and trust between the partners.
- Creating an open discourse based on effective communication, as a basis for producing a shared language and a sense of partnership for the future.

4. Commitment and implementation outcomes

- An agreed-upon design of a practical work plan – including tasks to be performed, timetables and implementation processes.
- Creating communication structures – a system for ongoing maintenance of relationships and intensifying interpersonal commitment. Although such discourse is sometimes done at an early stage, when it is difficult to foresee any challenges that may arise in the relations, early-stage joint design with long-range vision is extremely important.
- Recruiting senior management levels and work teams for supporting the processes necessary to realize the partnership.

- Agreed-upon measurements and the method of their collection, indices associated with objectives, information transfer and transparency mechanisms, conflict resolution methods and mechanisms.

At this point I would like to share my personal experiences, in order to illustrate the concept of the application process – in this case, as part of my activities as entrepreneur, CEO and owner and not as an external consultant and expert. In the most significant process of building a partnership in which I was involved, I was one of the partners in a merger between two leading organizations, a merger that was both strategic and dramatic.

Gevim Group was established in 1996 as a professional entity in the field of mediation, seeking to bring about change in the discourse in Israeli society. At that time no one had any idea what mediation was. Within a few years, the field of mediation was acknowledged and many centers were established, of which only a few had survived over the years. One such center, Gome, developed as a school for mediation and coaching and had become our main competitor. Both firms significantly stood out in the arena with regard to the scope of work, professional level, investment in development, professional team and reputation. In fact, these two entities played a central role in making mediation familiar to all within two decades. Training in mediation was considered significant to everyone and not just to those developing a career in the field.

Over the years, the field of mediation has encountered challenges and crises vis-à-vis the legal system and other players. Our real and shared concern for the future of mediation in Israel, similar interests and the ability to join forces and generate a significant effect initiated an alliance between Gevim and Gome and between the owners – Sharon Rendlich and myself. After several years, during which a foundation of personal trust and mutual appreciation was built, Sharon occasionally raised the possibility of a merger. I always responded with a casual smile, both embarrassed and conceited. In retrospect, I recognized that my consciousness was blocked by most of the same barriers which I identify in others and have detailed in this book, but I mostly realized that I failed to recognize the value element in this offer. In the middle of 2019, I surprised Sharon by letting her know that I would be happy to set up a joint meeting. We invited Yehuda Atias, CEO of Gome, and Hadas Dror, VP of Gevim, to participate in our meeting.

Coincidentally, on that very day my son Nevo, then a high-school senior, was spending the day with me at the office and was therefore present during the meeting, listening and observing. He was the first to instill in me a sense of confidence to seriously explore this move. Needless to say, to back up the initial move, I made sure to get some input from my daughter, Atalia, who since kindergarten has shown a curiosity and interest in things that went on in Gevim.

The first meetings dealt with questions of value. No progress could be made until we all identified precise and compelling answers related to the potential and reasons for entering this joint venture. Both companies were in good condition – each one with its strengths and capabilities, two competitors leading a growing professional market for a long time. In defining the value element, one defines the level of collaboration in which both parties are interested, although it is essential to revisit the definition when discussing the element of commitment. We considered coordination – creating links between our graduate communities. We also considered cooperation – creating joint training in mediation while pursuing the rest of our respective activities separately.

As we progressed, the issue of value became clearer. Understanding that training mediators is an overlapping and competitive field, Gome also developed the fields of coaching and NLP, and Gevim invested in the fields of negotiation and collaboration. We realized that a most unique opportunity had emerged, offering a range of advanced and complementary tools for managing relationships in the new and changing world while also providing a response for communities of training program graduates and professionals in the field.

We also identified great potential and value related to the marketing and sales aspects. Both firms were highly effective in their respective fields – Gome in working with private customers – B2C, and Gevim in working with business and public entities – B2B. In addition, we recognized that Gome has the organizational culture and infrastructure of an entity managed in an orderly, structured and calculated manner, while the organizational culture in Gevim is more chaotic, agile and innovative. We also realized that alongside business growth, we could accomplish significant savings in overheads and operating costs. However, had this been the main consideration, there is no doubt that this move would have dissolved into nothing.

Moreover, at some point I realized that the merger between the entities would immeasurably strengthen the impact I have been trying to create for a long time in the Israeli society – a divided and conflictual society, struggling to maintain a dialogue between diverse groups and build a communal life. Frustrated, I felt that we were only touching the tip of the iceberg of what could be done. I realized that my enterprise would continue in partnership with valued people who are committed to the same idea – promoting a vision that will not only be mine and in my image, but will be different, greater and wider in scope. With this understanding, alongside dilemmas related to management and control, identity and ego, my gut turned over and over until, slowly, it calmed down. Listening to my gut feeling, as well as to those close and familiar with my organization, was also part of the process.

This deep and complex stage, in which we dealt with potential, interests and needs, led us to choose a degree of partnership that combines the full range of capabilities and tools of the two entities into one shared array. Obtaining clarity regarding the value element assisted in making a decision as to the right level of collaboration and creating a foundation for the process continuity. The possibility of operating on one level for a while and then ascending to another was carefully considered. Since a "shared consciousness" had already been set up, at that stage it was decided to engage in a full merger of the organizations and establish "Gome-Gevim Group". Shared consciousness is an essential element in collaboration, one that we should aspire to create at an early stage. It can be defined as a clear understanding of the strategic direction and designation of the partnership – an understanding integrated with a desire to realize the shared designation. There is definitely an emotional aspect to this, the "sense of partnership", which includes affinity, trust and confidence, in the other as well as in the process.

In the next step we delved into two elements: structure and relations. We established a more personal and exposed dialogue, which opened the door to closeness and openness. We felt that everything must be expressed, even complex and difficult matters. We realized that there was no point in walking on eggshells, cutting corners or preserving a pleasant romantic feel to the relationship. We agreed to quarrel over everything at the initial stage in order to avoid doing so later. And indeed, we encountered some very challenging issues. Authenticity and willingness to be vulnerable helped in building trust. At the same time, we defined an outline for the process, with a clear sense of commitment, and formulated the structural agreements and the basic arrangement.

A few months later, we dove deeper into all the issues defined in the element of commitment and implementation – making clear and focused decisions regarding functionaries, new contracts, choosing suppliers, physical infrastructure, implementation, work processes and more. At this point the main challenge was to consolidate the legal contracts. These, by nature, bring forth future risks quite blatantly, making it necessary to make decisions in the most explicit and defined manner. These discussions generated crises that clouded the continuation of the process. However, we managed to overcome them mainly thanks to the infrastructure generated during the early stages, and with the help of the professional tools at our disposal, which particularly helped to explore personal interpretations, identify the potholes and hurdles of ego and fear, process gaps and burdens and insist on strengthening trust. At times and when necessary, we called for the assistance of a neutral professional.

Alongside our process as leaders, we designed an outline that included the professional teams and headquarters. It also included the four model elements, in a sharing process that involved some challenging, exciting and unifying moments. Objections and concerns were addressed mostly by means of maintaining a full, ongoing and open dialogue with everyone, at the highest level of transparency and cooperation, understanding that we need time and acknowledging that we may lose some of the people along the way.

On this basis, which reflects all ECP products, we performed the merger as planned in early 2020. We embarked on a gradual journey with the goal of completing and assimilating the joint venture in all its aspects. We knew it would take us a year to implement a full merger. The guidelines which served as our road map through this process are relevant to all processes of initiating partnerships and cooperations and are presented in this chapter in an orderly fashion, while the experience of those involved is both emotional and at times even chaotic, overwhelming and frustrating. This is precisely why systematic construction is required.

What are the guidelines of the process?

1. Win–Win

This concept can be realized when joint work takes place for the purpose of maximizing profits for all partners. One should realize that a win–win situation is only possible when complete clarity about needs and interests, both shared and separate, exists and when each partner truly aspires that the other parties involved also gain maximum satisfaction in the process. It is a strategy which defines the manner of operating, even when barriers and failures arise. It is the compass. The long-term damage emerging from the experience of being on the losing side in win–lose situations is devastating. No one wants a frustrated and resentful partner, but we are not always aware or able to sufficiently see the experience of the other. But as we all know, the road to hell is paved with good intentions.

2. Focusing on needs and interests

In order to build partnerships and a shared path, we are required to explore and accurately understand the needs of the people involved, of those who influence and are influenced, as well as the interests of the organizations. In our regular patterned conduct, most of us tend to communicate at the level of "positions", which entails demands, claims, suggestions and solutions. All of these render the precise understanding of needs and interests difficult and interfere with building mutual trust and understanding. The process is designed so that all partners can dive deep into needs and interests, guaranteeing that they will always be at the core of the discourse, as the basis for solutions. Conflicting and contradicting needs and interests exist and are given legitimacy within this sphere and may be more accessible and even solvable by means of adopting this approach as a process-oriented outline.

3. Working in a structured and supported layout

Complexity is the natural foundation from which many cooperations emerge. This is one of the main reasons why keeping a structured and supported process is so important, as it generates a safe environment that promotes openness alongside progress. Structurality enables constant focusing and confidence along the way, and guidance helps to release barriers and ensure that difficulties in communication and conflicts do not curb the process. At times, they may even constitute an essential opportunity to deepen mutual understanding; however, this requires a leader who is not afraid of conflicts. We know, both from research and field experience, that most managers choose to avoid conflicts; therefore, this is a significant consideration in how to lead the process.

4. Preparation and focus

Preparing for the process is crucial, as it allows us to enter a clear and focused layout in terms of expectations and setting boundaries. Part of the preparation phase includes defining the participants, which also has a great impact on the ability to later implement the outcomes. Using an ECA diagnosis helps in accurately analyzing the situation and planning the path ahead.

5. People, people, people

The core of the process is the straightforward, structured and direct encounter between the people involved. It may involve an initial or a long-term acquaintance between parties. Experience teaches us, time and again, that bringing people together in a way that allows them to converse, think, listen, express themselves and better understand each other creates the most profound experience of connection. It does not mean that everything will be "nice" in such encounters, nor is it the intention. People appreciate honesty and directness more than games or polite diplomacy. In addition to sharing perceptions, needs, concerns and challenges, a synergistic value emerges through the sharing of information, knowledge, experience and different perspectives.

Creating value in processes, in relationships as a whole and particularly in partnerships, does not require absolute consent on every issue. It is a mistake to assume that "consensus" means full agreement by all. The exact definition of the term is "to feel or think together". The goal is to produce dialogue, understanding and possible influence. It does not mean that everyone has a right of veto, nor does it necessarily mean that we will reach full agreement.

The original premise is that people involved in processes know what works for them and what does not. They have the ability to produce the most effective, practical and realistic responses to the challenges at hand. To accomplish this, they mostly need an organizing frame, professional guidance and an orderly process. The process must be designed to facilitate maximum participation and involvement of individuals and groups, at all stages, while preserving the effectiveness of decision-making and progress.

6. State of being

We are seldom offered the opportunity to stop the ongoing and intensive work and experience a shared state of being with the people we work with and conduct a dialogue about the relationships and interfaces we share. At the end of processes, managers often speak of these experiences as the most significant gains, as far as they are concerned. They derive very high value from the experience of just being, from sharing and listening, being part of a discourse about their shared path ("Talk the Walk") and translating the discourse into continued effective doing ("Walk the Talk").

7. Reciprocity

If we wish to encourage people to cooperate and jointly benefit from the fruits of this process, they must realize that they are also partners in the risks involved. One must be aware not only of the rewards but also of risks. People do not tend to cooperate or enter into partnerships when they believe that the risk they are taking is greater than that taken by the other party.

8. Simplicity

We are familiar with the expression KISS – "Keep it simple and stupid". A better principle for the KISS is "Keep it simple and smart". Either way, simplicity is essential for processes taking place in a complex environment.

9. The Pareto rule

We ask what is the 20 percent investment required to generate 80 percent outcome and impact. In dealing with long-term processes, it is important to achieve "quick wins" in order to show success, recruit those opposed or on the fence and strengthen the passion and conviction of those involved in the doing. During the first stages, we will aspire to identify the low-hanging fruits, those that are easy to pick. Success begets success.

10. Trust

Trust in the core of the partnership and therefore in the core of the process.

The process structurality

The rationale behind a structured process is based on the desired products and is affected by context and location. There are a number of affecting factors, clearly

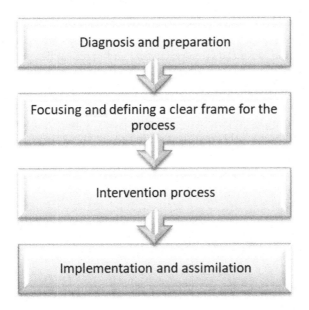

presented in the following table. It is recommended to make use of this table for focusing purposes during the preparation phase:

Sphere / State	Intra-organizational	Inter-organizational (bilateral)	Systemic (complex)
Initiation			
Existing			
In crisis			

Initiative / Your position	Initiated by you	Partner in team / decision	Coerced
Senior management			
Middle management			
Junior management/ non-managerial position holder			

Ex nihilo (out of nothing) – initiating partnership

Improving conditions in an existing partnership, restoring a partnership in crisis or establishing a new partnership – all of these are based on the same conceptual configuration, with the same perceptual and practical design. The order of activities is similar: we begin with the value element, then move on to simultaneously deal with the elements of structure and relations and finally take on the elements of commitment and implementation. When creating something "out of nothing", during the preliminary stage, each side must map his own elements and interests, subsequently creating a shared map. These are the most relevant questions for decision making:

- Why establish a cooperation/partnership?
- Why now?
- Who is it for?
- What is the purpose of the partnership?
- What is the vision and how does it relate to your personal mission as a leader?
- Who do we want with us? Who are the relevant partners?

- What can each of them contribute?
- What are the resources that each party brings?
- What are the barriers that each party brings?
- What is the set of power relations between them?
- In your opinion, what are the objectives, needs and interests of the potential partners? Why are they really here?
- What will subsequently keep them in the partnership and how can long-term sustainability be created?
- What are the historic and current relationships with the potential partners?
- What does it take to build and improve relationships?
- What is the level of trust between the partners at this stage, and how can it be raised?

In your organization/unit/side:

- What interests could the partnership address at the organizational level? What are the personal needs of the leaders that the partnership can address?
- How mature is the CEO/leader/organization/unit/leading team to enter the process?
- Is the partnership compatible with the vision, goals and mandate of the organization/unit?
- Does the organization have the resources to invest in the partnership? What are the resources at our disposal and what else is required?
- Who are the most suitable representatives from the organization side? Will these representatives gain support?
- What are the objections that may arise from within the organization?
- What will the organization gain from cooperation?
- What are the reasons against getting into this process?
- If the process initiator is not part of the senior management, is it necessary/possible to engage it? How?
- What other influencing factors exist in the environment, and what is their possible impact in the short, medium and long run?
- Do the required sense of urgency and necessity exist? If they do not, how can it be generated?
- How do I want to feel in the partnership? What will I feel in a successful partnership?
- SWOT Analysis – Strengths, Weaknesses, Opportunities, Threats.

Obviously, in this type of process, it is important to first examine each of these questions separately and explore whether any other relevant questions were left out.

The various models that deal with change processes emphasize the need to keep the influenced and influencing people informed regarding the change and share with them in the most transparent way what is happening and what is expected. The professional term "to communicate the change" is insufficient. The alternative and adequate term is "conversation" – creating a constant and authentic discourse during the process. The difference between the attitudes is quite dramatic, especially when dealing with processes affecting the people involved.

Foreseeing objections

It is important to be aware of objections that sometimes arise among participants or other players who are not directly involved in the process but have an effect on its implementation and outcomes. Some of the objections stem from the same fears mentioned in relation to the barriers described in Chapter 3, especially concerns about loss of independence. Change of the organizational culture or attempts thereof are a good enough reason for objections. Of course, there are the cynical and impatient participants, condescending in their attitude, who may consider discourse, or any process of this kind, as being part of the soft "touchy feely" world. Another source of objection may arise from those we identify as perfectionists and professional leaders, who fear that such a process may cause a lowering of standards and blurring of boundaries and responsibilities. This is how some people interpret collaborative processes. It is therefore important that the process be managed in a focused and assertive manner, all the while maintaining a sphere that allows for different kinds of dialogues, with determination and sensitivity.

Naturally, there is also an apprehension of organizational processes that lead nowhere. Every player has past experiences of processes that were unsuccessful and did not come to fruition. Most people arrive at the point where they examine the possibility or build a partnership with bitter experiences, bruised and disappointed. This must be taken into consideration and addressed. It is important that the discourse also includes the fact that alongside the potential for profit comes a cost or possible loss. This understanding may reduce cynicism and naiveté and build trust. Regardless, it is important to make sure that the profit outweighs the loss.

Objections should be expected, even if they are not stated or voiced out loud. Normally, people will be opposed to cooperations when they are too busy with other tasks and priorities, when they do not attach high value to what is about to be built, when they are distrustful of others and their motives, when they feel that they are unable to do their part well or when they are unsure that the profits justify the risks. Many simply fear change, are opposed to it and prefer the familiarity of their comfort zone. Sometimes it stems from the way they perceive the spirit of the organization and expectations from them, as described by an organizational development manager from a successful global company:

> Many managers want to strengthen cooperations, but they waver on the topic since they realize that it does not comply with expectations from higher up. There is no understanding of the need, neither the sense of urgency, not enough pain in the current situation, nor an understanding of the potential for more collaboration between organization divisions. They increasingly strengthen the competitive DNA, so even those who want to strengthen interfaces will avoid doing so.

Among those opposed to change processes, the ones capable of expressing their feelings are preferable to those who say nothing directly, only to turn around and plant contention in the office corridors, or those who simply wait for the implementation phase, knowing they will be able to delay, block or diverge the process in different ways, at their discretion. These are defined as "ghosts". You don't see or hear them, but then suddenly they appear and jam the process in its advanced stages.

Alongside objections, one should also expect enthusiasm and a wish to become part of the process and contribute to it. These will be defined as "harnessing factors" and "change agents"; they are managers and employees who understand the goals, identify with them, regard them as valuable for themselves and trust others. Sometimes we may even recognize them and recruit them in advance or will do so later in the process.

Stages in the change process

There are several fundamental stages in the process of building and implementing new cooperation or partnerships, each adapted to the relevant process:

1. Bonding discourse

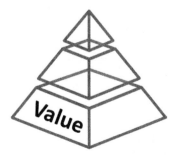

1. The value element
   - Clarifying the different and shared goals, mapping the interests of organizations and the needs of leaders. It is imperative to ensure the presence of those required to maintain effective promotion of the process and discourse regarding the needs of the partnership itself – trust, transparency, balance, equality, shared decision making and more.
   - A sincere and in-depth discourse about leaders' assumptions and ideas regarding the partnership in its formation stages – even in the absence of a clear path and action plans. Without discussion of expectations and agreements that are the foundation for advancing in the process, the appropriate infrastructure will not be created.
   - It is imperative to clearly define the desired path: coordination/cooperation/collaboration. Alternatively, it is possible to have different definitions for the short term and the medium/long term.
2. The relationship element

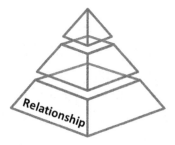

   - Acquaintance and reciprocal learning, both personal and organizational.
   - Developing an outward mindset – directing my perception toward others and caring about them and whatever matters to them.
   - Establishing relationships and setting up shared work teams.
   - Creating trust as a central goal. At this point, trust is built by the smallest of things, such as arriving on time to meetings and turning off cell phones for their duration, as well as authentically sharing everything that is relevant to the joint future, including concerns and deliberations. The more present and vulnerable we are, the more we will allow the other side to experience this state of being, and that is how trust is built.

3. The structure element

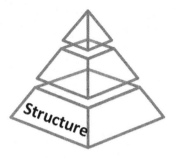

- Defining the organizational structure and leading position holders, areas of responsibility and authority.
- Orderly definition of work processes. Defining decision-making processes, at the policy and strategic level as well as the tactic and operative level.
- Determining the resources flowing into the partnership and defining responsibilities for them.
- Structure of forums and meetings.

  Needless to say that all the above is relevant even if we are merely aiming at tactical cooperation, without changing the organizational structures but with the clarity required for all formal aspects.

4. The implementation and commitment element

- Defining success.
- Marking objective criteria and goals. Making concrete decisions. Determining tasks.
- CKPI – Collaboration Key Performance Indicators.

- Setting operation plans, action items and timetables.
- Measurement parameters. Measurement methods.
- Designing and strengthening ongoing control processes.
- Determining mechanisms for negotiation and conflict management.
- Guaranteeing transparency in the process.
- Defining decision-making processes. This is the core. A person will wish to take part when he feels he can make an impact, and then he will be prepared to pay the necessary price. A person will let his territory be interfered if he knows that he can have an impact on other territories and on the overall enterprise.
- Reciprocity – the partners need to clarify the various interpretations of this concept and create joint clarity.
- Defining communication channels and transfer of information.
- Determining defined standards for various situations and contexts.
- Defining the time span in question.
- Discussing the questions: what happens if the need to disconnect the interface or disassemble the partnership arises? How does one party leave the partnership? What happens if one party breaches the commitment? What will be the future of the product/service created in the frame of the partnership?
- Clarifying boundaries of the joint activity.
- Discussing the question: are there any red lines regarding issues which the organizations will not cross?
- Determining definitions related to credit.
- The information issue: who transfers information, and how often? To which factors should information be transferred, within the partnership and outside it?
- What are the clear and acceptable standards in the work processes and control?
- How are shared learning, trust and relationships empowered along the way?

2. Operation discourse

After work begins, the degree of suitability and clarity of structure and relations must be jointly assessed. Interests and needs of joint work must be sharpened, trust deepened and the presence of the implementation and commitment elements must be verified, with all that entails.

3. Maintenance discourse

One of the most significant conditions for promoting a partnership is the existence of mechanisms facilitating open and effective communication (Gazley & Brudney, 2007; Leat, 2007). The ongoing negotiation between the players is the heart of the partnership. It is a dynamic and continual process, designed to achieve joint agreements and strengthen the partnership over time.

Maintenance discourse includes analyzing successes and failures and discussing ways to improve work processes based on mutual feedback and outcomes. Uniting other elements in the organizations involved should be ensured – both up and down – or attending to needs that arise and require engaging additional organizations to the process. Assimilation and follow-up processes must be intensified. In this context one should ask, is it advisable to increase investment and take more risks? It is crucial to engage in constant building of relationships, as well as establishing an organizational culture that can be defined as "the way we do things around here".

Given the way partnerships are built, it is fascinating to observe the startup arena. Prof. Noam Wasserman of Harvard Business School claims that 66 percent of the reasons that startup companies fail are related to the human factor (Wasserman, 2012). In his view, these companies are prone to failure neither because they have not succeeded in developing the right product nor because they erred in the market survey or penetration timing of the product in relation to the competition. The causes of failure are embedded in interpersonal relationships within the organization and its surrounding. Prof. Wasserman and other researchers studied about 10,000 initiators from 4,000 different startup companies in the last 12 years.

In mediation processes that we conduct with entrepreneurs and managers in this arena, we encounter countless disputes arising from breach of trust, communication difficulties, incorrect and unclear definitions of roles and areas of responsibilities and more. The "it'll be O.K" barrier is recurrent in startup partnerships, partly because connections are formed in close circles. Partners operate from an initial standpoint of trust that stems from acquaintance, not with deep and well-established trust that enables joint work. Wasserman claims that this is the Achilles heel of most partnerships in this field.

The state of abundant ambiguity and uncertainty, characterizing early-stage startups, encourages avoiding any discourse relating to all the issues that must be covered during the partnership-building phase. Beyond that, the "closeness assumption" we have with "natural partners" causes most of us to skip the stages of structuring that are proposed in the model as a systematic and critical move. We prefer to leave "gray areas" and allow "elephants" to roam the room with no interruption. In later stages, many conflicts that could have been resolved in advance will appear. All these could have been minimized, and sometimes even completely prevented, through proper structuring of the partnership by precise and consistent work of maintaining and building relationships from the very beginning. It seems that only professional and systematic tools can balance human nature and enhance the success rates of partnerships in this, as well as in other arenas.

Who are the process partners?

A dilemma relating to the partners from other organizations always arises as part of these processes. On the one hand, we wish to involve most of the stakeholders who possess relevant know-how and are able to implement decisions. We want people from various knowledge fields with a variety of reference points. On the other hand, it is important that the process be efficient; therefore, unnecessarily large forums should be avoided. It is recommended to create a first circle of discussions and decision making and another enveloping circle that includes additional stakeholders in organizations. In any case, it is essential to enable as much independence and legitimacy as possible to the expression of perceptions and opinions of different people in the process, regardless of their relative strength.

Another dilemma relates to the participants' level of seniority. We want people with a mandate to make decisions and with influencing and motivating abilities in the organization to be in the room in order to advance the process; however, it is necessary that they are available and accessible. Furthermore, we seek the presence of people with know-how regarding specific issues. If necessary, a senior think-tank can be created alongside the work teams.

An interesting study about cooperations in the Canadian medical system regarding AIDS (Maguire, 2005) showed that success in creating an effective inter-organization partnership resulted from a number of leading champions – all mid-level managers with strong informal influence. They knew how to create a deep level of identification and connection, both within their organizations and with leaders of the other organizations. Their success as champions was based on their interpersonal ability to sustain parallel processes that may involve potential contradictions. Not everyone is capable of doing so.

The study demonstrated that not only did the champions create the necessary connections but also showed that those who were defined as "skeptics" played a very significant role in the process. They introduced the right questions, created balance between enthusiasm for cooperations and the complex organizational reality and came up with concrete answers. They were the conscious voice in their relevant groups and responsible for realizing the various interests. The central applicable conclusion of the study is that the leading "champions" find it very important to mobilize the "skeptics", should they want to lead a full, accurate and effective process in the complex inter-organizational sphere.

Who is leading?

Every process includes a basic question: is it "top-down" or "bottom-up"? The optimal answer is "both". It's great but also rare. The key answer depends on the presence or creation of change-leading management that will connect the organization management to the field levels. A large food company is facing major growth challenges, including new global distribution, along with high sales and profitability objectives determined by the board of directors. These moves have led to the realization that positive synergy is required between the organization units as a condition to meet goals. However, the traditional organizational culture, characterized by hierarchy and separation of units, placed a big question mark regarding any possible process of change and adaptation to the changing reality. The urgent and acute need for creating change in work processes and the organizational culture were identified by mid-level managers, but they failed to harness senior management as a leading and involved factor.

In joint planning and in order to overcome the challenge, it was decided to create a team of 30 significant managers in the organization. The group included representatives from all units of the organization, with significant emphasis on the business units and supply chain. The team consisted of key people in the organization and was defined as "transformational leadership", in a way that clearly reflects that we are referring to leadership that promotes fundamental change. The senior management chose not to be involved but gave the team their full support to lead the process.

During the preliminary phase, ECA mapping was performed and the barriers were identified: excessive bureaucracy, absence of shared goals, managers' ego, dictations from the higher-up, a lack of definition regarding task prioritization as well as a strong silo structure. The defined strengths apparent in the mapping were primarily commitment, connectedness and great affection and commitment felt by employees and managers for the organization. Based on these findings, a new story was outlined, setting a collaboration strategy. Four cross-organizational teams were built according to the selected significant issues.

For example, one of the teams worked on connecting the collaborative strategy to the ERP (enterprise resource planning) system, assimilated two years earlier in the organization, mainly in creating precise work processes. It was clear to all that connecting to an existing and familiar tool is better than creating a new one and that integration with technology is critical to success in such a large organization. Another team chose the challenge of assimilating shared goals in work plans. It was determined that senior management would be connected later only for the purpose of approving the forum recommendations for creating a single global supply chain. In all other channels, team participants independently led processes to assimilate synergy while taking the risk that their managers might eventually stop them in place.

The aforementioned example illustrates how leadership can be generated in the field and the mid-level. It is feasible in the business arena but less common in the public domain. Recently, a number of mid-level managers in a government office initiated a process aimed at improving cooperations in the organization. The price that we, as citizens, pay for the lack of collaboration in this office, and between this office and others, is not only regarded as a tremendous waste of resources but is also consequential in matters affecting our lives.

Upon taking office, the CEO, a centralized and dominant manager, with a lack of collaborative vision, reduced cooperations between his office and other government offices. Efforts by middle managers to promote a significant move in the organization have been halted from above.

When it comes to inter-organizational collaboration, the question of leadership becomes complicated. Managers are accustomed to being in control, and this control is withheld or weakened when it comes to issues beyond their natural territory. At the same time, one should note the "autonomy dilemma" (Huxham, 1996), defined as a constant tension between the separate identity and organizational self-interest and between collective identity and shared interest of the partnership. Representatives of the units or organizations that are present in the collaboration arena with others will experience dilemmas and tensions arising from their responsibility toward the organization versus their responsibility toward the partners and the shared framework.

When the process takes place within an organization, the CEO's role is highly important. For example, one can note the significant and fascinating process of change that is taking place at this very time in the leading Israeli health maintenance organization (HMO) "Maccabi Health Services". Ran Sa'ar, CEO of Maccabi, testifies that for years he had been encouraging competitiveness in the organization, which led to impressive achievements. At one point he began to divert his mammoth ship toward a different route – not opposite but very different. And this is what he says:

> When competition has grown to such an extent, I realized that we are not taking advantage of our resources correctly, and we live in a world of limited resources. There is another type of resource waste that occurs – when you do not apply the right resource in the right place; for example, if you are evaluated by your qualitative performance in medicine, and in order to gain another point in your score, you decide to invest resources disproportionately. This also affects the organizational culture, such as concealing processes, both from

friends and colleagues. I do not reveal what I know to others, even as a downward message. All this stands in contrast to the organization values, including integrity and trust. We reached an extreme place, and I also saw other things outside the organization.

We have seen successes of cooperations at the Innovation Center we established and in other arenas in the organization, where all parties benefit and reach great achievements based on cooperations, at times even greater than we would have achieved in competition. We realized that we needed to take a "time out" and try to do something new. It has been gnawing at the back of my mind for years that change must be made. We started by strengthening the weak elements – still a task performed by each district individually. We changed allocation of budgets between districts, deducted budgets from two strong districts and diverted them to the two weak districts.

Today the focus is on changing the language and creating a structure which, on a practical level, will drive us towards a more collaborative perception. The entire organizational culture must be changed. Change of organizational culture is perhaps the hardest step there is. It entails language, structure, experience and process, and along the way you must make sure not to ruin everything that already exists in the competition and promotes us. We aspire to find balance, to produce a collaboration culture within a world of competition. It's a process that will take time.

The senior managers are testing me in the process of change, while they are also being tested themselves. We are all under scrutiny. I'm aware that not everyone is confident that I really mean what I say, so I must make sure they comprehend it. I will not be alarmed if for a time we pay a price in one criterion or another (relating to medical quality criteria and service criteria). As CEO I must be conscious of the example I give. "Walk the Talk." This is a very Top-Down change.

Sa'ar decided to divert his ship in order to strengthen collaboration. His choice to do so by means of dictating from above complied with the thirst that was apparent in the field and with initiatives of a number of key managers.

Whether the leading factor is the CEO or middle managers, recruiting senior management is a prerequisite step in the process. If senior management is not directly involved in leading the process, it should, at least, be aware of what is happening and back up the middle managers and the work teams by formulating responses and assimilating them.

When to say "no" to a partnership creation process?

Should we even go into the process? Managers need a systematic principle of action to help them make a decision. This is how they will avoid frustration and waste of resources for themselves and their people. They must take into account the costs versus the rewards of collaboration. Hansen (2009, 41) names it "Collaboration Premium" and suggests a simple equation, which is defined here as the "added value of collaboration":

1. The cost of investment in the collaboration – resources needed to create and sustain a valuable partnership, additional occupation of units beyond their normal work, energy and time invested in meetings, conflicts, and processes, and risks due to low performance and quality, budget issues, delays and more unknown challenges.
2. The cost of opportunities – the resources devoted to the partnership are usually at the expense of investment in other channels. We must set priorities and understand what is the best investment of organizational energy.
3. The value of return from the partnership – profit/impact potential.
4. The added value from the partnership – the outcome obtained by reducing all costs.

The equation is deduct from the cost of investing in a partnership the cost of other opportunities and the return from the partnership. The sum of all these elements entails the added value of the partnership. If the added value is positive with respect to the three elements, the partnership may be valuable. If not, it is preferable to avoid it altogether.

Research indicates that all too often partners choose to enter into cooperations and partnerships without examining them properly (Pisano & Verganti, 2008). The goal of any collaboration is not the collaboration itself but achieving better results. We must make sure that there is real value in collaboration and choose it only when we find it beneficial for us. Leaders must be capable of making a clear decision when to cooperate and when to avoid it altogether. They must assimilate into the organizations the notion that people should not cooperate for the sake of collaboration but will also be able to refuse it when the value proves to be non-beneficial.

In his study, Dovev Lavie (2007) specifies that during the decade between 1990 and 2000, the number of software companies that integrated into business alliances rose from 32 to 95 percent. These partnerships promote business growth through access to resources and markets, by creating new business systems, reducing expenses, sharing risks and strengthening flexibility. Many studies show that between 40 and 70 percent of these alliances do not produce the expected value. Lavie's research raises a substantial question mark regarding partnerships between entities of different magnitudes.

For example, let us refer to "Oracle's Partner Network", which consists of about 20,000 partners: independent software vendors, platform partners, sellers, marketers and more. Alongside those who wish to enter a partnership with "Oracle", some argue that in the end, the big company earns more at the expense of the smaller ones.

If so, managers need to choose partners more carefully and identify if, in the long run, the expected value for their organization is materialized. It is not always the rich partner with the resources and abilities that brings value to the partnership. Therefore, when a significant gap of power exists between partners, partnerships should be examined all the more carefully.

Chapter 7

Practical solutions for organizational internal and external collaboration

"So, what's the solution?" I am often asked by senior managers during the first hour of our meeting, as I become familiar with the needs and hardships of their interface. In most cases, my answer is: "I don't know. Together we will construct an accurate process which will help us consolidate the right solutions." In recent years the question of solution is heard less and less in opening conversations. Most managers understand the importance of the process and are engaged from an early stage in discourse about the journey.

Not many managers are aware of their contribution to the situation or of the barriers that characterize their management and organizations. I recall a case when a CEO asked to initiate a process with us. Following my talks with all the members of the organization management, and after understanding the severity of the situation, I reluctantly had to tell him, in the most respectful yet poignant manner, that as long as he held his position in the organization, there was no point in carrying out the process. Two weeks later he resigned, a move that was beneficial to the organization and its managers. Many managers experience a certain degree of blindness regarding their personal contribution to the state of lack of collaboration.

 DOI: 10.4324/9781003514992-7

The premise is that an accurate process will lead to accurate solutions. In fact, there is no prescription that can be drawn up in advance. Many practical solutions are presented in this chapter, for the purpose of illustration and inspiration. Just as each prescription drug comes with a sheet full of warnings, including possible side effects, directing the patient to consult a doctor if necessary, in this case too, it is recommended to be mindful in applying the solutions as prescribed. The effective response will always include a number of customized and integrated solutions while at the same time addressing its applicability and impact capabilities.

In the initial stages, we will prefer to use solutions that are relatively easy to apply – low-hanging fruits that are easy to pick. Twenty percent investment will produce 80 percent impact. We will try to generate a mode of "Quick Wins" in order to engage the people we need and generate the energy to support the next steps as part of a long-run move. Naturally, solutions that are identified as difficult to implement and with little impact will be irrelevant.

In this chapter I shall describe in detail the major practical solutions that were created and applied in organizations throughout long years of field work. Some of these solutions are focused and simple, while others are more structuralized and complicated to implement. Most of them are defined as "communication structures", supporting the integrated application of the four ECA (Effective Collaboration Analysis) model elements. This is a structural formal definition of a clear procedure or framework, designed to improve work processes and all aspects relating to relations between partners. The structures are translated into commitments, since they are assimilated and applied permanently over long periods of time. It is critical to formalize how communication is conducted within the structure, to create a real opportunity to effectively reveal and manage conflicts and strengthen the value of cooperation.

1. Strategy and organizational compass

The roots of collaboration lay in strategy and in the organizational compass. Throughout the book great emphasis is placed on the importance of the organizational culture, work models, tools and skills of leadership. At the same time, it is necessary to create a clear definition of a strategy of collaboration. This is an important statement that outlines direction. It stands in the forefront, affecting work plans and discourse in the organization. If such a definition does not exist, or requires revisiting, it creates an opportunity to leverage the situation and carry out a process in which employees and managers are involved. Alongside the integration of collaboration into the organizational strategy, a strategic plan of collaboration might also be structuralized, that is, creating a time-framed strategic move, setting up work teams and making decisions that are assimilated in a planned and organized process.

2. Work plans and shared objectives – CKPI's

As part of a process in a unique entity engaged in the field of leadership, the CEO defined a goal for the field managers for the upcoming work year. One of the three strategic goals they define every year must be a goal they share with a respective manager. The field managers accepted the instruction with understanding and commitment, as it stemmed from a year-long process of strengthening collaboration. Application, on the contrary, was challenging, since they were all used to preparing annual work plans separately and presenting them in a joint forum. Furthermore, implementing the joint work plans in the first year faltered. A year later, this move was already perceived as natural and easier to implement as a permanent part of the work plans.

Creating shared objectives for different units is a great lever for building organizational collaborations. However, it can be quite challenging for managers who are used to working with separate objectives. It is recommended to perform the shift gradually and take advantage of the annual work plans. In addition to defining a shared strategic or annual objective, other more focused objectives can also be defined, at the level of project objectives and KPI – key performance indicators, defined for the individual teams in order to improve joint operations. In this case we are offering a new term – CKPI's – collaborative key performance indicators.

These solutions promote a strategy of shared responsibility, joint ownership and a wide horizontal view by the managers. In other words, the processes of defining and creating the value cannot be performed separately in each unit but on the basis of cross-organizational consent. This is the exact opposite of how it is customary to design work plans and define objectives.

3. Changing the organizational structure

Until 2001, Cisco's structure had been organized according to segments of customer types and was later changed into a technology-focused structure. The main concern was creating internal centralization and distancing customers. A key solution to this issue was setting up a central marketing organization, which would connect the various technological groups and the customer-oriented sales units, as a move that would support the integration of products and technologies. Moreover, senior managers were appointed as champions for strategic clients, including the CEO, John Chambers, who was defined as Ford champion. In 2004, the company took a step up in adjusting the structure and created cross-organizational leader groups, which introduced the "customer's voice" in a number of critical processes. Cisco is an example of an organization that is constantly evolving in the creation of collaborative solutions compatible with the changing arena (Gulati, 2007).

Sometimes structural change is the most effective leverage, especially to the Silo barrier, so even if creating change in the organizational structure is unattainable, it is still possible to formulate interesting solutions for organizational change within the existing framework. In the process executed by "Maccabi" HMO that was mentioned earlier in the book, a hackathon was set up to consolidate collaborative solutions from the field. The selected group conceived the "houses". Six houses were created, each comprising sub-units from a number of districts. They consolidated in an ordered process of creating collaborations and acted to promote shared professional objectives. The purpose of the new substructure, which was pre-defined as merely a temporary move for one year, was to remove the walls created in the division between the five districts.

Another example refers to a leading organization in the defense industry, where challenges reached such a level that the individual divisions were helpless in addressing them. A forum was therefore created, consisting of innovation leaders. The R&D Vice President (VP) said, "Joint research and development between divisions has been an obscene word for years. Throughout the years this muscle was nonexistent. It's like taking a bone from your own flesh and putting it elsewhere." Emphasis was placed on creating trust and transparency in the process. The participants mapped all core technologies and created knowledge communities. Subsequently, they set up central laboratories with joint work plans and new solutions for customers. This process included designing business models in conjunction with making personal connections.

4. Point of contact – POC

This element includes defining people in interface junctions and selecting some to be official and clear one address. This person centralizes the various collaborative aspects from within his organization toward another. As an example, this model is applied in the Air Force Cooperation Unit. This unit includes air force officers placed in land force units, strengthening the collaborative language.

This solution is quite common in the business sector, although it frequently lacks accurate definitions of the responsibility and authority spheres, sector boundaries and communication structures. It is important to choose people of high collaborative intelligence and invest in creating an infrastructure of trust and shared language among all POCs involved in a particular interface.

A partnership created between a small municipality in northern Israel and a non-profit organization supporting impoverished families was founded during its initial stage on the close and good relationship existing between the Mayor and the non-profit's Director. When the parties wanted to expand the move, a partnership was gradually created with some senior position holders within the municipality, understanding that it was impossible to base the whole process on the mayor alone, and with the intention of generating wider processes. Many challenges and barriers were resolved using different tools, but the most significant leap occurred when a manager from within the local authority was designated as the non-profit's representative in the municipality and as liaison between the entities. Defining her as the POC broke down walls between the organizations and accelerated processes.

5. Relocation

The term "relocation" is familiar to us in its geographic context, yet in this case the concept refers to the organizational aspect. For many years a security agency experienced problematic relationships between the technological unit and the operational divisions which the unit was supposed to serve – including escalating tensions, conflicts and project delays. The most effective action performed by the organization, in an attempt to improve these interfaces, was to appoint to the technological unit a manager who was "raised" in the operational field. Many eyebrows were raised, especially among the tech people, who felt betrayed by the move. Organizations that initiate transition of managers between different units may pay a price in professionalism. Any head of a technological unit that is not a technologist may be less skilled to navigate the professional processes arising in the unit. He may not contribute to effectiveness, but he will certainly contribute to relevance – by bringing a different and more accurate understanding of the needs of other units and the means of cooperating with them. Within a short period of time, discourse between the divisions had changed. The technological unit became more relevant in the organization, and collaboration improved immeasurably and continued to be designed in the same way many years after the manager had completed his term. The phenomenon of transitionality is increasing among organizations, but it rarely occurs by itself. Creating a collaborative organizational culture strategy requires maximizing transitions.

If this solution is found to be suitable for the collaborative strategy, it should be assimilated in a structured and long-term manner – even if professional aspects are impaired in the short term. Some global companies have been operating in this way for a long time in order to strengthen their affiliation to the global organization and work collaborations between sub-units. An outstanding example is Unilever, a company that invests a lot of resources in order to ultimately produce a shared language, collaborative organizational culture and proper work processes between the company's units. Unilever invests in the mobility of managers between countries around the world. Seemingly, there is some risk and even potential damage involved in bringing in a senior manager from a different country, lacking any familiarity or perception of the local culture. Nevertheless, the value in creating an organizational culture as a global organization greatly exceeds the possible price.

6. Repositioning

Beyond the dramas that took place, the fascinating part of the popular TV program "Wife Swap" was expressed in the insights that emerged from the experiences. The saying "walk a mile in someone's shoes" is relevant in interfaces. The solution is repositioning position holders from two units for a period of one week. Even a day or two of repositioning helps to strengthen subsequent work interfaces. Consequently, a significant increase in the degree of understanding, recognition and empathy for the needs, concerns and reality of the other side occurs. It may sound marginal, but it is highly valuable.

7. Employee integration

The integration of employees in an organization concentrates on learning the needs of the unit to which the employee is designated and focusing on her/his tasks. Sometimes it may take years before the employee meets colleagues outside his unit team and learns about the other units in the organization. When this happens, employees will usually say that it should have happened sooner. Some organizations define a regular and binding process for employee integration, which includes a short visit and one-day stay (or longer) in other units in the organization, and visiting other units during the orientation days for a new employee. This move is extremely valuable for organizational collaboration, especially considering the minimal investment required in the short term.

8. Defining an urgency scale

The issue of priorities is a painful one, raising tension in many interfaces. A position holder from one entity is interested in addressing a need arising in another entity; however, this is not always compatible with tasks and priorities set for him by his managers – especially in the world of many tasks and few resources. The dilemma between our tasks and the tasks of others who rely on us occurs on a daily basis and is often unresolved. In this structured conflict, great significance is placed on the way partners conduct among themselves – between constant battle and on-going reciprocal communication, with intermediate solutions and compromises.

A clear definition of urgency and priority should be created, making it possible to operate under explicit procedures and agreed-upon shared language. The most common and simple definition comprises three levels of urgency: normal, urgent and very urgent. The terms and ranges vary from one organization to another, pertaining to its tasks. For example, the interface between a bank's business client-managers and its legal department experienced many difficulties and crises due to discrepancies in understanding the levels of urgency. Through joint work they determined that the most urgent level of response to each other's request shall not exceed a maximum frame of 24 hours, the second level was set at three working days, while the third and least urgent level was limited to a timeframe of no more than eight working days. This clarity helped to significantly improve internal collaboration and provide better solutions for customers. In hospital ward interfaces, urgency levels will be defined in terms of minutes. Some organizations define urgency using colors – red, yellow and green.

9. Cross-compensation

A VP at a technology company introduced a process of organizational change and assimilation of collaboration in his division as well as in its interfaces with other divisions. His directive was clear and was accepted by his team. However, as the process proceeded, they indicated that as long as their personal reward mechanism remains as it is, no change can take place. Each department operated as an independent profit and loss unit, and their managers received significant bonuses for their achievements alone. The managers were sincere in saying that because of the reward model, they would rather pay an external provider for a cheaper service, even if it involves paying a competing entity, despite the fact that it would be more sensible to obtain the service from a corresponding department and in doing so strengthen the organization.

The VP insisted that the change in work processes could be made even without changing the method of remuneration, based on the organization's vision and in the belief that its managers are imbued with organizational values and responsibility and not just by personal financial considerations. He was right, but so were they. That was the spirit of the discourse for nearly a year, with no significant change in organizational collaboration. Finally, the VP understood and made the required change, thus creating a cross-unit compensation model, in addition to the departmental remuneration. It did not take long before a dramatic positive change took place in division collaborations.

This compensation model can be illustrated through an example of a compensation mechanism between subsidiaries of a big business group in the construction field. The cross-compensation solution was a highly profound and significant perceptual shift. They realized that in the absence of this element, it would be difficult to assimilate other solutions, which were designated to advance collaboration in the group. The overall solution was complex and detailed and included a uniform cross-unit mechanism – a solution applied merely in the three senior managerial levels. The CEOs' first bonus was set at 70 percent of their product and 30 percent of the group product. The second and the third tiers in the companies were defined by a key of 80 percent company, 10 percent group and the other 10 percent personal goals. For years the CEOs relied on their product to account for 100 percent of the bonus, with full control of their sphere, so the change was dramatic for them and affected a whole set of work processes in the group. This kind of outcome, which seems virtually simple, is based on a process laden with conflicts and challenges.

A slightly different solution implemented in some organizations grants personal bonuses for managers only if the corresponding managers have also met their goals and are also compensated.

10. From supplier–customer perception to partnership perception

In recent years, and especially in large organizations, the perception of service is undergoing an ever-expanding process of profound change. Supplier–customer relations are gradually making a shift toward a definition of partnership. It starts with inter-organizational interfaces, with a process of creating an agreed-upon definition according to which units are run as a partnership. This perception increases the degree of empathy and reciprocity and reduces the familiar claims of the intra-organizational customer toward suppliers. In the extra-organizational dimension, the understanding is increasingly embedded that in the new era, it is necessary to establish an experience in which the customer feels that the supplier sees him as a long-term partner. This has many implications for work processes, sharing and transparency. The focus is mostly on creating value for the organization's customers.

11. "Share the glory"

It is very important for both managers and employees who participate in partnerships to receive credit for their success. If two organizations cooperate but only one is credited, it is expected that the other organization's managers will feel less committed. The need for recognition is fundamental and most certainly relevant to the personal level within an organization and the connections between various units and functionaries. However, for this need to be clearly expressed, discourse must be based on sincerity and trust.

Recognition of the other is the heart and soul of interfaces and partnerships. Consequently, people feel that they are seen and that their actions create impact. Recognition mainly requires mental focus and emotional capability. Receiving feedback from others, in a wholehearted and accepting manner, does not diminish our strength. Recognition of one's success is not reduced when the other partner's share is acknowledged. Managers with high collaborative intelligence fully understand this and leverage it to generate successes in cooperations. These principles can be applied as a structured and declared decision in all kinds of interfaces and projects, as well as part of an organizational culture.

Appreciation and recognition produce "positive contagion". Various studies show that whenever people choose to cooperate with others, they receive positive feedback and are treated more respectfully by their surroundings, and are subsequently more helpful and collaborative. Expressions of respect and appreciation toward contributors to collaboration strengthen it and have an effect on others (Willer, 2009). This is a good reason to use the Appreciative Inquiry method once in a while.

12. From NIH to PFE

In order to effectively deal with the barrier of "Not Invented Here", it's best to transition to the perception of "Proudly Founded Elsewhere". It is necessary that the organization management have a clear directive, assimilate the language and terminology as well as its application in the field, until the change permeates.

This solution is translated into work processes of collaboration between organization units or between organizations. One option is to create sharing and consulting platforms, collegian groups and "TED Collaboration" meetings that promote exposure and familiarity. Another option is to learn and adopt solutions created by other units, thus producing permanent frameworks encouraging curiosity and learning from others. It is not only the unit that reached the highest achievements that should be awarded but also the one that assisted the other unit to realize its goals.

13. Assimilation of method and shared language

Language affects consciousness and perception, which, in turn, form reality. To strengthen collaboration, this should be expressed in the language – spoken and written, internal and external, formal and informal. In order for a language to be practical and applicable and not be perceived as detached, an organizing model is required, one that integrates into everyday language and becomes natural and comprehensible. This tool is designed to produce a uniform reference point in the interface and help bridge the variance prevailing between the partners.

A method that confers parameters of measurement will strengthen the anchors of collaboration and the effective dialogue in its frame. It will create a legitimate space for a subjective discourse that maintains dialogue and connection. The ECA model provides an effective solution as an organizing model, and presumably, over the years additional models will evolve. Its main advantage lies in its simplicity. Those who have been exposed to this method find it very easy to immediately apply it as part of the language and discourse, assimilating it into more in-depth and specific processes.

14. Education and training – T-shaped management

There's a story about a coachman who drove a wagon pulled by four sturdy and strong horses. One day, while galloping, they tried to pass a deep mud pit on their way and got stuck in it. They tried and tried again but could not manage to get out – neither forward nor backward. When the horses and their master were quite exhausted, a wagon driven by an old coachman passed by not far from them, driving through the same mud pit. The older man's wagon was pulled by three horses, not as young or sturdy and impressive as those harnessed to the wagon stuck in the mud. To the coachman's surprise, and to the surprise of his horses, the other wagon passed the pit very easily. His surprise was even greater when the three horses came to their aid and pulled the wagon with its four horses out of the mud, with very little effort.

The coachman who got stuck in the mud asked his friend who rescued him to explain how he and his horses succeeded in pulling them out. "How is it possible that my horses, who are stronger, get stuck like this while you pass by so easily?" The other replied,

> You have chosen and gathered from different places the strongest horses you could find. Each of your beautiful horses is strong in itself, young and sturdy, full of self-importance. Yet they all grew up separately. My three horses spent their entire lives together and learned to work together from scratch. They learned from their very first days to cooperate, and so they act with humility and simplicity and manage to get out of even more difficult situations.

Cultivating a culture of collaboration rather than one of competitiveness is a change that requires an educational process. Training managers for collaboration, in terms of jointly learning the perceptions and practicality, is important at all levels of management. The emphasis for junior managers is team work. For all other levels of management, the emphasis is on leadership of the interfaces between the teams, as well as planning and performing horizontal, internal and external collaboration.

T-shaped management is a dual management concept embedded in training, which is starting to take place in many organizations. The vertical arm of the letter T symbolizes the manager's perception referring to his unit and its management. The horizontal arm of the letter T symbolizes the manager's width perception – his ability to successfully see and manage the interfaces and cooperations that prevail with other units and organizations.

Experience teaches us that integrated training for position holders from different units that sustain collaborative interfaces between them is more effective in terms of collaborative improvement, when compared with training in which each unit's representatives participate separately. For example, when a marketing department requests training that will help optimize interfaces with R&D, it is advisable to invite the people from the development unit as well. This will allow the creation of a unified and shared language and even enable them to jointly examine issues that concern the participants regarding their shared work processes.

In a security-business organization, a decision was made to provide the dialogue-based negotiation methodology training to all the relevant functionaries. The negotiation teams working with customers are from all the business units, but the request made by the divisions was to keep the training separate. In a strenuous process, lasting several months, the Business Unit (BU)'s heads were persuaded that it was more beneficial to conduct the training in heterogeneous rather than in homogeneous groups, since negotiation teams incorporate diverse disciplines and units. At the end of the training, all participants emphasized the high value created by the mere integration itself, both in terms of learning different perspectives regarding negotiation and in terms of creating one shared language for all parties included. Consequently, the business value that was created was extremely high.

15. Feedback and evaluation

When there is real intention to strengthen a collaborative culture in the organization, it is imperative that managers be evaluated on their ability to realize it. The annual feedback and evaluation talk held with each manager, along with the accompanying evaluation sheet, has a great impact on the assimilation of collaborations in the organization. When no section in the evaluation sheet relates to the manager's ability and motivation to collaborate with his colleagues from other units, it is as if the organization is making a statement that the issue is of no real importance. And vice versa: the appearance of such a clause indicates the importance the organization attaches to the matter. In recent years, human resource managers have increasingly assimilated, as part of the feedback and evaluation processes, the parameters of collaborations with other units – beyond engaging in teamwork capabilities.

16. Management meetings

Meetings and discussions in general, and in particular management meetings, symptomatically reflect the prevailing organizational culture. The issue of management meetings emerges as a significant subject in all processes relating to collaborations. Managers define management meetings as the lowest collaborative level – coordination, since it mostly involves a series of updates. It is not unlikely that participants find themselves busy with their laptops and smartphones, narrowing their involvement and responsibility, thus creating a "circle of waste".

When management takes upon itself the responsibility for creating change in the culture and organizational processes, management meetings must also be redefined accordingly. For the CEO this is a challenging discussion, as it confronts him with his managerial patterns. One of the best and most significant outcomes of this discussion occurs when managers come to realize that the forum constitutes a platform for improving interaction and relationships and creates a sense of shared responsibility in the organization.

The common and recommended solution is to define a different structure of meeting that significantly reduces the part of regular updates, leaving at least equal time for strategic discourse and substantial issues. The topic of discussion is selected and known in advance. Responsibility for the discussion and its preparation is assigned to managers by turn. During the meeting, proper time is allocated to relations between the participants, and during that time it is important that the table is kept clear of distracting digital technology.

Collaborations in local management teams or in global teams, integrating more digital meetings, are more challenging due to distance, relative isolation, time constraints and language. The use of technology not only helps and increases effectiveness but also maintains a certain level of built-in distance. Openness and intimacy will frequently be created only in teams that have been working together for a long time or in cases where cultural homogeneity exists.

A couple of years ago I facilitated an Effective Collaboration Process (ECP) with a global division management of a large high-tech company, where all communication, excluding an annual three-day session, was carried out via digital channels. At some point, during the process, the team members, all senior managers positioned at various locations, shared a deep pain – they expressed the great professional commitment they felt toward the VP while at the same time lacking a sense of security and intimacy in their relations with her. They described situations in which she took control over meetings, as part of her pragmatic and task-oriented management style. It was obvious that the VP was acting out of a very purposeful state of doing, while their need was in the sphere of being, creating a sense of inclusion and support in their complex struggles.

When referring to the VP's approach, the managers expressed themselves in this spirit:

> We've gotten used to being alone, but it's hard … My work today cannot be carried out without collaboration, and this is not really possible as long as there is not enough trust and confidence. Any real discussion will only be made possible when we agree to expose ourselves and be vulnerable … not if we are invariably focused on our performance and reports. How can anyone expect the "shared accountability" that you demand, when we do not feel this applies to us too?

The central decision made by this management was to forward reports in writing only and dedicate meetings to sharing challenges. The VP pledged to reduce her dominance over meetings and allow others to experience sharing and connection. It was agreed to create specific groups with a common factor, as well as intimate forums which they defined as a "safe zone", moves that they themselves were called upon to initiate according to the arising needs.

17. Delegitimization of collaboration barriers

What happens when a senior manager or any significant position holder in interface nodes acts in a manner that adversely affects collaboration? A wide range of responses exists – from denying the situation and accepting his conduct to parting with him. However, the response must be a conscious one, in light of its implications on collaboration and the organizational culture. A CEO cannot declare strengthening partnering in the organization, on the one hand, and avoid actions that validate it, on the other.

In an operating company, one of the VPs was conducting himself in a domineering, competitive and condescending manner toward his colleagues. In personal conversations, everyone complained about his conduct, noting the many costs the organization was paying due to this situation. However, the CEO regarded this VP as his successor. He was concerned that there was no other person suitable for the role and thus completely disregarded his shortcomings. Even in closed conversations, he denied the fact that the VP's conduct constituted a barrier for the organization. Due to the hierarchical organizational culture and high PDI, there was nobody willing to raise a voice in the CEO's ears, telling him the (future) king is naked. They all abandoned the idea that the organization could be run more cooperatively, and thus each concentrated merely on his own affairs. During these years, the company ran a successful and profitable business, so the costs incurred on the organization were not painful enough to stimulate any change. In such situations it is impossible to impact collaboration, and indeed the process was halted after several months.

There are many more examples in which the organization manager made a clear managerial statement in the face of non-collaborative behaviors. This requires awareness, courage and a solid position in the organization. There are various reasons why taking such steps may be difficult. The factors restricting collaboration can be powerful and veteran position holders, formal or informal; the CEO may be lacking in managerial courage; perhaps it involves people who produce very high value to the organization, and therefore, the CEOs are willing to accept almost any kind of behavior from them. These are all very common phenomena.

When an organization management sincerely chooses to create change, an unambiguous message should be conveyed to the restricting factors. In practice, it can be realized through termination of employment, a change of location or formal status, informally weakening them, as well as conveying direct and indirect messages regarding the illegitimacy of their non-collaborative conduct. Hence, the senior manager must demonstrate managerial courage and organizational maturity. In places where non-collaborative behavior was delegitimized and weakened, the other managers breathed a sigh of relief and promoted processes more freely.

18. Synergy/Integration unit

Large organizations can choose to establish a dedicated unit and, where it is less required or feasible, set up a cross-unit and cross-discipline team. Position holders and teams can be defined, solely designated for that particular job, or as an addition to their existing tasks. These units or teams continuously focus on creating and improving the work of interfaces dealing with cross-organizational issues.

19. Digital platforms

Digital platforms are evolving rapidly in many frameworks. An interesting study examined how the use of Dropbox affects collaborations in organizations (Pah et al., 2018). The study was based on information obtained from about 1,000 university departments during the years 2015–2017, with a total volume of about 400,000 users and many projects. Researchers compared ten percent of the best universities to ten percent of universities located at the bottom of the scale, especially in aspects of research and impact publications. They identified the characteristics of the organizations with the best performance:

1. Reduce the number of partners – in the top decile, the average number of partners per project was 2.3, while in the bottom decile, it was 3. Hence, one can conclude that it is advisable to keep a limited number of partners.
2. Take the time – in the top decile, the average time for project execution was 172 days, while in the bottom decile, the average time was 130 days.
3. Create team continuity – in the top decile, partners worked jointly on an average of 5 projects over time, compared with an average of 3.5 projects in the bottom decile.
4. Aim for equality – in the top decile, everyone seemed to be involved in a relatively equal way; however, in the bottom decile, it seemed that there was one person out of the whole group who took upon himself significantly more than the others.

20. Digital community

An intra-organizational portal is a well-known and relatively easy technological solution to assimilate. Many organizations apply it mainly for the benefit of accessibility and information about employees; however, the scope of possibilities is increasingly growing. The simplest example is creating a closed Facebook group in the organization, where employees can see each other's profiles, creating room for online informal discourse. Old-fashioned organizations will tend to avoid this – both in order to maintain boundaries between home and work and respect for employees' privacy and due to their concern about unmonitored discourse. Currently, there are more innovative and adjustable concepts, with a wide range of technological solutions.

Organizations must assimilate a culture of internal networks. The goal is not only to establish community, affinity and relationship properties but also to enable organizations to rapidly respond to challenges and changes, based on the free and natural flow of information. In addition, one of the most important conditions for employees to bond is their ability to express themselves – including expressing their personal position in the organization.

21. System unification – integration

Sears, one of the largest shopping chains, has been selling Michelin tires for many years. A difficulty emerged in the partnership between the two companies related to tension between supply and inventory. Certain Michelin products were missing in Sears' sales centers on a regular and continuous basis. Since the companies had been working relatively well together for over 30 years, it could be expected that they would continue to do so. However, in 2001, the managers of both companies jointly decided to explore options to change the existing situation.

The two companies established a collaboration that generated a unification of systems and a joint work process related to the aspect of the supply chain. The companies created and assimilated the principle of CPFR (Collaborative Planning, Forecasting and Replenishment. By creating a common system of inventory planning and systematic interface work, they managed to reduce total inventories by 25 percent and strengthen the supply and sales systems significantly. The decision stemmed from a genuine need and aspiration to improve business results, as well as from Sears' organizational culture, which maintains very close relationships with many of its suppliers (Steermann, 2003).

Integration of processes and information systems between different organizations provides a solution to many issues and barriers, but the required investment is often too high. Toward the end of 2016, ICL (Israel Chemicals Ltd.) decided to halt the massive ERP project it began in 2014, after an investment of about $225 million. The project was designed to integrate 13 different computer systems into one harmonized system, as part of the realization of the "One ICL" strategy. There is no doubt that halting the integration caused a delay in cross-organizational processes, but the decision makers assessed that the cost of continuation does not justify the expected value.

Following the events of 9/11, the U.S. Intelligence Community established a common information system called "Intellipedia", integrating all intelligence organizations into one technological platform. The name is based on "Wikipedia". Naturally, the older and more senior managers found the concept hard to digest, while junior managers and young employees assimilated it enthusiastically. Within a few years, the Director of National Intelligence significantly increased the budget allocated to this technological platform, due to the significant growth in users and information.

22. Measurement, audit, monitoring and control

Creating change through measurement and control is a rare move, being an endpoint marker from which we draw conclusions in retrospect. Nonetheless, at times it is the most effective leverage, as it entirely correlates with the organizational language. Numbers emerge from the page for all to see, enabling lateral and long-term comparisons. Measurement deals with products, and products are linked to the core of the organization's doing. The reference point is more easily understood by managers, as opposed to process thinking, which is often more challenging. Similarly, internal control units aimed at changing the organizational culture using critique as leverage can greatly affect the organization. Naturally, at both these levels, it is important to assimilate culture and tools that will enable performance improvement.

23. "Offsite"

"Offsite" is actually a code name for a communication structure based on taking a break from the ongoing and urgent work routine. You can leave work for half a day or three days, to the desert or to the sea, as long as the setting allows for a dialogue about relationships and collaborations. Imagine a vehicle driving on and on under heavy traffic loads. Once in a while the vehicle must be serviced in the garage, the hood must be lifted, the oils replaced, anything malfunctioning treated. If the car stays too long in the garage, it will not serve its purpose, but if it is not there at all, it will most likely be stuck somewhere on the side of the road.

> The result we have jointly achieved in recent days could not have been achieved elsewhere. The surrounding tranquility, the absence of phone reception, the simplicity and intimacy, were extremely vital for us in order to face the challenge we experienced here.

These were the closing words of the manager of a large association undergoing a complex and sensitive process, after two long days in the desert. Most managers understand the importance and value of such an experience after participating in it even once and incorporate this communication structure in their organizations at least once a year. At first sight this does not seem to play a part in creating collaborations, but it is a means that generates, by its very existence, part of the solution.

This definition, or any other name coined by the organization, may be used as a code name for structured processes in establishing new teams, projects and interfaces. It reflects the organization's clear understanding that one should not rely on "it'll be okay" and that an orderly establishment of any partnership and cooperation, with all they entail, is highly important. Once it becomes familiar and is found to be effective, everyone regards it as a natural part of the work routine.

24. Conflict management mechanism

Assimilating tools and mechanisms designated for conflict resolution as a communication structure of collaboration is an important response to the difficulties that may arise along the way. Agreeing in advance on the mechanism, the nature and method of its use, makes implementation easier. It is possible to rely on factors within the system in case of intra-organizational cooperation, and an external professional mechanism can be defined when it involves collaborations between different entities. In any case, it is advisable to predefine it in the outlines of the partnership.

A legal document that defines the partnership frame will include a "stipulation of mediation" clause, obligating the parties to a mediation process, should a significant conflict arise. In this case there is clear commitment of those involved to try resolving issues through the dialogue channel before any other procedure is applied. Naturally, the mediation outcomes are subject to the full consent of all the parties involved; thus, forcing a solution is not an option.

These responses are designed to prevent some conflicts and manage others, with no intention to create a conflict-free zone. Contrary to popular cultural perception, according to which conflict has a detrimental effect and should be avoided, the new paradigm in collaboration regards conflict as an opportunity for mutual learning and relationship improvement. Research performed by Gottman (Gottman, 1994) spanning over 20 years and including more than 2,000 couples presented his conclusions regarding the question of why some married couples hold out while others fail. The study found that disagreements, arguments and conflicts are inevitable scenarios in any marriage. However, stability and happiness are a consequence of the ways in which married couples discuss and resolve conflicts that arise between them. The "magic proportion" is 5:1 – the couple must share five pleasant experiences for any sensitive one (Gottman, 1994).

Research dealing with married couples can project on any relationship between partners. A conflict-free sphere indicates indifference or autocracy. Excessive conflicts consume energies and impair trust. Therefore, even if a regulated mechanism for conflict management is not defined, it is important to instill in managers, at all levels, the required skills and the managerial courage to settle conflicts, in general, and in collaborative processes, in particular.

25. Monthly date – interface meeting

A delivery company, focusing on an intensive and demanding operation in an attempt to provide their customers with high quality and accurate solutions, experienced a growing difficulty in their internal interfaces, as identified by the company's management. Over the years complexity increased, as did the intensity of mutual dependence between the teams. The need to strengthen collaboration was pushed aside, since all managers were deeply involved in the everyday routine and urgent matters of their work. About 50 team leaders participated in training involving the principles and tools of collaboration, discussions were held and an applicable outline was designed.

The most valuable decision made was to create a new "communication structure". Every team head defined two parallel team leaders whose tasks were influenced by their interfaces. A binding routine was defined, according to which once a month a one-hour interface meeting of two would be held – for each leader one meeting with whoever he chose and one with whoever chose him. It was determined that discussing current tasks during these meetings was forbidden, as the only topic of the meeting would be the interface itself: needs, structure, feelings, trust and work processes. The focus was placed on improving the interface and the ongoing impact on employees regarding the relationships they maintain with the other teams.

The main principles of these monthly dates related to communication structure operation are as follows:

1. Schedule a meeting anchored in a stable schedule with fixed day and time, thus creating a routine and habit. It is customary to set up a meeting once a week, once every two weeks or once a month.

2. Back up the managers and avoid situations whereby senior managers "take over" these meetings, as a means of conveying a clear message in the organization.

3. Define the topics for discussion at the beginning of the session, but be open for anything that will come up in the flow of the conversation.
4. Make sure to point out positive events taking place in the interface. Do not take anything for granted. Express appreciation for improvement on topics. Discuss issues that require improvements.
5. Analyze disputes and difficulties. Do not evade and do not avoid. Leverage it as an opportunity for deeper mutual understanding. Moreover, allow room for the expression of feelings and emotions.
6. Listen. Listening to one another is the most important condition for creating value in the relationship.
7. Conclude meetings with clear resolutions for implementation.

Following are a number of additional solutions created by Prof. Fishman, former Head of Obstetrics and Gynecology Department at Meir Medical Center, as part of the "Interfaces Project" he was leading for over a decade. It is his personal initiative to improve work processes between the delivery rooms, maternity ward, women's ward, neonatal ward and the gynecology emergency department. This is an irregular move, as the organizational environment of hospitals is saturated with complex collaborative challenges, which produce high costs, for both employees and patients. The three different disciplines – medicine, nursing and administration – represent different perceptions. If collaboration between leaders of these disciplines do not run smoothly, constant "circles of waste" emerge, including conflicts and escalations. Following are three examples of the communication structures created by Prof. Fishman and his staff:

15:15 Procedure: This is the time when the morning shift is replaced by the following shift. It is characterized by a long, cumbersome and, at times, ineffective handoff, mostly depending on the people involved, their professionalism and intentionality. Naturally, those who have finished their shift wish to complete the handoff as quickly as possible and leave, while those who have just arrived are still settling into the reality of the shift, which is often turbulent and stressful. The communication structure defined as "15:15" is exactly what its name implies. At that very moment the two teams gather – the staff leaving and the staff arriving. During the frame of this time, adhered to with precision, a briefing with an accurate and orderly structure takes place, including the use of a board concentrating all the parameters. This communication structure was created on the basis of all the needs, failures and solutions as identified by the staff, allowing for a full effective handoff between the shifts of all the various departments simultaneously.

"I am with you" procedure: This communication structure was created in the interface between the maternity ward and the delivery room and gradually expanded to interfaces between additional staff within the department. The clinical routine in each department in the ward is characterized by a parallel workload. Each team, in each unit, has priorities and precedence that are not necessarily synchronized with those of the corresponding department with which they must work, and there is no shared outlook by all departments. This phenomenon invokes conflicts between teams and often creates accumulated frustration, tension and hostility in relationships between the units.

To handle this situation, it is imperative to realize that interdependence between the units makes effective communication critical for the tasks at hand. A designated communication structure was formulated: "I am with you". This move is intended to promote sharing and build a joint outlook starting at the beginning of the shift. The nurses in charge of the staff in each ward contact their counterparts in other units, to establish personal acquaintances and share their relevant information and needs at the beginning of the shift.

Immediately following the 15:15 procedure, the shift manager, beginning an eight-hour shift in the delivery room, picks up the phone and calls the incoming shift manager at the maternity ward and says:

> Hi, my name is Ruth and "I am with you" for the entire shift. Please let me know your urgent limitations and issues and I will tell you mine, and for the duration of this shift please communicate directly with me.

Managers create a personal acquaintance and maintain direct contact, which allows for more effective coordination throughout the entire shift.

SBAR: Similar to other medical systems, the gynecological array in the hospital is characterized by emergencies, which produce urgency when the lives of mothers and fetuses are at risk. In such times there is no room for long and cumbersome communication. The message should be delivered fast and clear. For this purpose the communication procedure used in the U.S. Navy Submarine system was adopted – SBAR:

1. Situation
2. Background
3. Assessment
4. Recommendation

This communication structure is very effective in many work interfaces – not just in hospitals and not only in emergencies. It produces a unified, simple and clear language. However, it is very unlike the way we are used to communicating; therefore, a long-term structured assimilation period is required if we decide to adopt it.

The process of improving interfaces led by Prof. Fishman at the hospital has resulted in a number of measurable and clear products – including a decline in maternal and neonatal illness, a decline in the number of errors in treatment, an improvement in treatment safety as well as a decline in the rate of events ending in lawsuits.

26. "The Glue and the Oil" consultant

"The Glue and the Oil" concept is evolving in organizations, especially in complex project processes, aimed at ensuring more accurate handling of the "how" and reducing resources that may be required in the future caused by neglecting this part. Most position holders are very busy with their ongoing work, the "what", and less involved in relationships.

This consultant, either internal or external, helps to identify barriers, clashes and negative relationships and provides support at specific points of crisis or conflict. In this way, barriers can be identified in relatively early stages, before they intensify and are detrimental to work processes. Consequently, they can be handled more easily and with investment of fewer energies and resources than those required had their care been neglected and further postponed. The consultant serves as the "oil and glue" of the project management, or of the interface between teams, as a factor assisting the leading manager.

27. Influencers Forum

Emi Palmor, a former CEO of the Ministry of Justice of Israel, developed a unique program called Influencers Forum, intended for employees with up to six years' experience in the organization. There are over 5,000 employees in the ministry, with 40 units and divisions and about 70 different sites all around the country. This program is designed to create connectivity and continuity for high-caliber employees who have other alternatives, to help them express their voices, ideas and critical thinking, and create a shared organizational culture. Becoming familiar with other units is designated to create space for employee mobility and interest. Palmor's words on this move:

> Due to its size and traditional perceptions, at the time the Ministry worked as a collection of silos. Alongside the work I was doing with

the senior management, identifying shared interests between unit managers and creating cooperations between managers (Top-Down), I used the Influencers forum to help them get acquainted with each other and "discover" that interesting and important things were also happening outside their specific field. I made them start sharing challenges and knowledge, at a very early stage of their "lives" in the organization.

The significant stage in the process occurred when, towards the end of the program, they were asked to choose a topic they are engaged with and then present both the problem and its solutions to the management forum. This created mixed groups from various units, who realized they were in fact concerned about cross-organization phenomena. The process generated two topics: first, it resonated to management problems and challenges that the young employees are concerned with; second, it clarified how joining forces between different units allows to advance ideas. It is clear that when each unit handles its affairs separately it carries less significance vis-à-vis the management, the commission and the treasury, when compared with cross-organizational matters.

Emi Palmor created the move and personally led four rounds of the program. She further attests to the outcomes of this move:

The most immediate and significant value embedded is the ability to recognize and cooperate with position holders outside the parent unit, recognizing their accumulated knowledge and experience in other places, as well as the rapid accessibility created among a network of about 90 members. Influencers Forum has become a source of innovation in the organization, as well as a stepping stone for position holders, since graduates of the program soon became desired candidates for all senior assistant managers positions in the organization. This made them agents of change. An excellent example of the effect of the program was evident when seven deputies of the Attorney General appointed a forum graduate to the post of "planning leader", in charge of synchronizing the work plan of his department.

This brought about conditions that allowed for cooperation and coordination between the various departments in counseling and legislation to exist – a situation that had been very difficult to achieve before. The mid-level position holders were outraged over the investment and restriction of young employees devoid of managerial ranks in the organization. I found it important to ensure the absorption of more people who had not yet blended into the organization, and were thus able to observe it with a critical eye without fear of expressing criticism to authority figures, while at the same time open to other ideas and to thought and work patterns that are different from the closed unit DNA they had acquired.

28. COS – Collaborative Operation System

This solution includes a set of possibilities, based on creating work systems that combine a number of units in the organization or between organizations and practical work teams. It mostly involves projects, improvement teams and special tasks. This move includes a connection created by recognizing the challenge, agreeing on objectives and process, designing collaborative discussions, while eliminating hierarchy and consolidating work plans and their implementation. The emphasis is on connectivity and ownership of stakeholders in the organization with regard to the process.

COS or Collaborative Operation Systems is sometimes defined as "Fusion Centers". It refers to permanent or temporary situation rooms, which integrate relevant players for managing a particular issue or a temporary crisis. In the United States, they were set up in most states to create an integrative picture, to thwart and manage issues pertaining to crime and natural disasters. They integrate government agencies, security and intelligence, state governments, police, the business sector and more. The success of these centers primarily depends on a level of trust between the partners, since one of the central challenges is sharing classified materials between organizations. The concept of "fusion centers" can be applied in any subject and field that requires integration between organizations. We recently encountered a little integrative organization of this type during the pandemic crisis. Too little.

29. Collaboration standard index/mark

An organization with a higher level of collaboration will attain a higher level of trust toward it, as well as within it. A sector that will introduce a collaboration standard mark or even regulation regarding collaboration will devote importance and priority to this issue. These solutions are aimed at defining norms and standards, and although they have not been tried yet, there is no doubt that they will be very significant in the future.

30. Removing barriers

These ECPs concentrate on focused treatment of specific barriers that appear in interfaces between units and organizations or any organizational procedure that is designated to identify organizational barriers, reduce or eliminate them.

31. Collaborative decentralization – connected autonomy

The transition from concentration of information and decisions at the top of the pyramid to decentralization does not have to be an absolute move. The term "Connected Autonomy" was defined by Indra Nooyi, former Pepsi CEO, and appears in Hansen's book (2013). The goal is to allow units to work independently and alone when it entails the most beneficial outcomes. In this way it is possible to leverage the advantages of decentralization, with reference to the element of liability, reward for results, employee ownership of the process and more. Nonetheless, it is important to select processes and projects that require collaboration and to assimilate collaborative behaviors in a decentralized mode as well.

32. Matrix structure

This structure is a hybrid model that integrates units and organizational functions in different processes, both horizontal and vertical. The essence of the matrix is the solution to separation of various organizational silos – a separation that, in most cases, does not allow for an effective response to the challenges of the new era. Models sometimes produce managerial duality, power struggles, process delays, ambiguity in decision making and blurring the boundaries. Thus, successful assimilation necessitates a collaborative organizational culture and high capabilities of field managers for keeping an effective dialogue and creating mutual understanding.

33. The value management chain

Defining value is based on an understanding of the customer's perception of the maximal value for him. The various units are required to define the process and work together for the benefit of materializing this value – including setting goals, processes and tasks, which systematically produce a shared course to create the highest value.

Producing a value chain requires setting clear goals that will result in commitment and, at times, defining one person or factor that will be responsible for their integration. A prevalent mistake is that all units cater to one unit, such as a sales department. This may generate better service though not necessarily a strong partnership.

ISIS - Case Study

In his fascinating book, the *Teams of Teams* (2015), former General Stanley McChrystal describes the two main solutions he defined for the American forces fighting ISIS in Iraq. For months, the big, well-trained and equipped army could not effectively cope and wear down ISIS forces. He decided to remove all walls and separations between the special forces, seals, rangers, CIA and other units operating in that area. Another important decision was to abolish hierarchy. Life-risking operations that only he was authorized to approve were taken from that stage by lower-rank officers, including lieutenants. By these solutions he created collaboration, accountability, agility and relevance. This immediately affected the battle field and U.S. forces achieved all their goals.

This example is a success story of influential transformation, based on a sincere understanding of the barriers, collaborative leadership and implementation of accurate and structured solutions.

There are many other solutions circulating in the field, but it is especially important to remember that no solution stands on its own; one must create an aggregate of solutions that are accurate to the organization and adapt it to each situation. The solutions should be selected and created in accordance with barriers and challenges which are identified in the diagnosis. There is no doubt that the chosen solutions are of great importance for strengthening the element of commitment and creating conceptual patterns and work routines that may lead to practical changes in the field. The next chapter describes a new role, which can also be defined as a solution in itself, as well as a generator of solutions.

Chapter 8

CCO - Chief Collaboration Officer
The futuristic profession

In a reality in which many of the existing professions are about to become extinct, a new profession is likely to emerge: Chief Collaboration Officer (CCO). It is most likely that in light of the growing importance of the field, such a senior functionary will be present in every organization. This person will lead and influence the organization in issues relating to collaborations and relevancy.

Reality demands that an in-depth solution be created in order to professionalize the field of interfaces and partnerships. Part of the answer lies in creating this new role. It is advisable to avoid the title "senior collaborator" and aim for "VP of collaboration" or "partnership leader", or better yet, CCO. Many organizations use similar terms commonly acceptable by senior position holders: CFO, CEO and so on. Therefore, it is most likely that the title CCO will be accepted as the natural choice.

What does the role include?

- Assisting orderly and professional construction of interfaces and cooperations – within the organization and with other systems.
- Professional and preventive treatment of problematic interfaces and release of blocked nodes.

 DOI: 10.4324/9781003514992-8

- Assimilating shared language and organizational culture.
- Solving significant collaborative challenges in the organization.
- Identifying strategic opportunities for cooperations and partnerships.
- Assimilating orderly methodologies and measurements.
- Professional assistance in decision making related to entering into partnerships.
- Conflict management.
- Accompanying managers and various functionaries and providing consultancy for interface management, cooperations and crisis management.
- Long-term assimilation of orderly collaborative and methodological perceptions for cooperations, in systems where processes take place.
- Empowering and harnessing all the relevant factors for effective processes and resource efficiency.
- Accompanying external negotiation processes.
- Identifying new opportunities for cooperations and partnerships in order to strengthen the relevance of the organization.
- Empowering external cooperations and collaborations in the CCO network.
- Community management.
- Creating and managing network sharing of organization/community.

Imagine a group of senior government officials who use one language and one unified work model. When inter-organizational barriers arise, they are the ones responsible to come together in order to remove obstacles and optimize work processes. This vision will revolutionize the field of collaboration and leave an impact on many processes, thus creating value for us as citizens. The power of the networks that will be created, both within large organizations and between them, is a significant objective in itself.

Defining this role may also help to create relevance in those spheres that are still conducted in the traditional old-world conceptions. Take, for example, the role of the Ministry of Education inspector. The mere definition indicates most of all the perception of an old and irrelevant world. In practice, and in light of the challenges of this era, the correct definition should be "collaboration leaders". These are the people who should lead processes and bridge between schools, formal and informal education, education and community and the education system and parents. Until recently, this issue has not been defined and no tools were provided; however, there is no doubt that this is the direction for the future.

In many systems, managers are currently performing their tasks as defined in their job descriptions. It is expected that they manage their system and improve cooperations with their colleagues. Even if this is now more prevalent than before, it is still necessary to appoint a function that will see the whole picture and lead professional processes in the field. The managers themselves do not always have at their disposal the time and resources which are required to be fully dedicated to this task.

If the issue of collaboration is to be taken seriously, a senior manager should be appointed for the job. He should be connected to the strategic level and report directly to the head of the organization. That person should be an expert in his field, able to focus on the subject, with a systemic perspective and understanding of the eco-system. One may ask, then: Why not rely on existing position holders and just expand the definition of their role?

The most natural candidate for the role is the organization's human resources manager, the HR. Many of the features and capabilities required for the CCO position coincide with those of the HR manager, including profound under-standing of processes, high interpersonal abilities, evaluation tools and more. Another natural candidate is the organization's Chief Information Officer. This position holder should have a broad organizational vision and an accurate per-ception of interfaces between different units. Another option is to expand the role of the organization's Chief Operating Officer.

Integrating this function with an existing role will not allow for adaptive change. At best, collaboration will attain a lesser place in handling the main roles of the position holder. Significant change requires a similar move as facili-tated in new disciplines that have developed over the years – including adopting a clear definition differentiating between tools and training, and establishing clear positioning in the system. Today, unlike several years or decades ago, we are clear about the diversity and different clear definitions of the evolution of professional roles. Is it currently possible to think of the operation manager as responsible for quality assurance processes? Can the CEO deal with the issue of human resources? The answers are very clear. The same clarity will be obvious in the future regarding the role of the CCO. There will be a person with a defined role, who is an expert in this field. Very large organizations will engage a CCO group.

Even if in the upcoming years the position of CCO will be integrated with other roles in the organization, this appointment and responsibility will require special training. Such training will include gaining knowledge about a wide range of elements: professional models of cooperations, community manage-ment, tools of integrative negotiation and mediation, expertise in manag-ing dialogue processes and building consensus, profound understanding and capability of using social networks, conducting discussions and meetings and demonstrating high control of creating effective interactions. In the frame of this role, one must be in command of a deep understanding of innovation and opportunity management. This job description will be expanded and intensified over the years, making it clear to decision makers that this role entails a unique profession and discipline. One can assume that in the future, CCO training will be integrated as an academic track in universities. Almost three decades ago, we predicted that Mediation and Conflict Management would be taught in universities, at a time when only a handful of people knew what it was about. Since then it has become highly prevalent in the academic field. I predict that the same will happen with collaboration. It's just too important for our future.

In some organizations it will make sense to add to the title and role description Chance Management and/or Community Management. It's a nice coincidence that the two also begin with the letter C, just like collaboration, maintaining the title of CCO. But coincidence aside, they are both directly related to collaboration, in the internal as well as external organizational arenas.

Chapter 9

Collaborative intelligence
When needs and dialogue lead us

This chapter will focus on one of the most basic and important elements in any relationship and in any kind of partnership. It's a delusive issue – amazing in its simplicity and surprising in its complexity. I must admit that even after 25 years of in-depth practice in the matter of needs and interests, it still remains somewhat of a mystery to me. The professional working hypothesis claims that needs and interests can always be identified and comprehended. However, time and again I find myself in situations where – despite all the awareness, efforts and professional tools I possess – I still don't fully recognize nor completely understand the needs of the other.

The tools, language and perception dealing with understanding the depth of needs and interests are neither familiar nor customary in our arenas. We don't acquire this understanding in an orderly manner throughout our life, and therefore, this matter is mystifying and unfamiliar to most of us. Managers and position holders who believe that working with needs is the foundation for any effective dialogue and a necessary infrastructure for any partnership argue that this insight changes and clarifies fundamental perceptions of the manner in which we handle relationships.

Understanding needs is relatively simple. Why, then, is it also complex? To begin with, the T.O. pattern – "Task Oriented" – fails us once and again. This thought pattern, especially prevalent in managers, is based on a process of defining and expressing a position from which we quickly, automatically and directly shift toward alternatives and solutions. We are solution oriented; thus, we often lack the understanding and patience necessary for the process required in order to achieve the correct and most qualitative solution.

DOI: 10.4324/9781003514992-9

The position reflects our demand to achieve a particular desired result. For example, I demand that my employees get to work at a fixed time in the morning. I demand that my colleague submit a report containing certain data. I demand that my supplier provide a perfect product of high quality. Of course, they will express their positions and their demands. Sometimes, maybe even too often, we will be drawn to sway between these two positions, in a kind of "cha cha cha" dance, the principle of which is moving back and forth on one axis. The solution will be created in one way or another – aggressive or compromise – but solely on this axis. To illustrate, if one party says 100 and the other says 200, the solution will be located at some point between these two numbers, between the two positions.

One's position can have many different expressions – from an unspoken expectation, through a gentle request, to the use of force and even violence in order to realize the position. A legal procedure takes place in the space between the positions expressed in statements of claim. Each position is validated by explanations and justifications, and the judge grants his decision on the axis between the two positions. Alternatively, the judge may formulate a compromise, but the compromise will usually be made between these two positions. Our social discourse is greatly influenced by the adversarial legal approach, and that is why it seems natural and appropriate to conduct ourselves in this manner. The classic and familiar negotiation most of us were raised on is a chronicle of a predetermined dance between two positions. Therefore, it is often regarded as a kind of bargaining rather than a negotiation, which has depth and takes into account the ongoing relationships between the parties. We tend to use the bargaining pattern in relationships even with our spouses and children. This is the common and familiar language, and so, when conflict arises, positions become more solid and fortified.

We often invest all our resources in dominating our position over that of the other. Emotions have an increasingly growing effect, sometimes at the expense of reason and discretion. There is no synergistic vision or chance to identify a win–win solution. Attempts to create a discourse fade in the face of two different positional monologues that do not leave any room for a dialogue. Or, in the words of the Israeli comedian Shaike Ofir: "A monologue is one person talking to himself. A dialogue is two people talking to themselves."

We must delve into the sphere of needs and interests in order to create a dialogue. In this sphere, the best conditions exist to form the foundations for mutual understanding and agreements. Moreover, the discourse created allows for a more attentive, inclusive and respectful relationship. In terms of both outcomes and process, a dialogue about needs is far more effective than monologues about positions. "Position discourse" is less effective in its outcome, since it will usually lead to the domination of the strong party's position or to a compromise between the two positions. The process is often characterized by distant and ineffective communication, creating high levels of frustration and mistrust. Processes with no room for significant dialogue and work interfaces or relationships, which are mainly occupied by positions or solutions, will lose their potential depth and humaneness. When taking a position, we tend to extremize our own and attack that of the other. The other party is then more likely to respond with extremism and sometimes even aggression. Thus, we easily enter into conflicts, escalations and cycles of energy waste that generate a sense of frustration and stagnation.

A process that allows for expression, inclusion, understanding and, when possible, a response to needs and interests is a process that supports the value circle. In the organizational context, the organization benefits from the high value. This process is based on a high level of attentiveness and interpersonal contacts. Still, in the outcome test, this seems to be the only chance to promote qualitative, consensual and long-term solutions – even if in the end, it is impossible to provide a complete response to all the needs.

The key is to separate between "understanding" and "agreeing". When I listen to the other from my point of view only, and when I am preoccupied with the extent to which I can identify or agree with what the other says, or how much the other's words threaten me or are in contrast with my own needs, then I'm not free to really listen. If I separate between understanding and agreeing and focus primarily on an attempt to understand the other, then I will be able to afford the other the space to express his needs while giving myself a real opportunity to understand them. We usually don't bother to understand others, if we believe that there is no common ground or we cannot formulate any agreement with them. I suggest this is a fundamental error in interactions and relationships.

We use the term "needs" to understand what is important to people. The term "interests" is used to understand what is important to an organization or to any unit in an organization. For example, an individual in an organization can have a need for "maintaining integrity in work processes", which is essential for that person. At the organizational level, the corresponding interest can be articulated as "assimilating the value of integrity as an organizational culture". In this case, the need of the individual and the interest of the organization are totally compatible. Nevertheless, there are situations where contradictions may arise. For example, a need which is defined by the manager as "promoting my personal positioning and status in the organization" may be at odds with the organizational interest "to promote collaborative decision-making processes in the organization".

When personal needs do not correspond with the organizational interests, maintaining a dialogue regarding needs and interests is still essential. This process does not contradict the importance, and at times even obligation, to create clear boundaries. Making a clear "NO" statement when referring to matters that are defined as illegitimate in the organizational values and culture and/or unattainable in the current organizational reality is sometimes essential.

It is often said that everything is personal. Based on this assumption, when people in organizations represent the interests of the organizations or their units, it will invariably include their personal needs as well. An effective process creates space for both organizational interests and personal needs. The hypothesis of a collaborative perception, as demonstrated in this book, is that the most profound and effective way to engage partners, inside and outside the organization, is to identify both the personal needs of the individual who will lead the potential cooperation or collaboration and the interests of his unit or organization. After identifying the needs and interests, they need to be addressed. If only the organizational interest or the personal need is addressed, the interface will inevitably be weaker. When neither needs nor interests are given a response, there is little chance for real, comprehensive and effective cooperation.

Categorization of needs

Can needs be divided into different and distinct categories?

Everyone is familiar with Maslow's pyramid of needs. However, some say that the categories which Maslow formulated are less relevant today, since for most people the levels of the basic survival needs are already taken for granted, to some extent, and many of the tangible needs are already realized. Therefore, more attention is paid to the top of the pyramid – certainly if you consider the characteristics of the Millennial generation, for whom the needs of self-realization often outweigh material needs. The occupational properties of this generation clearly indicate that employees prefer to choose a workplace where they can develop and generate significant impact, a space of personal control with less authority, the possibility to realize their family and other personal needs in conjunction with those of their workplace – even if it adversely affects their salary, sometimes even significantly, over a workplace where they cannot satisfy these needs.

One should distinguish between two major families of needs: tangible and intangible. Tangible needs include resources, work space, time, salary, food, physical conditions, knowledge and information, definition of formal authority and more. Intangible needs include a sense of belonging, ability to make an impact, growth, independence, satisfaction, fulfillment and more. At times these needs are more emotional in their essence, related to the personal and interpersonal sphere, and more difficult to identify without awareness and appropriate tools. Often the stated position will be based on both types of needs. An employee requesting a pay raise strives to meet both the need for economic well-being and the need for recognition and appreciation of his work by the employer.

In most cases, the more significant needs are those in the intangible category. They motivate us to a greater extent; therefore, impairing them will be the main factor in creating rifts in relationships, conflicts and crises of trust. On the other hand, understanding and acknowledging those needs and certainly fulfilling intangible needs are huge levers for any relationship. However, there is a catch: these needs are more difficult to express and identify. They are perceived as our soft belly. In many organizations, especially those with an organizational hierarchical and task-oriented culture, their expression is not legitimized. It is also more difficult to ask about them and grasp their meaning. To overcome this obstacle, space, process, trust and application of precise skills are required.

Surprisingly, intangible needs are often easier to realize. Recognizing the value of a partner and acknowledging it are possible even in the absence of resources. Nevertheless, these needs are often much more challenging to address, especially when the arena is characterized by mistrust.

In the case of one especially difficult conflict, which involved three partners who are also brothers, our path was repeatedly blocked in an attempt to formulate a common and agreed-upon vision of the future value. The partner who repeatedly halted progress demanded that the others recognize his long-lasting hard work that currently brought the company to its great place, allowing them to enjoy the fruits of his effort. The others expressed their recognition regarding the value of his work and expressed gratitude and appreciation, but he was not satisfied and continued to obstruct any progress. At a certain point in the process, which was highly crisis ridden, the picture that I had not been able to decipher for hours became clear to me. I shared my understanding with him:

> What matters to you is not only that they understand how hard you worked and what achievements you brought to the company, and not just to express gratitude and recognition, you want them to understand the road you took. It resembles a high and dangerous mountain you had been climbing for years, gradually paving an unfamiliar path. You felt alone during many cold and dark nights, unseen by anyone. And once you reached the summit, they joined you and looked around in amazement. They are grateful and appreciative to you for all that, but they are not really able to grasp the road you took. This frustrates you. You want to relinquish this journey.

With tears in his eyes, he confirmed that this was how he felt. At the same time, the other partners understood that now, for the first time in many years, the real issue between them has been uncovered. At this stage I told him that his needs would never be fully met.

> No one can really imagine what you have been going through for years; the loneliness and the difficulty, the responsibility you have taken on. You have to acknowledge that the full recognition you so desire will never be given, even by your brother and sister.

This is one of the only times that I had to make it clear to somebody that he will not receive an adequate response to a central intangible need existing within him.

At this point I will introduce the four elements as a means of categorization: earth, water, fire and air. These elements are familiar to us from various spiritual dimension, and they can be used in highly rational and concrete processes. The use of these four elements may sharpen the understanding of the issue of "needs":

1. Earth needs – needs related to foundation, survival, body, space, frame and material aspects of our lives. This category may include several needs: physical well-being, safety, food, rest, suitable space, movement, touch, activity, comfort, stability, continuity, efficiency, order and more.
2. Water needs – emotional needs such as intimacy, empathy, emotional awareness, love, sense of belonging, compassion, sincerity, consideration, sense of partnership, reliability (the ability to rely and be relied on), trust, connection, link with others, closeness, harmony, the ability to feel and be felt and more.
3. Fire needs – needs related to instincts, creativity, self-fulfillment, relationships, our expression in the world in aspects of doing, influencing, meeting challenges, sense of competence, contribution to our surroundings, recognizing our value and its significance in the eyes of others. These needs include the ability to act out of a sense of movement, flexibility, control, passion, autonomy and independence, respect, pleasure and an interest in what "turns us on" and stimulates us to action and more.
4. Air needs – needs related to our perception, thought, understanding, intellectual stimulation and elements of imagination, vision, values, planning and conceptualizing about the future. These needs are related to the way we look at our actions in the world – in terms of choice, freedom, awareness, purpose, clarity, wide contribution, personal growth and development, self-realization stemming from integrity and a sense of self-significance and more.

This categorization can help us understand the issue of needs – both in the individual aspect and in understanding the organization. For the purpose of illustration, we can recognize the changes that have occurred in the issue of needs between different generations. In the past, complying with Maslow's pyramid of needs, more emphasis was attributed to earth and water needs. In contrast, in the new era, more emphasis is attributed to fire and air needs. It can be said that "Maslow has been turned upside down". This does not mean that the tangible needs cease to exist, but that the dominance of intangible needs is different from what it once was.

Why don't we express needs in a clear and direct manner?

People tend to avoid expressing needs – which makes it difficult to understand their needs and initiate a dialogue on this topic. It is important to realize this without judgment. There are several major reasons for this.

We truly assume and believe that it's all about positions. When holding a discourse about positions and in situations of conflict, we often "fortify" ourselves in our position, strengthen and empower it, strongly believing in our righteousness, and adhere to it. We make it clear that this is our demand, our desire, something we are entitled to. We may sometimes find it difficult to pinpoint and define what is the basis of this position and what it derives from and may even assume that it is irrelevant and unimportant to understand it. In order to understand our needs, we have to be aware of the issue, use suitable tools or ask for the assistance of another person.

For the most part, we do not share our needs and interests, because we are afraid that others will use this information in a manipulative manner against us. This is the commonplace conception characterizing negotiation: keep your cards close to your chest to prevent the other from recognizing your soft belly. These conceptions are still commonplace everywhere. Innovative perceptions, however, support the assumption that it is advisable to define and express needs and interests; otherwise, we may achieve the positions we have expressed but not those we really need – the very thing we concealed. The outcome will, most likely, be somewhere on the spectrum between the positions of the two parties. It goes without saying that expressing needs requires faith in ourselves and in others, a sense of confidence and the appropriate environment. This should be done in an intelligent and sophisticated manner and not out of naiveté.

Another reason why we do not express needs is that we are simply not used to thinking and speaking about them. We don't learn this from our mentors: parents, teachers and educators in the education system or managers. This requires a different mode of thought, manner of expression and level of attentiveness. Once we decide to look at this dimension, it is relatively easy to identify and practice it.

Long before we try to realize it in complex processes, we can observe situations, listen to other people and dabble in differentiating between positions, needs and solutions. This can be assimilated into relationships as well as organizational culture. It is the most essential point in the language of partnerships. Whoever understands it and controls it holds the most prominent key to the collaboration levers in his hands.

We often hope and expect that the other person will understand our needs without having to articulate and explain them. This is especially true concerning those who are close to us. We assume that because they are close and familiar, and assuming that they care about us, they will know on their own how to identify what is important to us. Once, during a tempestuous conversation with someone, she said to me: "I'm not telling you what's important to me and what I need. You have to understand it on your own." This statement probably also reflects a need, but beyond that, if the needs are not verbalized, the relationship will be less fruitful. These expectations are part of the "familiarity trap", also intensifying the "it's gonna be OK" barrier. It obscures our ability to identify gaps between the parties and invest in mutual understanding of needs.

Finally, many people do not express their thoughts, feelings and wishes in a clear, honest and accurate manner, because it is difficult for them to be vulnerable. It also refers to thought patterns, expressive abilities and even to internal obscurity and vagueness regarding their own needs. The ability to define and express these needs effectively and accurately is a challenging task. It is easy enough to articulate positions and solutions but much more difficult to do so with needs. Even when it is not a personal or emotional issue, it's still highly challenging; for example, defining the interests of an organization preparing for negotiations with another organization, especially when there are various interest groups in each organization. The processes of articulation and expression of needs and interests, when carried out in a systematic and accurate manner, greatly increases the individual or the organization's potential to manage partnerships, negotiations and conflicts. Clarity regarding our needs is extremely reinforcing and empowering – even in difficult and complex situations.

Identifying and understanding the need

How can one identify and understand the needs of the other? Positions are found above surface level; they are tangible, declared and clear. In contrast, needs are often found below the surface. An accurate process and the right tools are necessary in order to identify needs. Of the whole array of tools at our disposal, the most accurate and effective one is the seemingly simple tool of asking questions. The following are the two most basic simple and significant questions:

1. "Why?" We pose the question "why?" about the position. This should be a simple, clean, non-judgmental and non-defiant question, asked out of curiosity, true interest and with sensitivity. We may have to ask this question several times during the conversation – at various times and different contexts.

   There is a known folktale about an orange that best simulates the transition from positions to needs. My version is that of a father who returns home after a long and arduous day of work. He is a manager, so his days are full of decision making. From outside the house he can hear shouting, and when he opens the door, he sees his two children arguing loudly about an orange. The father wants to know what's going on, so his son answers that there is only one orange, and he wants to eat it. Immediately, his daughter bursts out and says she wants the orange for herself and that it is only fair that she should get it, because she took it first.

   When I asked managers in my workshops what the father should do, one answered that the father should take the orange for himself. Indeed, this is one possible solution, familiar to all of us from our own life. Another participant answered that he should run to the store and buy another orange. In the story, similar to most of the answers given in workshops, the father cuts the orange in two halves and gives half to his son and half to his daughter. This solution placates them both. But, to his surprise, the father sees that his son takes his half and squeezes it into a glass and drinks it up. His son's need was the juice, since he was thirsty. The daughter takes her half of the orange, peels it and cuts the peelings into small pieces, to make delicious, candied orange peels. Because they did not progress from the "position discourse", and because they made a rapid transition to "solution discourse", the process that the father chose led to a mediocre outcome, not as good as the optimal result could have been. Each of them received only half of the full potential of the orange. If only the father had asked them "why" they wanted the orange, thus discovering their real needs, both children would have received a whole orange rather than having half of it discarded to the garbage.

   Although life is not an orange, in many situations, much more than we can imagine, it is possible to detect this component of the orange, which utterly alters the way we see the situation and ultimately generates a more effective process and solution. Evaluation, expression, identification and discussion of needs are an important step in every dialogue, relationship, partnership and collaboration. This stage is often skipped because of the rapid transition made from expressing positions to seeking solutions.

2. "What is important to you?" is the second question, precisely aimed at understanding the needs of the other. It is a very important question in ongoing relationships as well as in short interactions. Formulating the question correctly, especially at the right timing, may work wonders, curtail anger and weaken resistance when it arises and aids in trust building – provided it is asked sincerely and authentically. If, during a dialogue with a colleague, the manager asks him, "Can you please explain to me what is important to you in the work interface between us?", he will probably receive a number of needs as an answer. For example: "Full transparency between us is important to me … It's important to me that in case problems arise, we will solve them between us rather than repeatedly turning to the CEO." These things will be said directly and clearly, or in a complicated and extensive verbal sequence, and at times even emotional.

It should be understood that often one need overlaps another and may even reach deep psychological levels. Reaching these levels isn't necessarily advisable or possible. Managers and partners are not psychoanalysts. It is indeed recommended to try and understand what generates a need, if that is relevant. For example, if we understand that somebody had a need for recognition of his professionalism and contribution, we can ask why or what is important to him in this context, discovering that what is important for him is a sense of certainty regarding his position and future promotion in the organization. It is irrelevant for us to examine his need to prove himself to his parents or to himself, even if it is deeply connected to his needs.

When engaged in partnerships, one must make use of additional tools and present an important point of reference, based on the willingness to be open to learning, curiosity and attentiveness.

Mindset of "unselfing"

What does this strange title mean?

In order to be as accurate as possible in identifying the needs and interests of the other, there are a number of essential things we need, in addition to the aforementioned questions. The foundation is our point of reference during interacting with the other person.

Our usual state of mind is based on "knowing". Not of humbleness and learning. We have answers, information and often solutions too. Most of us hold onto assumptions which are not tested in reality. This pattern, adopted by many of us, is unfortunately not mitigated by intelligence, experience and seniority. It affects our listening to such an extent that, in fact, we usually don't really listen. We mostly wish to be listened to.

Much has been written and said about listening. For our purposes, we shall refer to a division into levels of listening.

1. Responsive listening – I act in relation to the other from a reactive position, not entirely conscious and controlled. The classic reactions, especially if I feel threatened, are "Fight, Flight or Freeze". Even if I seem to be listening, I'm mostly preparing my response to the continuation of the conversation.

   One of the greatest challenges in dialogue and listening relates to our ability to identify and suspend reactions. When interacting with another person, we are in a state of reaction. Our reactions stem from the other person's words, his body language, our mutual past and more. Reaction is exacerbated when that person speaks about issues over which we disagree. We may interrupt and stop that person, or we may let him speak, while at the same time we are actually planning our response, completely inattentive to him. On the other hand, while reactions such as identification or avoidance may not appear to be aggressive or contrastive responses, they will also interfere with our ability to fully listen.

2. Judgmental listening – I listen through my perceptions and interpretations. I "know" what is right; I have the answers and the solutions. I am not really attentive. My energy is focused on trying to show the other that I am right and that my solutions are correct. Even when my interlocutor speaks, my attention is directed to myself and not to him, thinking how to convince him that he is wrong and I am right.

   Within the frame of these two levels of listening, it is difficult for us to be attentive, especially in situations of conflict – partly due to the assumption that quiet, contemplative listening contradicts our desire to correct the other and advance our agenda in the conversation. "Admission by silence" means that if I allow the other person to speak without raising any objections, he may believe that I concede to his ideas. However, this assumption is wrong. Full attentiveness to the other, in an attempt to understand his needs, perceptions and narrative, does not necessarily mean that I am relinquishing my own needs, perceptions and narrative. In every relationship I can find the proper time and manner to express what is important to me and not at the expense of listening to the other.

3. Factual listening – I am engaged in facts, information, implications and solutions. This is a rational cerebral form of listening. It can also be defined as operative listening. I am in a complete state of Doing. My level

of attentiveness to the other is partial at best, with the objective of moving toward a solution or action. When working toward finding a solution, the other has no real sense that he is being invited to express his needs, definitely not intangible ones.

On top of that, at this level of listening, I will find it difficult to listen to the other and understand his needs if I assume that I am incapable of offering him a solution. Knowing that in no way can I assist him in meeting his needs, I see no point to invest in a dialogue. But this assumption is wrong, since creating solutions may ultimately be found. Beyond that, merely being heard and understood is very significant to the person sharing, no less than a practical realization of his need; this is doubly true for long-standing relationships. The essence of the discussion of needs, even if impractical, is central and important in any relationship. For example, among cooperating managers, when one of them feels that the other is not attentive and empathic to his needs, it is very possible that he too will feel alienated and demonstrate apathy toward his partner and, moreover, toward the partnership in general. Dialogue about needs creates a bond between partners and may motivate them. Frequently, the very act of listening, asking questions and showing interest in the other's "story" may meet a very central and important need: the need of the other person to successfully voice his ideas and opinions and thus feel respected.

In the context of operative thinking, it is only after fully understanding the need that we can really examine whether we have the option of offering any solution or not. The more we improve our ability to listen and understand needs, even if we do not accept them or meet them, the more humanity we bring forth, in terms of our ability to manage effective communication and work with other people.

4. Empathic listening – listening from a personal standpoint. Attention is paid to emotions and relationships. I listen from my heart, I am open and non-judgmental and I accommodate the other and make an attempt to understand his viewpoints. This is a state of Being, where I am completely attentive, removing from my center of attention all aspects of action and solutions.

5. Present listening – it is difficult to find a precise definition for this level of listening, mostly because it is relatively rare. It refers to a high level of presence and of sensing the other person while completely halting my own set of reactions. I'm observing reality as it is (similar to Buddhist Vipassana), connecting head and heart, clear mind, present and quite consciousness and in a state of Being and devotion to what is happening, as something that is made possible because I myself am irrelevant in these moments.

The thoughts and feelings of the listener are not present, at least not while he is listening. This is the meaning of "unselfing".

A true and accurate understanding of needs requires the two highest levels of listening and is not possible at the three lower levels. Sounds simple? It is and it isn't. These levels require lifelong learning and practice. We are required to relinquish the familiar screens of interpretation, judgment, criticism, reactivity, prejudice and paradigms that we bring with us to any interpersonal situation. If I really listen to the other, through pure learning, I may ultimately understand that I need to change my perceptions and behaviors. Choosing to listen requires courage.

Another challenge relates to the lack of humbleness and the assumption that we "know", something that may even be defined as a major "flaw". Even if I understand the importance of conducting conversation about needs, there is still a great risk that I will assume that the other person's needs are clear to me. When I know him well, or have already seen thousands like him, I may feel that I am encountering him from a place of "knowing". By doing so I will not be able to recognize his real needs, even if my intentions are good. My assumptions about the other person's needs may hurt him and our relationship, no less than an action designed to intentionally do so.

We commit these "sins", in a sense, mostly with people we know and are close to us – spouses, children, employees and colleagues. We are sure that we know them, and when they express a position, we definitely believe that we know how to interpret their needs by ourselves. When it involves managers, who are required on a daily basis to "know" and offer answers and solutions, these patterns are particularly strong. Although the "all-knowing" manager is not as popular as he once was, it is still very common. In extreme situations we even define this behavior as "hubris" – the sin of arrogance.

The unknown is very challenging and even frightening for us all. It is a position that is foreign to the Western culture and to most of the organizational cultures. But we must remember that when we enter the interpersonal space from a place of "knowing", we minimize this space to a great extent. The ability to not know is a key element in what we define as unselfing and profound attentiveness.

A work premise including an attitude of humility and curiosity is a necessary element for adhering to an accurate and effective process of listening and understanding. This makes it possible to deal with the enormous complexity in this space – including situations where my interlocutor does not really know how to identify his own needs, as well as situations where people find it difficult to express their needs directly. The experience of really being listened to may produce for that person a significant transformation. When real attentiveness and dialogue take place, one may experience a more precise understanding, growing awareness, feeling of reciprocity, a willingness to jointly solve problems and more.

One of the main tools in this type of dialogue is the tool of reflection. This is how I make sure that I understand correctly and precisely what the other person is saying. I do not trust my detection abilities, which are influenced by many factors that may impair my understanding. Reflection helps me reformulate positions as needs. Although this tool is sometimes perceived as strange for practical and T.O. managers, it has penetrated the organizational cultures of a wide range of systems. As a result, many managers who learn and practice it describe the fundamental impact of using this tool on their relationships with others. Reflection helps to shift from a state of monologue to dialogue, and practically demonstrates the listener's humility and humbleness, thus helping to build trust in any stage and form of relationships that were previously lacking.

Should needs be expressed

So far, we have mainly dealt with the importance of listening and identifying the needs of others. Is there reason and relevance to expressing our own needs and interests? The answer is that it is both desirable and significant, for a number of reasons:

- As aforementioned, the classical and traditional conceptions of negotiation encourage the concealment of needs and interests, while newer perceptions support the assumption that needs and interests should be expressed in order to realize what is important for us. Unless we express our needs and interests, it might be difficult to realize them in the process. Realizing our needs and interests should yield high value both for us and for our organization. This is highly important in work interfaces and long-term partnerships.
- Making a clear distinction between needs and positions mainly helps us to focus on realizing our needs and interests rather than adhering to a position. Our ability to mediate this to the other party will help create a more expedient and effective process. At every level of collaboration and at each stage, we must experience full clarity about what is important to us. For the most part, it is preferable that things are made clear to the other party as well.
- Establishing an accurate specification of our needs and interests, both at the personal and the organizational level, aids in the establishment of

prioritization and a clear order of preferences. All of these may guide us in the right direction later in the process. This focus empowers and guides us through the early stages of building a partnership or in situations of conflict that produce chaos and uncertainty. When we operate within or on behalf of a medium or large organization, there is a wide range of interests of the various units and different needs of position holders. It is important to analyze and grasp the whole picture from the get-go.

- There are specific practices we must learn and use in order to create an effective dialogue which encourages the expression and understanding of needs. One of the important practical ways to allow this is to invite the other person to express his needs before we express ours. Managers should adopt the practice of being the last to speak. It is not easy. More tools are the right questions as described and the reflection.

- It is important to establish processes that include a clear element of reciprocity. When meeting with other partners, we do not wish to focus the entire process solely on their needs. Furthermore, expression of needs and interests on our part creates "modeling" in the process and advances openness and trust. This is often the most significant catalyst that will encourage the other party to share his needs and interests.

- When we decide to express a need, timing and phrasing are of great importance. First of all, it is advisable to do so only after engaging in the needs and interests of the other. This will enable him to be more attentive to what we seek to express. It is also important to formulate the need in a positive rather than negative way. For example, instead of saying, "I do not want…", it is better to say, "It's important to me that…"

- It is best to open up these spaces gradually and in a sophisticated way. It is best not to share all the needs and interests at the very beginning of the process. Rather they should be woven further down the road in an intelligent and sensitive manner, at the right timing and dose.

What do a needs-oriented dialogue, leadership and collaboration have in common?

The Full Range Leadership Model (Bass & Avolio, 1994) defines a number of leadership styles. Some of them are defined as less effective: "laissez-faire" (a leader that sits back and relaxes, allowing things to pass by him); passive corrective leadership (the leader exercises authority in extreme situations); active corrective leadership (the leader is engaged in preventing extreme situations and is more active); and rewarding leadership (rewards and punishment according to actions and performance). The styles that are defined as part of the characteristics of formative leadership, and are perceived as more effective, are inspirational leadership (a leader who bestows inspiration on his people); leadership based on intellectual stimulation (perpetual intellectual stimulation as a driving force); value leadership (based in part on ideals, mimicry and identification); and finally, leadership based on personal relations.

The latter style, which is perceived by various researchers and practitioners from the field as extremely challenging, is entirely based on needs. It involves a leader who identifies needs and, on the basis of his understanding and attitude, also recruits people and motivates action. He invests energy in personal relationships with each individual and is attentive to the unique needs in a way that produces a significant feeling of empathy. This principle, attributed to the employee motivation model, is also relevant regarding motivating colleagues and partners.

The paradox is that many leaders are positioned in the basic listening spheres and arrive at many situations from a standpoint of "knowing". Managers and leaders occupy the position they do because they are required to know, and it seems they do it well and correctly. They are required to solve many issues, and therefore, they are naturally solution oriented. The outline proposed here, suggesting a focus on needs and interests, requires learning and muscle-training, which are less familiar to us as leaders and managers. The first steps in this path will surely result in pain, but it is also guaranteed that the following steps will be lucrative and rewarding, because this move creates high value for the organization and for all involved in interactions and interfaces. Many who have chosen to move forward on the path to humility path describe implications and effects on other relationships in their lives, far beyond the workspace.

The issue described in this chapter constitutes the essence of collaborative intelligence. It is the ability to work effectively and productively with others for the benefit of realizing goals – in hierarchical interfaces too but especially in those which do not allow the use of coercion or authority. This is not about kindness and a positive attitude toward collaboration. These are important, but there are also dogmatic people with a tumultuous and even vulgar personality who possess extremely high levels of collaborative intelligence. This is not about charisma, although it is always helpful and may even mitigate situations that require the recruitment of people toward a common goal.

The key elements of collaborative intelligence, beyond the capacity for listening and working with needs and interests, are as follows:

- Empathy – the attempt to understand the other regardless of whether he tries to understand you. This understanding differs from agreeing with the other party. At the collaborative level, empathy includes the desire and curiosity to understand the viewpoint, cultural perception, personal needs and organizational interests of the other parties in the partnership.

This element, naturally, contains attentiveness and an understanding of the essence of a needs-oriented discourse.

- Positivity and a mindset of abundance – in our lives we have all encountered people that bring a competitive win–lose approach to every interaction while promoting their own agenda at the expense of others. Even among people who focus on problems, those who tend to say "it will not work" do not possess high collaborative intelligence. An optimistic approach allows for long-term vision, with prosperity and abundance of mutual profit options for all partners involved. A mindset of abundance recognizes opportunity in complex situations and advances processes more quickly and effectively.
- Authenticity and vulnerability – a willingness to share feelings, perceptions, needs and interests and express them in a sincere and direct manner. These features have the greatest impact on any relationship. The wisdom is to allow such authentic expression without hurting the other, certainly not intentionally.
- The ability to build trust – this approach is characterized by trust in others, emanating from a willingness to take risks rather than out of naivety.
- A.Q. – Adaptability Quotient – the ability to adapt to and thrive in an environment of change, complexity and uncertainty – a high performance potential in dealing with complex issues, making decisions and advancing tasks in a chaotic arena. We have already emphasized the importance of attentive presence and a state of Being in contexts concerning various aspects of dialogue, but without the dimension of Doing and without a high level of performance and application, there is no value for joint work.
- High EQ and high CQ – an emphasis on the importance of emotional and cultural intelligence. Deep curiosity and sensitivity at the interpersonal and intercultural level are an essential part of collaborative intelligence.
- The ability to generate the right energy – the ability to inspire others, influence creative energy in intimate or broad, easy or challenging forums and accommodate manifestations of cynicism and resistance, recruiting key players and infecting them with the right energy.

Following are some leading questions we may use to examine our collaborative attitude and intelligence:

- Do I have any interest in collaboration? And if so, why? What is that interest?
- How do I work in a team?
- What is my attitude toward shared responsibility?

- Which personal abilities and resources can I offer to the collaborative processes?
- How do I benefit from these processes?
- Which concerns do I have about collaboration?
- How do I deal with situations of conflict?
- How do I deal with situations of uncertainty?
- Do I have high enough AQ? If not, how do I develop it and/or who in my team does?
- Do I have the understanding and ability to merge and balance leadership and collaboration? In other words – Am I a collaborative leader? Am I humble?

The premise of this book is that collaboration is a space that can be learned and applied in practice, including the various perceptions, methods, models and tools. Not all of us have an awareness of our collaborative abilities and limitations. Although not every person has a natural tendency toward collaboration, every person can strengthen the skills inherent in him. It is a muscular system we need to be acquainted with, develop, strengthen and maintain. To do so, we need a basic willingness and a choice of direction. Collaborative intelligence is the core of collaborative leadership. In the new era, leaders and managers need it more than ever.

Chapter 10

Collaborative leadership

August 5, 2010. A disaster strikes the San Jose copper mine, which has been operating since 1889 in the Atacama Desert in northern Chile. A group of 33 miners are trapped deep underground following the collapse of hundreds of tons of rock into the tunnels. It takes six hours for the dust to set, before the trapped miners are able to gather in a small space, where they will conduct their lives for the next 69 days. It is fascinating to examine the team's leadership and the way decisions were made in the group. However, with regard to our context, we will focus on the leadership of those operating above ground.

Those operating above very quickly realized that there was no solution. Experts estimated that the chance of saving the miners was less than one percent. There was no way to dig anywhere fast and deep enough to save those trapped inside since the rock was too hard, nor was it clear what was their condition and where their exact location was. The Chilean government understood that the mining company, which in its negligence caused the accident, will not rescue the miners. Chile's president, Sebastian Pineira, nominated Andre Sugart to run the operation. Sugart, an engineer from a different mine, had 20 years of experience in the field and was known for working well under conditions of chaos and stress. He gathered a group of 32 professionals from various fields. The operation leaders primarily focused on the task of locating the miners and, later, on the task of rescue. In both parts of the operation, they encouraged creativity and innovation, cooperated with many factors, exhibited control of the situation and strived for fast performance.

Seventeen days after the collapse, during the eighth drill, they located the trapped miners, 688 meters below the ground. The moment the drill picked up the note written by the miners, saying "we are fine in the shelter, The 33", it

DOI: 10.4324/9781003514992-10

became clear that everyone was alive. From that moment on, they were called "The 33". For the next 53 days equipment, food and communication were maintained, all through a 15-centimeter wide opening.

The journey to their rescue entailed reaching out to anyone who might be relevant and examining every response or idea arriving from close and distant arenas. American mining experts who operated in Afghanistan, an Australian mapping company, a Canadian mining company and many others contributed knowledge and ideas. A team based in the capital Santiago checked every angle – including ideas generated by civilians from all over the world. In the field, Sugart ensured that a collaborative work system was established and refrained from creating a hierarchy, in order to maintain an uninterrupted flow of ideas and ensure they receive his full attention. At the same time, he demarcated the collaborative space. For example, he distanced the families from the professionals while still making sure that they are continuously updated.

An important breakthrough occurred by the introduction of mining technology, which emerged from somewhere in the United States. This knowledge was provided by a young engineer from South Africa, who arrived at the location independently. Sugart was attentive toward him, as to all the others. The mining process was eventually carried out by three teams working in parallel – each applying a different technology. At the same time, NASA and the Chilean Navy prepared a metal capsule which they named "Phoenix 2", to aid in the eventual safe rescue of all the miners.

The trapped miners survived thanks to leadership that encouraged cross-sectoral cooperation of disciplines, countries and organizations. The leaders realized that they had no answers, and in this given situation, they should act humbly and attentively, raise questions rather than provide answers and be willing to embrace any help offered. This action is embedded in the concept of PFE (Proudly Founded Elsewhere), rather than the concept of NIH (Not Invented Here). Humility combined with curiosity and an urgent need to find solutions created a state of readiness to invest and take risks by listening to others. It takes self-confidence to act in such a way. It is difficult to learn if we think that we know. Curiosity about what others bring forth generates a generosity toward them. This is the essence of collaborative leadership.

Harvard researchers who studied aspects of management of this event correlated it to the organizational world and to the manner leaders act in times of crisis. Uncertainty, time pressure, risks and survival can all be found in many arenas. According to the researchers, in such situations – especially when emotional tension is involved – leaders ask themselves whether they should act authoritatively, controlling and managing their people, or whether it is preferable to empower, invite innovation and explore different directions. The Harvard researchers argued that a dichotomous choice between the options is wrong, as both should be executed at the same time (Rashid, Edmondson & Herman, 2013).

This study defines the solution as "Control & Empower". It is especially true when involving people and factors under the authority and responsibility of the leader. However, in many cases, including that of the mine in Chile, the challenge is to collaborate with others over whom one has no control. A more accurate expression to use may be "Control & Collaborate". The difficulty lies in the fact that we usually relate to the matter as a dichotomous choice out of two different courses of leadership styles.

The basic question is: how do we define leadership? This directly affects the issue of collaboration. I believe that today (unlike the past), leadership is based on the ability to create collaboration, to connect different parts of the organization or eco-system, in order to achieve goals.

The dilemma encountered by collaborative leadership is how to enable people with diverse opinions to take part in realizing and creating a common goal. The *Wall Street Journal* published an article titled "The best bosses are humble bosses" (Shellenbarger, 2018). This article, like quite a few studies conducted in recent years, describes managers who act out of humility – those who best promote the work of their team, the organizational and inter-organizational collaborations. The definition attached to this phenomenon is "H Factor", a combination of honesty and humbleness. However, it is doubtful whether we would state the H factor as the central characteristic of most leaders we are familiar with. Why do many managers still lack this trait? And if its effect is so valuable, why do managers have a hard time embracing it?

Humility and sharing are perceived as "soft" and intangible, while the challenges of the organization are perceived as "hard core" and tangible. It is difficult for many managers to see the possibility of bridging the apparent contradiction, and some worry that they would be regarded as weak and vulnerable. For some, reaching the rank of senior manager is construed as a legitimacy to tell people what to do. They find it difficult to accept the concept of collaboration out of humbleness. However, in reality we see a need for a change of perceptions. While it may be said that the arrogant ego attracts attention and headlines, humility, in its wisdom, succeeds in achieving results and generating real change.

The Covid-19 crisis that broke out in the spring of 2020 created an opportunity for a fascinating comparative study on collaborative leadership and its impacts. *Forbes* pointed out that in female-led countries, the crisis was managed much more effectively and with better results, compared with male-led countries (Wittenberg-Cox, 2020). Countries with women leaders are New Zealand, Taiwan, Iceland, Germany, Finland, Norway and Denmark – some are isolated islands and others are relatively small countries. There is no doubt that leadership had a significant impact on the actual results.

The first to act was Tsai Ing-wen in Taiwan. Even before the pandemic was defined as such, over 100 guidelines and restrictions were imposed on the citizens; consequently, it created complete control over the spread of the coronavirus. New Zealand's president, Jacinda Arden, completely closed the borders and forced home isolation at a time when there were only six infected patients in the entire country. Two weeks later, she restored routine life in the country. From the very beginning of the pandemic, Iceland's president, Katrín Jakobsdóttir, allowed all its residents to perform free tests and created patient follow-up, thus preventing the need to shut down the economy and school system.

The way these leaders expressed themselves in the media uniquely combined an acknowledgment of the situation, transparency, sincerity, humility, empathy and sensitivity while taking responsibility and making brave and quick decisions. These are the two integrated muscle systems we refer to regarding collaborative leadership. Many of the male leaders invested a great deal of their energy and media airtime on finger-pointing or boasting that they are saving the day.

The most effective leaders and managers in this age do not claim to have all the answers. They understand that the world is too complex and that their job is to distill from their experts the best responses through a process of shared dialogue. These leaders know that their constituents need a different kind of leadership – one that empowers them, strengthens their resilience and interrelations and helps them to conduct in a state of uncertainty and constant change.

These leaders and managers recognize that the time when wisdom was enhanced by climbing up the hierarchy has passed. In the past, the tribe Chief was the only one who could read. Today, things are altogether different. Decisions should be made at the lowest possible stratum in the hierarchy, provided all the information is made available. The price of decision making at the level of organization heads is the time invested and the quality of the decision. The head of an organization can only spend a minute or two on an issue that a junior manager can spend a whole day on, giving it much more in-depth consideration. It is irrational to conceive that a more intelligent decision can be made in one minute than a decision arrived at through a day's worth of work. The price is also in slow reactions and actions and less agility.

In matrixial arenas, which are becoming more commonplace, managers have to create a space that promotes sharing and harnessing others, since they cannot rely on authority to promote their projects. Leaders also need to identify and lead the interests of the various partners, inside and outside the organization, with a long-term vision. They must understand the possibility of acting within a complex reality through dialogue and from a standpoint of mutual acceptance. They are required to produce clarity and stability alongside flexibility and the ability to change. Most of all, they must be committed to perceive the importance of relationships and the organizational culture and take full responsibility for nurturing them.

Why is the collaborative leadership style still relatively rare? Many managers developed a leadership style that worked well for them along the way, and when they stepped up the hierarchical ladder, they assumed that it was because of their managerial style. Hensen's study (Hensen, 2009) identified five central personal characteristics of managers and leaders that make it difficult to adopt a collaborative style of leadership:

1. Hunger for power – some leaders base themselves on ambition for power and a desire to have others depend on them. These leaders are also reluctant to collaborate with others, since they regard collaboration as a relinquishment of power.
2. Arrogance – managers whose attitude is "I know best", who are sure that they are smarter than others, tend not to involve others in their decision-making processes. And they are right. Why collaborate with others who understand less and waste their valuable time? This factor has been found in research to be the biggest hindrance to collaborative leadership. These managers enter the discussion room assuming they possess the knowledge and the best answers; thus, they are fundamentally less attentive to others.
3. Defensive approach – this approach constitutes a significant barrier. Defensive leaders find it difficult to accept criticism and tend to see problems as arising from anything other than themselves. The more defensive a leader is, the less open he will be to collaborate with others, especially due to the recognition that he might be wrong.
4. Fear of failure and defeat – this fear mainly leads to clinging to one's personal agenda, since hurting it becomes personal.
5. Big ego – surprisingly, according to the research, this factor is found to have the least impact on the ability to adopt a collaborative leadership style.

A leader who works collaboratively must prioritize the needs of the system over his own or at least keep a balance between them. Collaboration strengthens consensus, which, in return, empowers collaboration. When I was asked by a department manager in a government office to lead a process with his managerial team on issues of strategy and collaboration, I identified during preliminary conversations held with him that what he was interested in was creating a "fig leaf" rather than generating real change or value in the process. I reflected back to him his competitive and combative conduct in the office. He confirmed that this was no coincidence, as his main driving need was to be promoted. When we focused on the gap between his needs and the interests of the organization and found that his priorities were unwavering and clear, we parted as friends.

Can leaders change? It seems that if the non-collaborative characteristics are deeply rooted in the personality of a leader, change will rarely be possible. However, if a leader is aware of himself and of the need to make a change, then change is possible. John Chambers, CEO and Chairman of Cisco, said in an interview to the *New York Times* in 2009:

> I am a man of command and control. I like to be able to say "turn right", and find that 67,000 men turn right. But this style is old-fashioned. The world today needs a different leadership style. More cooperation and teamwork.

There are definitely managers who change along the way. Charismatic, dominant, opinionated, authoritative, veterans and experts, revered and every possible variation between these elements gradually change their style and become more attentive, sharing, consulting, processual, trusting, empathic and facilitating. They realize that these qualities do not come at the expense of charisma or effectiveness. These managers understand very well that good relationships are an underlying condition for good outcomes and products. They recognize a need to revisit the idea that competitiveness improves achievements. They also understand that an organizational culture in which one party wins and the other loses does not allow for the creation of a collaborative eco-system. Some managers perform the change quickly, as soon as they perceive its value and realize that sharing empowers them as much as exercising familiar administrative power. At the same time, there are those who adhere to their ways, which inevitably affects the processes and results.

Managers who choose to embark on a journey of change have to make the transition from autocratic decision making to joint decision making. This transition is directly expressed by the manner in which discussions and meetings are held and the nature of their interfaces with others in their senior management team. It involves highly challenging aspects, such as the willingness to develop sincere openness to other perceptions and unfamiliar alternatives, the need to establish psychological security among managers and employees and express different attitudes and perceptions and the ability to generate sensitive attentiveness and genuine interest in what others say out of an empathetic and interested attitude. Managers who make such a change, for example, will redesign their conference room, replacing the long table, where they once sat at the head, with a round table. This change carries great symbolic meaning, as it represents more collaboration and less control.

I first met Tzvika Schechterman, CEO of the Israel Shipyards Industries, in his office. He proudly showed me all his mechanisms of control as CEO, including an updated and a very tight operational control system which appeared on a huge screen in his office, next to a screen running camera feeds from different locations, as well as his corner office from which he could see all the platforms and beyond. I met a motivated, charismatic and razor-sharp manager, who generated the company's growth and impressive business results in less than a decade.

Led by a powerful CEO, his subordinates, who reported directly to him, had no reason to build any collaborative relationships between them, due to his "star" network. This resulted in conflicts that adversely affected the organization and created a situation in which senior managers took very limited responsibility upon themselves. Each manager operated in his own territory, with no common vision and no responsibility for the interfaces. At a certain point, Schechterman decided to initiate organizational change, which was enormously risky and required a lot of courage on his part. The success he describes here is a good example of the maturing process that CEOs and managements must undergo prior to leading profound changes:

> In the early stages we had a solid startup character. As a small group, our central motivating factor was based on personal relations. It is necessary at the starting point, but the drawback is that the business can only grow to a certain threshold. Once you reach that point, your former identity as a leader no longer produces the value required for growth. In the early stages we attained far-reaching achievements in a very short time and became one of the busiest ports in the world, in relation to platform length.
>
> Transformation is a huge challenge – my personal development and change as CEO, getting others accustomed to operate differently, and especially understanding that the change must be implemented, even when it is done without my presence. The structural change we made at this stage created more accurate definitions of roles and processes. Things that could not work during the first decade of our operation were now the right course of action for the organization. Operation was divided into two separate departments, entrance (unloading ships at the waterline and transfer to storage) and exit (customer inventory management and delivery). We merged them into one unit, which now handles the entire process. In this way the unit manager can see a comprehensive system and the work is performed more accurately. At headquarters we also joined a number of units under one management and reduced the number of people reporting to me.

The structural change has created a much more collaborative managerial and organizational system, and at the same time we are working on changing the organizational culture. We have created a different format for management meetings and for processes that include the intermediate ranks and those working on the front line. We are investing a lot in our organizational climate and assimilating more defined working methods.

My personal process is a significant part of this change. Work methods that were pertinent during the early stages are no longer suitable. For example, refraining from getting involved in all the nuts and bolts. It's very challenging to put it into practice, because the habitual response is to provide a solution to every problem. Change is manifested in asking others for their suggestions and ideas on how to lead towards a solution. Even if I know exactly what needs to be done, and it is clear that if I take the lead the outcome will be quick and correct, managerially it will impair the creation of the system required to enable the organization to keep growing. It took me a while to realize that I did not have to say what needs to be done, but rather listen to what the others are offering. Currently, managers at all levels initiate and lead processes due to this change in approach. They are much more involved and carry greater influence on the organization. For example, a manager who coordinated a strategic program was the one to stand on a stage and introduce it to the owners. This left a very significant impact. There is no doubt that this approach substantially increases the managers' involvement and is no less motivating than a paycheck. The picture is not all black and white and not always so romantic. There are some who really want to improve, and others who mostly want to improve their own comfort zone. However, this is a very significant change that seeps down as well.

It is impossible to move others even one inch forward if you do not connect them to the organization's objectives and to their actions in it. The point is to give the employee what he needs most: satisfaction. Feeling good about oneself is one of the most motivating forces. Higher financial reward has a short-term effect. Collaboration that allows the employee to make an impact, will harness and connect him much more, with a long-term effect. If you fail to do so, then no matter how talented you may be as CEO, you will not be able to generate any sort of movement, unless you do it all by yourself. You cannot let go and motivate only through collaboration, you have to also lead; both should be integrated. The challenge now is to have the change seep through and assimilate downwards, to all levels of management.

For senior managers seeking to make a change, we can use the image of two muscle systems for illustration purposes. The first system, the one we are familiar with and educated on, is the authoritative, centralized and consequential system. The second system is collaborative, dialogical and processual. These two muscle systems work in parallel and are both necessary and should not come at the expense of one another. Another analogy that can be used is a body that is very strong but not flexible – which inevitably leads to injuries and physical disabilities. The opposite condition, of a very flexible but weak body, also leads to physiological problems. The healthiest condition combines both strength and flexibility. A leader who deeply understands collaboration is the one who also deeply understands authority and control.

A significant part of the ability to integrate both features depends on the leader's experience and confidence. Ran Saar, CEO of one of Israel's big HMOs, and former Senior Commander at the Mosad has this to say on the subject:

> Leaders are leaders are leaders. Those who succeed in positioning themselves as leaders, in any field, possess leadership qualities which aided in their success. The more a leader acts with personal and organizational independence and charisma, the better he will be able to realize the goals he wishes to achieve. He must define collaboration and the creation of a different work culture as a goal. Leadership and collaboration do not contradict each other. Even as a competitive person I must know how to share, delegate, hear opinions, change my own opinions and compromise. If you are driven by fear this may generate contradictions. The right combination comes from a stance of power.

Leadership that limits collaboration does not only stem from hierarchical perceptions and patterns of control. Sometimes it is the desire to strengthen cooperation that may cause managers to over-centralize. As part of a process carried out with the operational layout of a global industrial company, a group of factory managers that included three Chinese, a Dutch, a German, an American and five Israelis sat in the room. In analyzing the state of collaboration between them and their units, once they felt confident enough to share, the reason for insufficient levels of collaboration in the organization gradually became apparent. The global operation manager is a strong charismatic Israeli who has gained the trust of all the other managers and the one with ties to everyone. When one of them has a question, it is their manager who has all answers, since he has already heard it from the other managers. When one of them is in need of raw material, he knows which factory can meet his needs. He held the same level of control and dominance in the process we conducted. It took him time to let go and allow for the creation of a collaborative discourse without constantly dictating and intervening.

This is a great example of a senior manager who believed in collaboration and was willing to do much more for it to develop, but could not understand why a higher level of shared doing among managers did not arise. Eventually, he realized that while he himself was the main catalyst, he was also the main barrier, in coordinating and centralizing cooperation by himself. Only then did he realize that managers should be allowed to take responsibility for practical implementation of collaborations. They created a mechanism of information transfer and mutual visits between factories for the purpose of learning and understanding the potential of mutual assistance, alongside additional solutions.

On the other hand, there are CEOs whose absence makes it difficult for managers reporting to them to cooperate. These managers can be defined as "present-absent". In a medium size financial company, the process of creating cooperations between units did not come into fruition for more than a year. Managers acted as they wished and would not heed the CEOs' request to change attitudes and work better together. During one of the outdoor sessions, I observed their dynamics and realized that they perceived the CEO as weak. His soft and fatherly attitude was great for the ongoing operation, since every manager did his part independently and distinctly, but it was not sharp enough to move them out of their comfort zone. Once the CEO understood the cost of his approach within the non-cooperative organizational framework, he adopted a much sharper and more focused stance. He demanded that his managers cooperate and did so in a way that made it clear that he was serious about it. The change in his approach created a significant turnaround in the organization.

There is no doubt that the outlook and actions of whoever is positioned at the head of the system will bear a crucial impact on the possibility of promoting all applicable solutions and initiating deep processes of organizational culture change. He is the leader, or at least the most significant partner for transformation. He can bring about changes that are nothing more than a line drawn in the sand washed away by the waves or hew a line deep in the rock that will last for years. His stated directive is critical, and no less important is his very pursuit of its implementation.

A CEO of a leading food company decided to enter a one-year process aimed at strengthening collaboration between the business units, thus breaking a profitability glass ceiling. He agreed to take his senior management on a three-day offsite in the desert in order to create an intimate and quiet setting. The distrust prevailing within management required in-depth work, and due to its intensity, seclusion was necessary. Since it involved a charismatic leader, with experience and reputation, intelligent and assertive, dominant and solution-oriented, it was clear that seclusion in itself would not be sufficient. He made a commitment to be in a state of learning during the process. Based on this commitment, he sat quietly for many hours and listened to his management team in an open and intimate discourse. He soon understood the value of such discourse, and during those three days he mostly listened, asked, learned and observed. The outcome of this approach was the emergence of a completely new and different type of communication among the management team. This constituted a basis for building trust and a very successful process of collaboration in the entire organization – a move which led to a significant leap at the business level.

Senior managers don't always succeed in creating the required change. As part of a process of generating cooperations between a number of companies belonging to a leading group, the VP of Human Resources was able to recruit the CEO to support the process. He participated in activities and conveyed clear messages up to the point where change was needed. The CEO in question was post-retirement age, with many years of senior managerial experience, greatly appreciated by all. However, he belongs to an older generation. In personal session, his managers said about him: "He has excellent strategic vision, but does not explain and share"; "He does not regard others as partners"; "He is not built for such processes"; "He is a dominating figure"; "If a problem arises between us, he will definitely resolve it"; "He is the only one who has an in-depth understanding and clear vision"; "He has a comprehensive understanding, but on issues he doesn't understand, it's almost impossible to change his mind." And indeed, these are his conceptions, which were formed over 50 years of command and management. In this organization, our attempt to bring about significant change had failed.

Uri, the CEO of one of the most interesting and fast-growing financial companies in Israel, was easily convinced to go with his team to a desert offsite. I asked him how spoiled his managers were and how much they would object to rough living conditions with no cellular reception. "Omri", he said, "leave it to me. It will be no problem." During the offsite I understood what Uri meant and why he was so calm about it. The reason is that whatever he wants, happens. His ability to create intimacy is rare. In a very quiet and humble way, he attracts people around him, creating strong bonds. They want to please him and win his appreciation. But this is a double-edged sword. Uri openly shared with me that he can influence only those who are close to him but not others. Some managers shared their feelings on this matter, revealing that those close to the CEO benefit but those who are not walk around with a deep sense of frustration.

On the whole, the atmosphere among the company's management team is excellent. For the most part, their interrelationships are good, and this is the foundation that allows for the generation of cross-sectoral integrative processes. In fact, it is the only source. Any new member of the organization's management will have no chance of promoting any issue before building friendly and close relationships. Anyone not personally connected to Uri and to some of the dominant managers will become an irrelevant figure in this environment. It is important to understand that this is not an atmosphere of scorekeeping, nor is it organizational politics. On the contrary, we are dealing with a very high-quality group that has created a certain organizational culture in which things are simply conducted as they are. There are hardly any instances of issues emerging in a structured and defined cross-sectoral process.

During a deep discourse about the value element, one of the VPs said the following:

> Friends, if we are honest here, then I would like to say that this cannot be realized [the perception of collaboration]. There are priorities and pressures that do not really allow me to assist others if it is not part of the job description allocated to me, if it is not in my priorities and if I get nothing out of it. If there is no reciprocity it will never happen.

In response to these words, the CEO replied: "This is exactly what I expect of you as senior managers. To see beyond your units and help others, even if it does not appear in the definition of your job. In my perspective, this is managerial accountability."

In the calm and simple discourse that took place in the desert, Uri delved deeper into describing his perception. According to him, his perception stems from the fact that he trusts every one of the managers and their ability to personally exercise the responsibility imposed on them. He does not believe that it is his job to tell them how to work with each other. His words were said from a positive and appreciative point of view, stemming from a perception of authentic leadership. Nevertheless, the managers asked for more orderly definitions and a clearer statement from him as CEO regarding interfaces between the units. During the process, everyone found out another important thing: they lack the ability to conduct a dialogue without friendship and closeness – neither a seemingly clean and "cold" work dialogue nor a dialogue for resolving disputes. That is why they have a tendency for avoidance. In the work process with this management team, the focus was placed on translating perception into action and strengthening the dialogical tools.

***

"Where there is doubt, there is truth. Doubt is the shadow of truth," wrote the author Ambrose Bierce. Indeed, my experience has taught me the power of doubt. For over two decades, I experienced myself as a leader undergoing constant change and was also fortunate to work with many leaders who agreed to put aside for a moment their knowledge of what was right. Those leaders agreed to place question marks about patterns they were familiar with, leave their comfort zone, and were confident enough to choose a stance of humbleness and strong enough to understand that they do not possess all the answers. Those who agreed to undergo a personal process and managed to lead an accurate organizational process, created the most significant impact. This is probably one of the strongest characteristics of leadership in the new era, adaptive leadership, and it is what distinguishes between managers who are only managers and those who are leaders too.

Chapter 11

Coopetition
Competing and cooperating

The highly complex relationship between competitors, albeit with the most significant advantages, occurs when competitors also cooperate. In the new era, this is one of the most powerful leverages for creating relevance, effectiveness and innovation. In the VUCA world, it is often the sole condition for survival.

The word "Frenemy" is an oxymoron made up of two conflicting words: friend and enemy. This word describes a relationship between two countries, or two organizations/groups, which are both competitors and collaborators. This word seems to have originated in texts and films by the writer/filmmaker Jessica Milford. In this context she was quoted:

> It is a very useful word, coined by one of my younger sisters, which she used to describe a girl that lived next door when we were kids. While my sister and her "frenemy" would always play together, they disliked each other with all their heart.

(Milford, 2010)

Today this term is widely used in diplomatic arenas, understanding that in the complexity of the new era, it is no longer clear who is a friend and who an enemy. Coalitions of cooperations are created even between enemy countries. The war in Syria exemplified this in an extreme way – when for a short time, Syria, Iran, the United States and Hezbollah fought on a quasi-common front against ISIS.

Another example is the relationship between the United States and Russia and many more illustrations of this theme in international relationships.

The corresponding oxymoronic term, which is rapidly gaining a central place in the business arena, is "Coopetition" – a combination of cooperation and competition. Although the seeds of coopetition began to appear decades ago, this is one of the most prominent phenomena of the new era. It reflects a profound perceptual shift by blurring the clear and dichotomous distinction between competition and collaboration that characterized the old world. From the dawn of time and for survival needs, as well as part of a competitive culture, people had to learn who was considered a friend and who was a danger to them. "Are you friend or foe?" – you were either one or the other. In recent years, this dichotomous line has blurred, leaving us with unclear boundaries. It is a strange hybrid creature that corroborates neither the standard win–lose concept nor the classic win–win concept, which is easier to realize between complementary rather than competing parties. Coopetition represents the reality of creating value for two organizations that are also competitors.

A form of conceptualization that widens the appropriate view of players that we define as competitors is based on the perception of value (Brandenburger & Nalebuff, 1996). A player will be defined as complementary when customers place higher value on your product when they also have in their possession the other player's product, in relation to the value they would assign to your product alone. A player will be defined as a competitor when customers attribute lesser value to your product, when the competitor's product is in their possession, in relation to having only your product. A player will be defined as complementary when a supplier is more drawn to provide you with resources while also

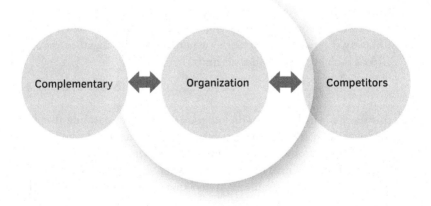

providing resources to the other player rather than to you only. A player will be defined as a competitor when a supplier is less interested in providing resources to you, while he provides resources to the other player, when compared with a situation in which he would only provide resources to you.

The high-tech arena illustrates the change in perception over the years. It is affected by a swirling pace of change more than any other arena, and so, agility, innovation and collaboration are its existential conditions. Hence, the adoption of coopetition is more natural despite its complexity. Business models in the high-tech field change rapidly. The traditional structural separation between software, hardware and infrastructure companies has completely changed, as most companies are turning into providers of solution packages – in accordance with the changing environment and the need to provide a more flexible and relevant solution for customers. Google and HP provide customers with shared solutions. Oracle and Microsoft compete and share the server and cloud arena. The decision was made after the decline in Oracle's business success and Microsoft's defeat in their competition for the cloud environment against other entities. This situation brought about a unification of the two opponents.

Coopetition also exists in other arenas. Aviation alliances have been around for decades: Star Alliance, founded in 1997, is considered the best and largest aviation alliance in the world. Lufthansa and Swissair not only compete with each other but also benefit from cooperating with each other, as well as with 25 other airlines – as demonstrated, for example, in connection flights, in gaining credit points that produce higher value for the customer, in negotiations vis-à-vis local regulators and more. Another example is the establishment of the first and largest online university in the world: EDX, enabled by a partnership of competing universities – Harvard, MIT and Stanford. Other well-known "Frenemies" are Apple and Samsung that are both competing business partners for many years, as Samsung is a key supplier for Apple.

These and other examples are not about creating cartels. The boundary is clear, but in certain situations it is also narrow. In these processes it is very important to maintain the legitimate discussion sphere and legal boundaries. An interesting process took place between two large educational networks, competing with each other. The struggle between them caused mutual damage to their reputations, an investment of many resources in the competition and damage incurred on both staff and students. Board members were unhappy about the outcome of the tough competition, yet they all saw no other alternative. In a brave step taken by the two CEOs, an in-depth process was performed with both managements. The most significant achievement was in building trust and relationships. It was agreed to discuss the issue of competing in a respectful and respectable manner, explore the possibility of joint procurement and define a number of shared activities and processes for staff and students from both networks. After a thorough examination, it was decided to strengthen the pedagogical differentiation between the networks rather than connect this sphere. In a clear and pre-defined manner, the issue of tenders over which the two networks competed was left out of the discourse and did not come up for discussion.

How does the growth of coopetition relate to the intra-organizational sphere? After all, there should be no competition between units within an organization. However, this is not the case, especially not in the face of the separate silo barriers and competitive organizational culture. Organizations consist of many units, which are often required to compete as well as cooperate with one another. This paradox constitutes a particularly significant challenge, especially in the aspects of information sharing and organizational learning. Research shows that a strong and centralizing organizational hierarchy adversely affects coordination between competing units – "the more control is exerted on the units by headquarters, the less willing are the units to share information and knowledge between them" (Tsai, 2002). In his study Tsai discovered that when hierarchy decreases and informal relationships take place, learning and sharing between units competing for external markets will increase. However, this is not the case when it comes to competition between units over internal resources.

Internal competition is about resources, standards, qualitative manpower, budgets, management evaluation, comparative compliance with goals, bonuses and more. External competition is about similar markets, products, services, reputation, market shares and more. Internal competition does not generate real interest in units regarding what occurs in other units; therefore, it is less important for them to invest in learning and transferring knowledge. The higher the overlap between units regarding the market, the stronger the desire to cooperate with each other (Baum & Korn, 1999). In contrast, external competition, especially in the business sphere, is a source of knowledge and experience that may improve their work.

Organizational researchers point out that organizations are based on certain coherent logic. Only in recent years have they begun to analyze, research and try to crack the capacity of an organization to be managed with conflicting rationale. These studies do not provide any understanding about the parallel existence of two leading and contradictory logic systems. Profound contradiction between competition and collaboration, toward the same players in the arena, may produce built-in tension with costs for the organization and its people (Scott, 2013).

The most significant question concerning both the intra-organizational arena and the relations between organizations is: how can one manage a relationship that is inherently contradictory? These are particularly complex relations, as they contain and combine two contrasting worldviews. It is the opposite logic of relationships: a combination of possible hostility due to conflicts of interest and competition, along with potential camaraderie due to shared and complementary interests. How can such internal contradictions be perceived in the personal and organizational rationale?

Part of the solution is embedded in this question. People find it very difficult to simultaneously cooperate and compete with others. A very high level of awareness, experience and capability is required to conduct such a dual relationship. Some leaders, specifically those who have a systemic vision coupled with collaborative intelligence, demonstrate such capacity; consequently, this paradox can be easily managed by the organization. However, it is important to engage the complexity of internal conflict between perceptions in the discourse of any organization, and in this framework employees and managers must be provided with tools and support to manage it.

An adequate example of leadership that promotes this trend is demonstrated by Satya Nadella, who was appointed to the position of Microsoft CEO in 2014. Shortly after taking office, he initiated cooperation with Apple, with an objective to integrate Microsoft's operating system into Apple's computers. Nadella made it clear that Apple was and will continue to be a large and significant competitor, alongside the cooperation designed to produce higher value to customers. There is no doubt that value to customers is also value to companies.

Leadership can redefine reality. It is faced with an extremely complex move to advance the possibility of recognizing the potential of working together with another organization, which had been perceived as a competitor for years. If senior managers in an organization, especially the stronger ones, are prone to maintain competitiveness, it will be difficult or even impossible to practice collaboration. This is a fundamental change in the rules of the game, a deep transformation. It is a necessary and relevant move in the new era, especially among entities operating in a very dynamic and rapidly changing environment.

This complex move can be carried out with the assistance of a third party, as is taking place in the case of Sweden's beer breweries union, which is helping to promote cooperation between two large breweries. The companies compete in marketing and distribution and cooperate in the collection and recycling of bottles. The importance of self-distribution stems mainly from their desire to sustain good relations with their customers and arrange their beverages in a prominent manner in order to affect sales. In terms of distribution and sales, the interface between the companies is perceived as a competition. However, when it comes to returning the bottles, the interface with the customer is irrelevant. The two companies created a parallel and identical packaging system so that it would be simpler to cooperate in returning empty bottles. This partnership reduces expenses, and its implementation is assisted by Sweden's beer breweries union.

Another example, also from Sweden, is related to the upholstery and coating industry. Two major companies that manufacture and market plastics used for protecting various products are experiencing harsh competition for every customer, as well as for market lead. Cooperation was initiated in their development laboratories in order to reduce R&D expenses. The companies' development staff formed personal relations and met on a regular basis. This is what the development manager said:

> We experience a good atmosphere of cooperation in the technical sphere. Competition and resentment exist only in the market arena. We jointly fund development programs, and have a plan for further development. We share our work with four academic bodies and sometimes present our results in international publications.

On the other hand, the sales manager emphasizes the element of competition: "When we win a customer from the other company, we buy a cake and celebrate..." This difference in attitudes results from the fact that development position holders worked in harmony, free of competition, while position holders in marketing and sales competed with each other, with no element of collaboration (Trish & Hinings, 2009).

These examples and other cases clearly show that the closer you are to the customer, the more competition will exist between organizations. On the other hand, the more distant you are from the customer, the more cooperations between rivalries will prevail. The key to managing the complexity and conflicts is inherent in structural separation between people and units that are in competition and between those that act collaboratively. This is an important principle for designing cooperation between competitors – unless it involves small organizations.

When we analyze our competitors' arena in order to examine potential cooperations, the simplest mapping is based on interests and impact:

We will prefer to explore possibilities for cooperation with competitors who share a larger measure of identity of interests with us rather than those with whom we are in conflict. We will choose those with higher influential means to strengthen our relevance and impact. Naturally, this exploration should take into account the arena in which we operate, including additional competitors, as well as the way customers and suppliers may perceive our association with competitors. Just like any other cooperation, the leading question is the potential value, without ignoring the history and relationships between the companies.

Disturbing changes, and certainly "black swans" with the challenging risks they present, also bring about opportunities in the connections between competitors. Sometimes there is just no other alternative. In April 2020, Google and Apple created a new shared technology, which was integrated into their operating systems, alerting users of their adjacency to a Covid-19-diagnosed patient. The goal was to assist in reducing the virus spread by providing alerts to users.

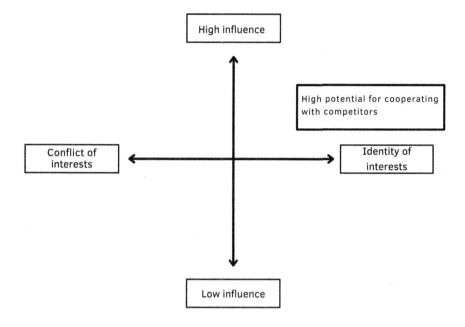

This capability was based on information submitted by the health authorities. In a joint announcement, the two competitors said, "We at Apple and Google believe that there has never been a more important time to work together and solve one of the world's most pressing problems" (Bloomberg 10.4.2020).

At the beginning of the Covid-19 crisis, Medtronic – one of the largest manufacturer of medical technologies – publicly shared the specifications of its respirator machine design, in order to enable manufacturers from all over the world to quickly manufacture similar machines. The limited number of respirators in many countries was one of the most difficult challenges during that period. "This is an unprecedented move," stated Yaron Yitzhari, CEO of Medtronic Israel.

> The company has many patents for respirators, and the demand for these machines are currently skyrocketing. I am proud to be part of a value based society that operates and is guided by a mission to save and prolong life. In this move, Medtronic placed the public good over its business benefit and exempted all manufacturers around the world from paying royalties on patents, and also published the full technical specifications, including assembly instructions, so that all over the world, every manufacturer will be able to start producing high standard machines in order to save lives.

> *(Israeldefence, 2020)*

Allowing competitors to use business knowledge is not trivial and reflects a new conception of competitiveness. Of course, this move was not just about value. Medtronic has gained wide and sympathetic media exposure, and its shares have significantly risen during that period – both for this reason and due to the increased production of respirators.

The new era and the understanding that many more challenges are expected force us all to re-examine every arena and consistently create an eco-system with all the relevant players, including competitors. Imagine for a moment that health systems in each country would adopt this concept and promote cooperations between parties currently perceiving themselves as competitors (mainly referring to HMOs, employers' associations, hospitals, universities and private and government agencies); would medicine in the national and international periphery change as the result of such collaboration? Most likely. The question is whether the necessary leadership needed to carry out such moves exists in health systems. The ability to generate an eco-system that incorporates competing organizations requires the highest level of collaborative leadership.

A groundbreaking example of an Israeli coopetition model is the establishment of "Momentum" – an NPO (non profit oganization) founded in 2016 with the initiative of "Beyachad" Foundation, in partnership with 16 vehicle import companies and the Importers Association. "Momentum" strives to ensure that the automotive industry, with specific emphasis on mechanics and diagnosticians, becomes a desirable field of education and training, offering young men and women the possibility of self-fulfillment and quality employment based on a differentiated profession, with promotion options and adequate pay.

The organization's goal is to strengthen the Israeli vehicle industry and economy while cooperating with factors from the public, business and social sectors and creating a socio-economic value for all the partners and the Israeli society. It is an active partnership of competing organizations, investing in education and professional training of new and existing employees, through permanent organizational infrastructure and professional work processes. This move does not entail any commercial cooperation between the companies.

"Momentum" mainly operates to increase skilled manpower for service centers while improving the profession's image and reducing turnover, integrating women and orthodox men and improving academic training. Competitors in the industry act in cooperation, among themselves and with the technological colleges and relevant government ministries. Trainings and certifications were adjusted, and an employment portal was created.

Hagit Elias, recruited to establish and manage the organization, says:

> The partnership began with building trust and finding a passionate champion who can easily harness additional forces, and who is

highly regarded by stakeholders in the field. In the automotive world it was Joel Carasso. He initiated the move and realized that introducing the desired change could not be done by himself alone, so he harnessed the owners of the vehicle import companies. They joined forces with him because of their respect for him, but also because of FOMO (Fear Of Missing Out) – that feeling that "if a big and innovative move is taking place, I cannot afford to miss out on it."

The first meetings, intended to establish the organization, naturally involved some suspicion, extreme caution and skepticism. Each participant guarded himself from exposure, even in areas where a shared interest was apparent. The initial establishment process was accompanied by a lot of ego, which derived from fear as well as the desire to fulfill the professional needs and wishes of each partner. There is also the sensitivity of protecting professional information. From the very beginning we are mindful of maintaining full transparency and are working closely with a lawyer, who is constantly overlooking the process regarding everything pertaining to the aspect of business restrictions. This increases trust.

Each partner brought to the table a story that was somewhat different, therefore, in the first stage we focused on creating consensus. I was asked to construct a strategic plan, and was aiming for a jointly built strategy. Each partner defined his vision of successful activity, after which the purpose of the partnership was defined through full consensus: raising a future generation of workers in the automotive industry through promoting the workers' welfare in the industry. The insistence on consensual decision-making consolidated a culture of shared responsibility and strengthened the commitment of each of the partners. The partners realized that it is impossible to solve the problem of manpower shortage from above. Furthermore, if the industry does not take responsibility, the situation will not change. Yet, it is impossible to take responsibility and make a change alone. A document of agreement was issued stating a prerequisite for joining the partnership – a payment that consolidates commitment, assigning a senior vice president from each company to the board of directors, a commitment to be present in all committees and work teams, and commitment of every importer to adopt an academic institution in the field, with responsibility and influence beyond the venture operations.

In the early stages, tension arose between the different commercial companies, as well as between the companies and the philanthropic partners. Through a process a new language was created.

Now we are a desirable club, one that others want to join. It is a locomotive that will pull the entire industry forward, creating impact on thousands of garages that are not included within the partnership. The regulator – the Ministry of Transport, the Ministry of Education and the Ministry of Labor – are also players in the arena and form part of the complexity. The regulator delays complex and lengthy processes in bureaucracy and cumbersome decision-making processes. We are producing an ecosystem with a long-term holistic and strategic vision.

The partners fell in love with the process. They are enjoying themselves, creating connections and a new value. There is still a fear that workers will be "stolen" from one another. When the need arose to expand the circle of influence and hold an unmediated meeting with employees, and not just with senior managers, they were concerned about workers from competitor companies meeting. The challenge is to work with the objections and explain in a rational way what we are doing, constantly keeping our eye on the big picture. Once they understand it, they are totally committed. The fact that VPs involved in the process are the service leaders and not the business leaders and the companies' competitive arena leaders, helps to separate between the competitive sphere and the collaborative sphere. The CEOs themselves talk about the partnership as a generator of added value alongside the competition that exists between them.

"Momentum" is a unique and innovative example of creating an eco-system that includes the business, government and academic sectors. This is an example of what is needed in all industries and sectors worldwide. Regulated construction of these moves – as an eco-system with shared responsibility, leadership, collaboration and innovation – will lead to creating a profound change in our society. This transformation is significantly based on the perception and ability of competing entities to collaborate with each other.

Chapter 12

The public sector
The eco-system challenge

I would like to open this chapter with a personal note. During all the years that I have been assisting leaders from all sectors, it has always been the public sector in Israel that I considered to be the most important and challenging sphere. It could be merely because as a citizen I myself am affected by this sector, combined with the inclination to influence it from a stance of professional responsibility. Moreover, it is possible that this sphere constitutes a professional challenge for me since it explicitly necessitates the application of the eco-system perception. In fact, collaboration or its absence in the public sector affects our lives more than we can imagine. The review presented in this chapter aims to reflect reality in this sphere, as I know it from my fieldwork. If this review seems too harsh, it could be the result of my attempts to generate change in this reality, hoping that the sector leaders will read it and lead the necessary changes. If it seems as a local example, it is, but it reflects the characteristics of the public sector in many countries.

Governments aim to produce positive outcomes for their countries and citizens; however, even the best intentions can also fail along the way, as a result of countless factors, including those characterized as VUCA. Pandemics, natural disasters such as fires or floods, armed conflicts, immigration and refugees, social protests, cyber-attacks – events of this kind are escalating in pace and intensity all around the world and are unpredictable for the most part. The responsibility to cope with all these factors lies in the hands of the public sector while also addressing known and familiar challenges such as social mobility and poverty, racism and violence, at-risk youth and more.

DOI: 10.4324/9781003514992-12   **191**

The resilience of a country and its society depends on its capacity for quick adaptation to change, whether predictable or not, as well as the manner in which long-term and complex challenges are managed. These challenges require systemic thinking, strategy and a capability for integrated action. The question one must ask is: to what extent do the characteristics defined in the first chapters as provisions for leadership and influence in a complex world, such as agility, accountability and collaboration, exist in the public sector? The answer to that is complex.

There are examples of good cooperations existing among organizations in the public sector in Israel. One such example is "360° National Program for Children and Youth at Risk", a program based on cooperation between five government ministries and other entities, promoting care for at-risk populations in collaboration with local authorities. Furthermore, the fight against organized crime is carried out by a highly effective cooperation between all law enforcement agencies: The Anti-Money Laundering Authority, State Attorney's Office, police and Tax Authority. The housing headquarters was established in 2015 in order to coordinate and integrate the various entities and activities in the field, to increase housing production and reduce the duration of construction. A subcommittee on construction and regulation in the Planning Administration is responsible for advancing Planning and Building Regulations. It includes five government ministries, representatives of authorities, academia, engineers and architects. The Child Online Protection Bureau is based on cooperation between the police and six government ministries.

These examples, however, are not indicative of the Israeli government system. During the Covid-19 crisis, the public was exposed to a lack of cooperation between government ministries, even within the health and education systems. It is clear that without collaborative infrastructure and leadership, which promote the eco-system perception within and between systems, they only function partially and deficiently and, during a crisis, will mainly depend on those in the front lines (in this case mainly medical staff, military and education). During the crisis, the public was directly exposed to government inter-ministerial struggles, as well as struggles with other factors. Each ministry and organization was focused on important public interests. This is what was expected of them. But in the absence of collaboration and an organized mechanism for finding balances, making decisions, creating agreements and effective headquarter work, the outcome adversely affected the public.

A lack of collaboration adversely affects public interests on a large and broad scale. "Lack of cooperation between government entities regarding essential issues constitutes one of the most acute problems of the State of Israel," says Prof. Eugene Kendall, who served as Chairman of the National Economic Council in 2009–2015. He explains his perception and indicates two reasons:

1. Lack of trust – we do not feel as if we are all in the same boat. Everyone is looking at things from their own point of view, unwilling to see the big picture. Every regulator has his own rules; every public servant has his own goals. Most of them are in a hurry to take advantage of every opportunity to advance their office interests; there is no mechanism that demands cooperation. Collaboration takes place despite the system and not because of it. The method is based on a lack of collaboration and a perpetual power struggle. The strong enforces his authority. The main cost of such a reality is that important issues get clogged for long periods of time. There is no mechanism for creating solutions to disputes.

2. Politicians have no perception of accountability, in the sense that the public does not punish ministers for poor performance nor grant credit for good performance. Distrust prevails in the country from every direction. Politicians are experts in destroying trust. After all, the word "party" derives from the word to part, and politicians are masters at it. The government does not trust its citizens, and the citizens do not trust the government. Ministers do not trust officials. They all go through sections of hell to carry out any move.

A number of commonly recurring patterns pertaining to lack of collaboration in the public sector can be identified, in accordance with the following points:

1. Leadership and statehood – in a private conversation, a CEO of one of the ministries described how a huge budget, pertaining to a particular national issue also relevant to another government office, was defined. The minister and CEO of the other ministry chose not to pool resources and jointly address the national challenge, simply because they wanted to clarify that this issue is handled solely by them. This is a very common approach, reflecting the great disparity from adopting a national interest perception and collaborative leadership.

   Ministers naturally tend to act according to a mixture of statehood and professional considerations pertaining to their personal political agenda as well as that of their parties. Many of the office CEOs are totally committed to their ministers and their agendas; therefore, in many cases, considerations of professionalism and statehood will not always be at the top of their priorities.

   Furthermore, in recent years leadership in public sectors and in the political arena has been evolving almost in contrast to the business sector. The latter has a growing appreciation for leaders who represent humbleness, inclusion and sharing. In most organizations in the business sector, traditional power and respect are less valued. On the other hand, it seems that the political system in many countries appreciates above all else hubris, arrogance, forcefulness, ostentation, hierarchy and control. This affects ministry CEOs as well as the empowerment of internal and inter-organizational collaboration barriers. During the last decade, only a small number of CEOs truly recognized the importance of such collaboration, beyond the level of making public statements.

2. Strategy – defining collaboration as a goal, as policy and as strategy is very random and partial. The processes aimed at maintaining a greater degree of internal and inter-ministerial collaboration are slow and limited, certainly in view of the needs that are arising. The importance of assimilating collaboration in a systematic and structured way is yet to be recognized. In addition, intra-organizational policy easily creates "blockages" in work processes, to such an extent that it is almost impossible to release them in the current situation.

3. Separate silos – the government is used to working with hierarchical structures, completely separated from one another. This phenomenon, which has long been considered impossible in nearly all business organizations, constitutes the foundation for all public service organizations and is perceived as both the natural and the exclusive layout. Traditional perception of management glorifies control and territorialism. Consequently, when organizations lack managerial innovation, collaborative leadership and cross-sectorial accountability, managers will achieve greater benefit through competition and struggle than by means of collaboration.

Absolute division between territories, different objectives, impacts of political interests and different organizational cultures are all indicative of how things work within and between government ministries. A director in the Ministry of Education shares her outlook on this matter:

> After two years of work on the development process of an education program, we discovered that at the same time another program, almost identical, was developed and implemented by another unit … School principals find themselves dealing with conflicting guidelines issued by various functions in the ministry, and often from the local authority as well. The less coordination exists between us, the more the school principals suffer.

4. Systematicity – structured, systematic and planned interfaces in and between government ministries are rare. Actual relations are formed subsequent to interpersonal acquaintance, crises, conflicts and any necessity that arises. Managers are not inclined to create work plans taking into account

other ministries and their integration, even when cross-organizational issues are involved. Lack of systematicity in successive interfaces intensifies conflicts and escalation processes; these crises require involvement of senior officials. The need for more inter-personal connections in order to create a shared language, demonstrates the need for more programs designated for managers in the public service. These are also translated into networks of work relations, within which personal ties are created that assist, to some extent, in interfaces between the organizations.

5. Governance – making joint decisions by all institutions and guaranteeing their implementation. Governance is based on actions and processes and largely depends on coordination and collaboration between organizations. The difficulty in its implementation is related to a lack of compatibility between office holders and the frequency of their turnover. On the one hand, one finds managers holding their position for many years, who despite their incompatibility cannot be removed from their positions. On the other hand, on average governments last for a three-year period, necessitating renewed and constant building of relationships between managers in different ministries. Temporality produces frustration and erosion among some of the managers. The turnover of ministers and CEOs brings about changes in directives and priorities, thus undermining long-term partnerships and processes.

6. Evaluation and reward – with time the tendency to evaluate managers' functioning increases, with regard to meeting goals and work plans. In contrast, there is no evaluation or reward for internal and inter-organizational cooperations. The Ministry of Transport is indifferent to successes of the Ministry of Economy, even if it means a significant contribution to the local market and vice versa. The perceptions of accountability are limited to a single division within a government office and not beyond that. The governmental work-plan book perpetuates separateness since it does not include objectives and evaluation on an inter-ministerial level.

It appears that often enough managers in public service act under the assumption that separate and territorial action is more rewarding than cooperations. Prof. Eugene Kendall remarks on this subject:

> In business everyone has one goal, and unless you reach that goal, people will ultimately recognize it and drive you out. There is no single shared goal in the public arena that can be evaluated and rewarded. It doesn't have to be this way. For example, in Singapore ministers are rewarded for meeting goals, so consequently they have every reason to put their egos aside. As far as

the government is concerned, credit is usually the reward, and often many compete for credit. There is a common misconception that the credit is either mine or yours.

7. Resource management – in the absence of joint processes and integrated quality solutions, an inevitable waste of resources will emerge. No one is held accountable for this as long as one adheres to laws and regulations. When disputes arise, waste becomes even greater due to delayed decisions and investment of resources in conflicts. In the business sector, managerial responsibility, in terms of expenditure and utilization of resources, is absolute and uncompromising, aspiring to pool resources wherever possible. This permeates into the social sector too.

   As a gross and broad generalization, it can be assumed that many decision makers in the public sector are less concerned about wasting resources when encountering failures. This is one of the reasons why investing in planning, building and improving cooperations is insufficient. The prevailing assumption is that "if it works it works, and if doesn't – fine." The personal cost and the organizational cost are negligible.

8. Bureaucracy and centralization – often enough, managers who wish to lead joint processes discover that they are restricted by the four strong players operating in the public sector: the Civil Service Commissioner, the Accountant General, the Attorney General and the Head of the Budget Division. These are the gatekeepers of the public sector in everything related to law and proper administration. They greatly affect decision-making processes within the offices and between them as well as the organizational culture of the entire public sector. Government division managers frequently describe the feeling of having their hands tied in the face of the power these players hold. Some claim that the absence of balance in power distribution between the players creates bottlenecks and complicates advancing collaboration processes.

9. Managerial courage – when compared with other sectors, the public sector is characterized by a high level of PDI, a lack of managerial courage and considerable difficulty for employees and managers to create impact on their superiors. While this claim may be a gross generalization, this reality is well known to those who are familiar with the sector. Managers are not always able to recognize these attributes, as they experience them on a daily basis and are accustomed to them.

   Many managers avoid conflicts with other managers in the interface spheres. Therefore, issues often remain unresolved and vague, or the conflicting parties may settle for partial and mediocre cooperations. Another delaying factor stems from the need to harness higher-level managers for inter-organizational collaborative processes. Since they are likely to object, many middle managers relinquish. When they are required to "choose their battles", they will naturally prefer the ones that will grant them recognition and appreciation in the future. They will not necessarily choose the ones that also promote other government ministries.

10. Absence of a decisive or inclusive factor – a major difficulty in managing the Covid-19 crisis in Israel stemmed from the absence of any inclusive factor handling the campaign and convening the various disciplines and approaches into one strategic procedure. Decision-making processes were problematic and slow and only exacerbated the public's sense of uncertainty and distrust toward the government. A time of crisis clearly reflects the issues that were attended to beforehand and those that were neglected. One organization is not capable of incorporating such a complex move and certainly not the Ministry of Health.

The picture is more complex and troubling when reviewing routine decision-making processes. Udi Prawer, former Deputy General Director for governance and social affairs in the Prime Minister's Office, describes the aspects of relative power and decision-making processes:

> Creating cooperations between government ministries requires a landlord, someone who will act as a center of gravity. If a number of ministries need to be convened for the process, then the Prime Minister's Office carries a lot of weight, even though it has no real official authority. Both the Ministry of Finance and the Ministry of Justice can serve for this purpose. Other ministries encounter difficulties in convening their counterparts, unless it involves a familiar and appreciated person appointed by the government. If, for example, the Ministry of Education and the Ministry of Welfare are involved in a process that requires cooperation, it will entail greater complexity and will necessitate strong resolve and good-will from both parties to reach an agreement.
>
> Part of the problem with the system is that it has no inherent figure that can make decisions. In accordance with the current legal state, only the government has the authority to settle unresolved disputes; however, raising such issues comes with a price tag. Consequently, you either initiate cooperations, or you remain in your place without paying too high a price. The decision to create cooperations requires a group of believers, time and energy. For example, there was a time when the Planning Administration,

Israel Land Authority and the Ministry of Housing joined forces almost voluntarily, and this move generated many important agreements.

This set of patterns and characteristics affects the organizational culture, which, in turn, empowers each of these points. A senior VP in a government office incorporates these aspects as follows:

> The issue of the organizational culture is a very problematic one. As an anecdote, my staff members sit in a room next door to another unit's staff members. They neither knew each other, nor did they know that they were working in parallel on the same programs. Everyone is doing their own thing ... It is a common problem in the entire public service domain. We each have our separate objectives. I am here now, but in two years I may be elsewhere, so why should I care? The problem is deep rooted. The organizational culture does not correspond with the needs in the field. There are a great deal of divisions and overlaps.
>
> It is much harder to make changes and demonstrate them within the public sector. Everyone is tied down in all the bureaucratic systems. The organizations are large and you feel like a cog in the machine. There is not enough familiarity between people and units. Government ministries are built in silos. No one connects them. There is no shared assignment. Within each ministry the head of administration merely sees their own task, and there is no shared task. There is no apparent need to cooperate. There is no integration that allows one to observe assignments from start to finish. It is also a matter of management. There are CEOs who are more invested in promoting change, and others who are not. Ministry offices are driven to insanity by over-centralization, leaving no room for cooperations.

In light of the unique complexity, managers who wish to promote collaboration are required to thoroughly understand and know how to manage the processes. "The National Economic Council operates without authority, although its essence is to create cooperations," says Prof. Eugene Kendall.

> At first they did not want to cooperate with us. How was cooperation eventually made possible? Only when you prove to people that you are truly cooperative, that you are not going to take their credit, nor penetrate their territory, and that you are professional, reliable

and discreet – will they begin to cooperate with you. Needless to say that they must understand the value of the move.

There are also attempts to create systematic processes, as Udi Prawer describes:

> In the Prime Minister's Office we developed a methodology whereby we convened everyone for a meeting that we named "a resolution to initiate a process", to which we invited the broadest staff possible. We realized that it would take a year to implement the process, including key events aimed at accelerating collaboration, public participation and data collection. For the most part the procedure started out with objections. One should really listen to one's partners. If you know what you want in great detail, you may paradoxically find yourself as far away from building consensus as possible. If you do not know what you want, and you are open to go on a learning and trust building journey with all the participants in the process, then you are in a different place altogether.

There is a strong worldwide trend to try and improve collaboration and trust in the public sector, through changing basic assumptions and understanding that decisions should be made together and carried out accordingly. An example is an entity called SEP, operating in the Netherlands. It consists of representatives of workers, employers and the public – in equal share – while the state functions as an observer. In this forum agreements are formed regarding all legislation and regulations relating to labor, which are subsequently passed on to the government and parliament as a joint and advisory body rather than by means of the sectoral lobby method. Over 90 percent of the recommendations are accepted.

The process taking place in the public sector is not a revolution but a rather slow evolution. The public system needs to recognize the complexity of this era and change accordingly. It responds rather rapidly to emergencies but is still slow and cumbersome in relation to the agility and relevance required in a changing world. The most important and urgent change is creating an overall system that maintains a very high level of collaboration. In order to realize it, substantial changes in perception, abilities, definitions, plans and work processes are required, realizing that knowledge does not merely exist in one place and that it is necessary to assimilate an orderly method and a shared language. New mechanisms are needed to formulate systemic solutions supported by existing knowledge in various organizations, so as to generate shared actions.

It is imperative that managers in public entities recognize the need to become relevant factors within a larger eco-system. A structured and legitimate mechanism is required for dispute and conflict management. It is a vital need for each government ministry and government company to have one CCO at the level reporting to the CEO, who will also be a part of a network consisting of his counterparts. It is important to create small and committed groups of functionaries from all relevant entities for each significant issue, in order to consider future challenges and provide relevant responses. Some must be distanced from present and near future management and be capable of meeting unexpected scenarios and creating ties transcending present territorial struggles between organizations. The management of each entity should define collaboration as a strategy and act accordingly – including introducing change to organizational cultures and development of a shared language with the corresponding entities.

In local authorities the picture is similar and yet different. Local authorities are characterized by an organizational culture similar to that of government ministries; however, in this sphere change processes take place more rapidly – mainly due to the introduction of new leadership and direct contact with the public, demanding a more relevant and adaptive form of leadership. Avi Ketko, Director of Tel Aviv-Jaffa Municipal Corporations Bureau, which includes 26 companies, is quoted on this subject: "Since we all operate under one roof, and are ultimately required to strive for a goal stemming from municipal policy, there are overlapping areas in which cooperations are feasible, thus gaining a larger advantage and saving resources" (Authority portal, 2019). Cooperation between the corporations has led to savings in investments at the main soccer stadium, including a lawn that was provided by the company responsible for the city park; joint activities of the Cinematheque and the Tel Aviv Museum for Art; as well as integrating employees with special needs in various corporations, with the cooperation of "Rehabilitation Employment Center" Company.

Another example of a systematic and thorough application of collaboration is the establishment of municipal policing units. Such a move involves creating high value and pooling resources, orderly construction of definitions and authorities based on legislation, creation of trust and relationships in integrated teams and adjusted application unique to each authority. Even during the Covid-19 pandemic crisis, local authorities had a more rapid and adaptable management capability to the local needs – from command and control to rehabilitation and growth.

Collaboration also develops between local authorities, mainly in the form of regional clusters. Thus, for example, the ultra-orthodox sector authorities, unique in their needs and characteristics, established together with the Ministry of the Interior, a forum that jointly operates for a public consisting of about one million residents. Local authorities and regional clusters constitute the largest potential platforms for empowering relevant and effective collaboration. Although they are affected by political considerations, change of discourse in the local arena promotes important public issues, such as education, environmental issues, demographic growth and more. Combining forces – including involvement of the business sector, which is usually detached from social issues – helps to leverage processes and improves the quality of life of residents. Quite often, regional and local collaboration produces significant public cooperation, thus increasing resident involvement and their ability to impact their own lives. Promoting the local and regional "eco-system" is a significant opportunity for any society.

The level of collaboration and trust in the public arena affects the resilience of any society. The Israeli society is challenged as a divided and split society, resulting in low levels of trust. Throughout the years its citizens have been able to join hands in a sense of comradeship only in the face of external dangers. Even in these cases, this sense of solidarity usually excludes the Arab and the ultra-orthodox public. Therefore, an effort should be made – as a vital social need – to integrate these groups in the fabric of collaboration and trust. If the lever for change is inherent in current political leadership, and in its direct and indirect effect on the public sector, then it seems that the characteristics of lack of collaboration, apathy and lack of trust are expected to intensify. Only if strong and effective forces arise from within the civilian population, promoting the values of collaboration as an alternative to the existing leadership, a significant effect on government will emerge.

Chapter 13

Cross-sector collaboration
A possible mission?

"Inter-sectoral partnership" is a term referring to the advancement of goals in the public sphere, assisted by cooperations between the public sector (first sector), the business sector (second sector) and civil society (third sector) – or at least two of the three. These processes stem from the current shift between traditional governance and integrated governance, or as it is acceptably termed: "new governance". It is described as the "emergence of alternative models, defined as a different form of political and institutional organization, for the purpose of promoting collective activity" (Peters & Pierre, 2000). The inter-sectoral partnership is designed to produce higher value than can be realized by the separate operation of each sector.

In essence, this model differs from the bureaucratic governance model, whereby the government holds an explicit position of seniority in relation to all other players. The government serves as both the authoritative sovereign and the entity that engages other sectors in processes designated to promote objectives and issues that are important to the public. In the meeting between different sectors and organizations, substantial differences in identity, language, rhythm, logic, rationale of operation and perception exist. There is a gap in the perception of each sector regarding its place in the partnership and the way it is seen by the other sectors. Thus, the perceptual conflict is embedded in the core of the connection between the sectors and affects the level of trust.

DOI: 10.4324/9781003514992-13

The government introduces regulation, budgets, expertise and access to additional government agencies to the partnership. The disadvantages of the government's part in the partnership are manifested in slow and bureaucratic conduct and the involvement of various political considerations. The business sector provides resources, employees, performance capabilities and influence, yet its drawbacks usually lie in the fact that they involve interests concerning profitability, even if only indirectly. The third sector mainly contributes passion, expertise, connections, affiliation to the field and legitimacy stemming from civic motivation and is usually free of other interests. Its disadvantages may be the subordination to agendas, a narrow focus, the interests of the entities themselves, a lack of resources and reliance on philanthropy.

The public sector introduces its logic to the inter-sectoral partnership: supervision and bureaucracy, hierarchy and control, legality, procedures and standards; it is identified by the concept "guard" or "defender". As far as this sector is concerned, any degree of sharing undermines the perception of governance and the ability to fully realize its responsibilities. It is concerned that external interference may alter government priorities due to the introduction of external resources and political ties. The challenge of maintaining autonomy of the players in the inter-sectoral arena exists both in terms of the government and the other sectors. The business sector, and especially associations and funds, may experience a threat to the integrity of their designated path and value system due to their relationships with the government and their dependence on it.

These partnerships represent a substantial dissonance. Public service decision makers are first and foremost regulators, with a clear responsibility to uphold the law. At the same time, they understand that many processes need to be conducted on the basis of dialogue, understanding and harnessing others to the process. Some feel there is no room for dialogue, believing their role is clear and responsibility absolute. Frequently, their approach will consist of the traditional conception of the relationship between a sovereign and the citizens it controls while ignoring the civil empowerment that has transpired over the years. Encountering such position holders maintaining such an approach raises frustration among leaders of other sectors.

Other factors in the government sector adopt and promote a different perception, according to which they are required to constantly generate relevance and serve the public. From this stance emerges the great importance they attach to recognizing the needs of various populations and maintaining a dialogue with whoever represents them. Naturally, other perceptions exist in between, raising the need to find correct balances and make appropriate decisions. The mere existence of discourse on this issue in the government sector is both fascinating and important.

Udi Prawer, former Deputy General Director for governance and social affairs in the Prime Minister's Office of Israel, and the founder of the multi-sectoral "Round Table", said the following in relation to his activities in the Prime Minister's Office:

> The value of inter-sectoral discourse is now clearly understood by all, existing by its mere potential to be a driving force for processes. The NPO's see what the government cannot see. The government has authority and power, while the NPO's see the ones over which this power is exerted in an insufficient and inadequate manner. Whenever the government plans a process with an underprivileged group, it sits down with its community representatives. Currently, when designing social procurement tenders, the civil society associations are also consulted. We have not yet managed to achieve full cooperation, but we have shifted from its utter denial to the understanding that it is Ok. The Round Table has been able to achieve a more egalitarian discourse, as was planned in the Prime Minister's Office. This generates a more symmetric dialogue; however, at the end of the day one should remember that responsibility lies in the hands of the government. In my experience, the government not only listened to this discourse but also internalized it and acted in the spirit of the issues that came up at the Round Table's meetings. The government system pertaining to public participation, which includes all sectors, fluctuates from "respond to the final matter" towards a discussion held between a third to two-thirds of the way. The phrase "listen with an open heart and willing mind" will have a greater significance when it follows the initial stage of listening. I believe that the mere fact that in recent years sharing and listening has been taking place during earlier stages – is of unprecedented importance.

In order for this type of collaboration to take place in the scope necessary to effectively treat complex issues, players need to develop innovative concepts and strengthen unique potentials. The new relationships can easily confuse the parties, compared with the natural relationships with the sovereign. The government is mostly regarded as a source of finance and a factor that generates the rules and framework for partnerships wherever it is involved. Therefore, government representatives are the first ones who must change their attitude, regarding themselves as partners who share chance, risk, responsibility and resources. Many of them have already adopted this new concept wholeheartedly. However, the greatest challenge emerges from the fact that they are affected by political and bureaucratic constraints and limited by legislation and guidelines that restrict their freedom.

Inter-sectoral partnerships mostly revolve around knowledge and synchronization: coordination and sometimes a kind of cooperation too. Rarely are collaborations or partnerships involved. "Value Alliance" is a model of meaningful partnership, as described in the book by Mike Levitt, who served as Governor in the state of Utah and Minister of Health during the Bush administration (Leavitt, 2013). Levitt initiated an important process by creating a database for the "American Health Information Community". In his view, such alliances are formed as a result of shared pain. Problems are a stronger catalyst than opportunities in forming value alliances. When the alliance partners manage to overcome the challenges, they begin to recognize that the context is not just negative but also positive. According to Levitt, success depends on the partners' ability to prioritize their shared values over ego, personal and organizational agendas, biases and styles.

The value in alliances is evident in a variety of aspects: higher effectiveness, pooling of knowledge and tools, creating value in networking, multi-dimensionality, reducing economic risk with the help of joint investments and diminishing regulation and litigation. Many different perspectives allow us to paint a broader and more accurate picture when dealing with a complex problem and create a wide range of possibilities and solutions. One organization alone, certainly a governmental organization, will act in a limited way from a perceptual aspect ("this has always been our way"), and its activity will involve the absence of diversity necessary in dealing with complex issues.

In 2011, a similar model was developed in the United States – "Collective Impact" – as an evolution of the working model "Consensus Building", which has been utilized alongside mediation in the last few decades. The working assumption is that in order to cope with complex social problems, a shared action by relevant stakeholders from different sectors is required, unlike the differential impact involved in the activities of each organization in itself. The basis for joint action is agreeing on the nature of the problem, formulating a shared vision and platform, a binding definition of required goals and actions and clarity about the indices and evaluation methods. One of the interesting terms in the model is "Back Bone Organization", designed to support the overarching work process and guarantee direct and continuous communication. As part of the model, the players continue to operate independently, as long as they are coordinated and synchronized within the framework of the joint program and assignment. The aim is synergy rather than uniformity.

The greatest realization of a government and business partnership is manifested in BOT projects (Build-Operate-Transfer), such as national roads, as well as in PPP frames (Public Private Partnership) or PFI (Private Finance

Initiative). These definitions apply to operating and maintenance systems of agencies as police and military training facilities. Once an operating supplier is selected by tender, the engagement is defined as a long-term binding partnership.

An interesting example is the Training Bases City of the IDF (Israeli Defense Forces), which was built a couple of years ago in the Negev desert as a PPP. The main challenge in this project results from the very different nature of the three partners – the IDF, the operating business company and the Ministry of Defense. These three entities have totally different organizational cultures, whose features affect the challenge rooted in creating a shared work culture and a shared language. Officers find it difficult to conduct their daily tasks alongside factors not under their command. Furthermore, they regard the business entity as a service provider rather than a partner. The ministry is the legal client but is not in the field and part of the ongoing interaction. Although these three entities hold very different perspectives, they all understand the need to create a collaborative relationship and maximum mutual commitment to overcome such a complex challenge. This kind of a move requires much flexibility, high level of trust and transparency and ongoing maintenance of the relations to accommodate the tension inherent in such a partnership.

Research and practical experience show that in most cases, inter-sectoral collaboration does not work (Barringer, 2000). Rarely is there any compatibility between project objectives and the personal interests of the various functionaries; moreover, at times contradiction in identities between the various parties hinders any potential for realization.

An interesting distinction exists between an instrumental partnership and a transformative partnership. A study examining cross-sectoral partnerships in several countries (Aveling, 2013) found that when a significant imbalance between stakeholders in a partnership ensues, especially in the case of a government entity working with civilian factors, the partnership tends to be more instrumental and less effective. When stakeholders are more balanced, on the contrary, the partnership will be more transformative in nature, producing higher value. The level of connectivity, commitment and mobilization is weaker in the former than the latter. According to the ECA model, even if the first three elements exist, the absence of the fourth element – commitment and implementation – weakens the entire pyramid.

Inter-sectoral partnerships inherently hold a structured tension that can be described as the "value paradox". On the one hand, there is potential for high value in integrated and shared work by various organizations with different resources, expertise, perceptions and cultures. On the other hand, a profound and structured variance exists between the organizations, inevitably affecting definitions of target, value and, in fact, all aspects of joint work. This paradox creates an inherent condition of great practical difficulty in achieving consensus concerning goals and processes and certainly in their realization. The most accurate and effective response to the value paradox is to conduct in-depth dialogue about understanding the dissimilarities and different goals, achieving clarity regarding issues having a common denominator and those that do not. At the same time, it is important to create structured collaboration, managed and supported by a professional external neutral factor.

Hidden agendas are an integral part of any cooperation. The more they are exposed, the better will cooperations be managed. The more hidden they remain, the more destructive they are to the process. The government has a structured interest in any cooperation with other sectors, by virtue of being the regulator. Consequently, it is easier for the government to assimilate and implement decisions through cooperations with civil society entities. This interest must also be transparent and overtly expressed in inter-sectoral processes.

Hagit Elias, CEO of "Momentum" (as mentioned, a public benefit corporation established in 2016, initiated by "Beyahad" Foundation and in collaboration with the vehicle import companies and the importers' association), says:

> The public sector is not yet fully prepared to lead cross-sectoral, broad and significant processes. For years it mainly consisted of junior clerks. A gradual change is taking place in both attitude and performance. Initiatives in the business sector are beginning to trigger dormant areas and change part of the agenda within the public sector. We need them to play a part in the process and speak the same language. I do my best to enlist them as full partners in processes. They do not think strategically, but when we focus and work on strategies together it succeeds. Moreover, the fact that we bring money to the partnership is very helpful. However, it is imperative to understand their needs and how to create value and meaning to what they do. Today they consider us full partners.

One such example is the Equal Rights Commission for People with Disabilities in the Ministry of Justice and the Equal Employment Opportunity Commission in the Ministry of Welfare. The roles of these entities, acting under the auspice of the law, guarantee that the rights of the citizens they represent are fully adhered to. For that purpose, they have effective tools for enforcement and punishment. However, the relevance of these entities is in promoting disenfranchised populations. This includes changing perceptions, recruiting relevant factors and assimilating tools and processes, based on dialogue rather than enforcement. The dissonance inherent in the work processes of those units is highly challenging. As they obtain clear recognition and status, emerging from a position of strength, they become capable of strengthening their cooperation with relevant parties, alongside enforcement. This move requires both power and maturity.

There are similarities as well as differences between the business sector and the social sector in their interface with the government. "Catch 22" is a suitable definition for the government–business interface, as described by Prof. Eugene Kendall:

> There is a very high degree of regulatory uncertainty. Many regulators assume that they are being cheated and that supervisors cannot be trusted. That is why regulators want to intervene beyond what is desired, sometimes even beyond the requirements of the law. This increases costs and, in many cases, serves to protect the regulator rather than the public. On the other hand, the industry does not adopt self-regulation, since it does not believe it can make a difference. This is a cycle of distrust that complicates doing business, lowers investments and raises costs. Nobody takes upon himself the task of trust building. I do not see any constructive steps towards building trust between the government and the business sector. This is one of the main reasons for lack of cooperation between the sectors. This is a clear case of "Catch 22". We arrived at a ridiculous state whereby anyone who strives to achieve profit is perceived as illegitimate. We, as a country, are wasting the asset called trust, and it comes with a great price tag.

In the interface between the social and government sectors, the dilemma of trust assumes a completely different property, as described by Michal Cohen, former CEO in the Ministry of Education, and later CEO of Rashi Foundation. By virtue of her roles, she holds a dual perspective on the inter-sectoral interface:

> It's all a matter of trust. When you want to cooperate and you are led by distrust – because maybe someone is out there to take your place, or perhaps is even better than you – then you are not open to cooperation. In the past, the prevailing notion in the Ministry of Education towards the third sector was that of mistrust, as if they were trying to take our place, thinking they were better than us. Our people clung to the notion that "we are the Sovereign." I told them to be confident in their position, to leave room for more partners. When you are clear about your identity, you have no problem accepting others. Those who are self-confident know how to create cooperations. The public sector often suffers from insufficient confidence. It is an abused and battered sector. Ask anyone about the

educational system and they will tell you what a "lousy" state it's in. People love to hate the public sector, everywhere in the world, referring to them as "freeloaders". For many this is far from reality. The issue of tenure is a recipe for mediocrity, because no matter how good or bad you are – your job is secure. Those joining the public sector are considered to have fewer options outside it. Therefore, people in the public sector are less confident about their place, constantly feeling they have to prove themselves.

I believe it is the government's job not only to set policy, but also to enable cooperations and leverage the strength of its civilians. In practice, only a small number of things work out, because there is neither a shared goal nor a shared definition. Consequently, power struggles ensue. The allocated roles are unclear and hard to understand. The government treats civil society as a service provider. It is not really familiar with the language of partnership. The civil society, the third sector, also faces difficulties. Anyone bringing two million dollars to the table is certain that he has the best solution to a particular matter. However, when the connection between sectors occurs, then perceptions, resources and capabilities are shared. Some of the tools – such as taking an external coordinator, an integrator – are critical, because it conveys a message that no one wishes to take control over the discourse. This is one of the keys to success. The matter of trust is so fragile that unless routine and conscious maintenance takes place, it will not hold. You really have to believe in it. Unfortunately, the professional venue bends in the face of reality.

One clear insight emerges from analyzing trust patterns of government interfaces with other sectors: a lack of sense of power and security within the government, combined with mistrust in the public arena, directly projects on inter-sectoral collaboration. In order to materialize value and potential, internal confidence as well as internal and external trust must be strengthened so that it will affect organizational cultures as well as work processes in the sector.

Udi Prawer describes a process of gradual change:

> In the past we had a weak government and strong civil associations and foundations that enjoyed "getting the government pregnant" at will. Today the government is strong and inter-sectoral partnerships are being built at its initiative. The government and the third sector still have something to learn, but both also have something to teach. When you say: both the government and civil society initiate, and people on either side of the table are allowed to meet, it is much

more beneficial than entrepreneurs who assume that these fatigued government clerks understand nothing. Furthermore, today's clerks, especially in light of training efforts held in the last decade, are players in the field of creativity and innovation. This happens with the government too.

A somewhat different angle is presented by Inbal Dor Karbel, CEO of Elem (Israeli Association for Youth in Risk):

Each sector plays a very significant role. One is in charge of development, one of performance, and another of the engine. One cannot exist without the other. For many years the third sector was able to provide quick and effective solutions where the government was not present. That sector had the know-how to develop and deliver solutions, raise money and get things moving. Over the years the public sector has recognized the capabilities of the third sector and identified opportunities to create partnerships. This process joined the privatization of many social services from the public sector to the third sector. As part of this transition, relations between the sectors have changed. Today there is a whole sequence of partnership varieties. You can find organizations that are cooperating with the government only for the sake of development, others are there to provide a response to dead zones neglected by the government, while other organizations initiate and carry out projects with the government.

Partnership with the government is not a partnership of equals, but one that is carried out by recognition of the value each party brings to the venture. In many projects everything is in fact carried out together, but still the State is the sovereign. Regardless of the association's influence, in the end, responsibility over the citizens lies on the State. This needs to be acknowledged. It does not mean that the partnership will consist of a controller-controlled relationship. Some government representatives join steering committees and decision-making processes with a partnership approach. On the other hand, sometimes this is not the case.

Elem association maintains partnerships with the government as well as local councils. It is clear that the government ministry or the local councils are the dominating entities, in control of the budget. Still, acknowledging the association as an expert and leader positions it as an equal partner at the table. Often the local council recognizes that it cannot respond adequately, therefore, an external professional factor is required. If each recognizes the value of the other – as was the case with the Ministry of Welfare and the Tel Aviv Municipality on the issue of commercial sexual exploitation of minors – then it works out perfectly.

When does it fail to occur? For many years and to this day public service has suffered a very bad reputation. In recent years, for those who tried to generate change and received no credit the ego arose and stumped the process. Senior government officials say that when problems arise all fingers are directed at the government, yet, when things go well the associations receive all the recognition. This does not contribute to partnerships, and the associations have some responsibility in this matter. This discourse is gradually changing for the better.

Associations often articulate sharp and direct criticism towards those working with them. Many associations maintain their positions, either lashing out at the system, or merely serving as providers of service, since they depend on government tenders. Associations should be continuously reading the map in order to understand what are the trends and who are the relevant players. For example, in recent years the sphere of local councils is becoming an increasingly relevant partner.

Philanthropic foundations are different from associations. Philanthropy has undergone changes over the years, and its relationship with the government has changed accordingly. Its activities require increasing involvement of large business donors, who introduce more innovative managerial concepts, creating a highly complex fabric of interests. Traditional philanthropy has contented itself with raising funds for associations and government activities; however, the new philanthropy strives to increase its control over financial goals and gain greater involvement in policy design. The government recognizes the philanthropic players as most significant in dealing with complex social challenges. On this basis, significant inter-sectoral partnerships and cooperations emerge. One of the most important conditions for exercising such partnerships is their degree of compatibility with the priorities and policy of the governmental ministry.

A fascinating study performed by Michal Almog-Bar and Esther Zichlinsky (2010) presented an analysis of "Headstones" – a partnership that was defined as successful, compared with one that did not – "Yaniv Initiative". In both cases the main characteristics were similar: they both entailed convoluted and complex relationships between the funds and the government; in both cases the government had reservations about the degree of influence the funds held, regarding them as a threat to its activities, and in both cases the government demanded to act as the leading partner.

The factors they identified as conducive to a successful partnership are identifying mutual added value, recognizing a defined and clear problem, harnessing players in the government and political arena, maintaining the professional status of government representatives, attributing continuous meaning to the partnership itself, the existence of communication mechanisms, mutual legitimacy among the entities, a preliminary in-depth study of the field by the fund and keeping a gradual collaborative structuring process, which also includes addressing the essence of the partnership. It emerged that these factors contribute to overcoming conflicts between the parties. On the other hand, the factors found as inhibitors, leading to unsuccessful partnerships, are a lack of structure, perception of the partnership as a technical–financial means, difficulties in governance, a lack of procedures and definitions, avoiding discourse regarding the meaning of the partnership, as well as interpersonal elements, including a sense of vulnerability and mistrust, which complicate discussions and decision making.

According to the researchers' analysis, the main challenge in both projects emerged from the government's difficulty to view the philanthropic players as a legitimate factor in policy making. They were regarded by the government as people of wealth who can assist in executing its tasks but not as a source of professional knowledge required for decision making. In the successful venture, the government regarded the foundations as factors that could introduce new ideas and help translate them into change of perception and policy. The foundations perceived the government as a cumbersome entity in need of external assistance due to its failure to provide systemic solutions to social issues. In the end, in such processes it is imperative to disarm the government's inherent apprehension and the philanthropic players' sense of patronage.

In light of all that was discussed in this chapter, what are the conditions required to successfully navigate the great challenge inherent within the gaps between the sectors? A number of conditions must be met in creating connections between them: mutual acquaintance, identification of a defined problem and understanding that it is impossible to deal with it alone, establishing trust, creating a clear structure, identifying the value in the partnership, formulating a structure process and participation of the relevant players. Time should be devoted in order to deeply understand the perceptual differences between the sectors, stemming from a position of trust and mutual appreciation. It is important that the structure and decision-making processes are clearly defined. Recognition must be given to the activity of the professional rank in the government while developing discourse regarding the essence of the partnership, defining roles and authorities and establishing mechanisms for dispute resolution. All players in the arena should participate in processes of analysis and strategic thinking. One should bear in mind that the government is not interested in being told what to do nor feel as if it is about to lose its sovereign authority.

Within the social field

Inbal Dor Karbel, CEO of Elem Association, openly shares her thoughts:

> The sector in itself does not know how to cooperate well enough. We could have created much greater value in policy design, impact, as well as value for the associations, had we worked more in unison. There are cooperations at the level of shared learning, how to work with the government etc., but not as much shared work and doing.

It is only natural for social entities to cooperate with each other in order to advance their goals and strengthen their impact; however, surprisingly enough, there is a very high level of competition within the third sector, far more than in other sectors. Mostly, cooperations are confined to coordination only, which includes transfer of information, limited professional sharing, coordination related to regulation and more.

Why are cooperations and collaborations so limited in social entities? First, it seems that for those involved, the high level of personal investment in setting up and operating of the undertaking results in emotional attachment and conduct. Moreover, it appears that these entities are in their comfort zone when they accumulate power and rely on large and fixed donors. They do not necessarily perceive cooperation as a necessity. At the same time, the recent shift in perception in the philanthropic world, whereby foundations and donors demand to see outcomes and results rather than just inputs and activities, greatly challenges social entities and creates an unprecedented pressure system that was unfamiliar in the past. There is also a struggle for professionalism, and acknowledging it is an important element in the conduct and perception of non-profit organizations. Furthermore, the social arena is still characterized by a mindset of struggle for limited resources, in accordance with the limited pool of donations, as opposed to the business arena where it is increasingly perceived that the possibilities for innovation and growth are abundant, as a blue ocean, with no real limitations. Moreover, among social entities competition exists over public awareness and credit for activities, as a necessary and at times even crucial condition for support from philanthropy, the public and government.

More than ever, today the social sphere requires high-level cooperations and collaborations – both in the intra-organizational aspects as well as in the inter-organizational and inter-sectoral aspects. As far as the intra-organizational level is concerned, in recent years social entities have become more professional and complex. Similar to any other organization, the ability to fulfill their vision and succeed in achieving their goals largely depends on the quality of interfaces, internal synergy and the ability to handle conflicts effectively. It is a misconception to think that altruistic values and social goals constitute in and of themselves a shield against organizational failures resulting from damaged relationships, inadequate work relations or a lack of sufficient attention for the quality of interfaces within the organization.

It should be acknowledged that outside the organizational aspect, the social field is saturated with players: government offices and public institutions, local councils, non-profit organizations, business companies, philanthropic entities, social movements, communities, parents' committees, academic institutions and more. The point of contact between the various agendas and interests not only enriches the field and enables growth of ideas, initiatives and a great variety of doing but, at the same time, also creates conflicts and ongoing struggles and impairs the ability to lead profound and long-term systemic and adaptive changes. The local council or municipality, which is for the most part "the landlord", depends on budgets brought in by the foundations and other external entities, some of which have overt and covert interests. Even without addressing unnecessary conflicts and struggles, the multiple factors operating in the field – often without coordination or cooperation – lead to the existence of overlapping zones – blind spots, that is, untreated issues – waste of resources and lack of effectiveness.

Managing processes and promoting initiatives in the social field require a broad and complex systemic vision and high capacity for interface management, cooperations and collaborations in inter-sectoral and inter-cultural contexts, within a dynamic and challenging arena. In recent years, awareness of these issues has grown and more frequently expressed, although all players testify that realization is still far-off. The various program integrators at the national and local levels (nearly every program has a local coordinator) are mostly experts in the field of content. They lack expertise in structuring processes and creating effective synergy between the various factors. Due to the mere fact that in a complex inter-organizational partnership, no one leads or forces his will, a local integrator and a structured process are highly important. Consolidating their identities and abilities as CCOs – experts and leaders in the field of collaboration – is still premature. Once the social sector systematically and expertly leads partnerships and collaborations, it will have greater value in the eyes of the other sectors, and naturally, the effectiveness of the processes and products will also rise accordingly (Gefen, 2012).

Chapter 14

50 shades of uniforms
Collaboration in the
military system

There are not more than five musical notes, yet the combinations of these five give rise to more melodies than can ever be heard. There are not more than five primary colors, yet in combination they produce more hues than can ever been seen. There are not more than five cardinal tastes, yet combinations of them yield more flavors than can ever be tasted.

Sun Tzu,
The Art of War

As strange as it may sound to speak of musical notes, colors and flavors in a military context, it is the defense arena in particular that constitutes a fascinating sphere for learning about rapid change processes in the various aspects of collaboration. The natural environment of these organizations is chaotic and constantly changing; thus, in order to remain relevant, they are required to undergo constant change. The external dynamic threat is the most significant catalyst for collaborations in these arenas; hence, the cost of stagnation is extremely high. These are the characteristics of this trend:

1. In recent years, the defense systems have tended to adopt advanced business management practices, including innovative and matrixial organizational structures, which, in turn, have an impact on the organizational culture.

DOI: 10.4324/9781003514992-14

2. Rapid adaptation and flexibility are required in this arena, which, in turn, have an impact on the ability to generate change.
3. The hierarchical structure, often perceived as adversely affecting collaboration, may actually constitute an advantage in its creation and assimilation – as long as the head of that hierarchy really aspires for it.
4. Large bureaucratic organizations tend to introduce changes following disruptions. Naturally, these occur from time to time in defense systems. An inverse trend also exists, according to which crises may cause a setback rather than encourage a readiness for development and change. In the military jargon, when encountering difficulties in navigating, we must return to the point where we began to drift away. Such was the case in the aftermath of the Yom Kippur War (1973). In the face of the Sager missiles that could be launched by a single soldier, rather than questioning if the tank was still as relevant as it once was, more armor units were established. The culprit for some of the Second Lebanon War (2006) failures was the military language, which is said to have regressed in the absence of a new and relevant language that must be developed.
5. History proves that in military systems, cooperations are critically important – from the Normandy landings in 1944, where General Eisenhower had full control of the U.S. Air and Naval Forces, to the concept of the surgical strike that was developed in recent years in Israel and around the world.

If the need is clear and tangible, where are the application gaps?

The East German intelligence organization, the Stasi, employed about 90,000 people, whose job was, among other things, to open every envelope and listen to every conversation. However, the Stasi did not foresee the fall of the Berlin Wall despite clear indications. It was found that the Stasi operated in separate silos in order to maintain compartmentalization and prevent a situation whereby too much information is centralized in one place. Many years later, approximately 3,000 people were killed in a terrorist attack that none of the intelligence agencies in the United States could have anticipated. As aforementioned, the 9/11 attacks would have been prevented had it not been for the issue of NIH (Not Invented Here) between intelligence agencies. No intelligence organization predicted the Arab Spring that began at the end of 2010 and its consequences. Alongside many examples illustrating a lack of collaboration, an infinite number of examples of its success can be noted too; however, there still are, and will be, many barriers and discrepancies.

Naturally, the need for high-level collaboration in the Israeli defense systems is real. In the 1950s, General Sharon had absolute and sole authority to mobilize the famous combat unit 101 to night operations; today, however, no one unit can operate independently without coordination with a large number of factors. The degree of effectiveness and relevance increasingly depends on integrated work between various organizations and disciplines. The pooling of knowledge, capabilities and resources is formed in a collaborative manner, as an inevitability.

The main emphasis in this discussion relates to the intelligence field in the defense system, since this sphere stands out in assimilating a collaborative culture within the last decade. The central need for change derives from changes in the nature of the conflicts and threats. Brigadier General Baron, former Head of Research Division in the Military Intelligence Directorate, describes this reality as follows:

> Integration in the defense system stems from a need related to two significant changes – the enemy and the nature of war. The enemy penetrated the spaces existing between organizations in the previous operation configuration. An example illustrating this situation occurred when Israel attacked an ambulance in Gaza in 2002. It was assumed that rockets were placed inside it, when in practice it was a stretcher. Upon investigating the case, it was found that there was no one in Israel who was capable of deciphering and identifying the difference. At the time, we knew how to analyze tanks and other objects related to war. The second Intifada (Palestinian uprising) in 2000, had a traumatic effect on the system, since we realized that we did not know how to handle it separately, each entity on its own. It had the dimensions of war, and the need overcame the organizational ethos. An understanding arose that the existing structure does not know how to deal with the changes, and that we should work in unison, within and between organizations. Connections began to form.

The ambulance image symbolizes the increasing rate of changes and surrounding threats and the difficulty in predicting the future, which is the core of the intelligence community. This reality carries broad implications on all military units. The phenomenon commencing in 2010, defined (mistakenly) as the "Arab Spring", disintegration of the regime in Iraq, the bloody war in Syria and the expansion of Iranian involvement – all of these resulted in a fundamental change in everything related to the intelligence situation and the challenges emanating from it.

In the past, the focus was clear: the Arab states. Among the community organizations – Military Intelligence Directorate, the General Security Service and the Mossad – responsibilities were clearly divided, in an outline that was referred to as the "Magna Carta". The main division of work between the entities was according to the different geographical arenas. However, past agreements are no longer relevant, especially in light of threats of Islamic terrorism from dozens of organizations, in activities occurring in many arenas simultaneously. The intelligence community is required to a higher level of collaboration than ever before in order to remain relevant. On this basis, the Cyber Defense Division was established in 2015, introducing many additional changes. This is a great and complex challenge for organizations that generate part of their basis of power and perceptual nature on the gathering of information. Its division and distribution among parallel organizations are not compatible with the concept of their basic operation.

"Jointness" is one of the hottest and most controversial terms in the defense system. The term "jointness" was coined in the 1980s in the United States. Zvi Lanir refined the definition as follows: "Creating a new systemic ability, based on the fusion of the unique assets of various factors, indicating deeper affinity than coordination or cooperation" (Lanir, 2005: 20). Following is another detailed definition created in the IDF (Israel Defense Forces) and the intelligence community:

> Jointness is an overall concept crossing organizations and levels. It begins within the consciousness of individuals in the organization, carries into combat theory, procedures and organization; in fact, it is a state of consciousness (individual and organizational). Jointness deals with inter-organizational affinity, expressed in organization agreements emanating from a shared interest to work together and achieve shared goals, while effectively integrating and utilizing resources and means. The goal – improving operational relevance and efficiency to perform tasks in the best way while using minimal resources. The challenge – the ability to construct the "bridges" between isolated armed structures and the need to think and act jointly, with the understanding that we will continue to exist in organizational, military and service differentiation, stemming from a real vital need. Jointness represents an organizational culture expressed by a state of mind (mindset / I believe) that creates organizational consciousness, and as such, its effect extends beyond action in time and data sphere.

> **(Michael et al., 2017)**

Major General Itai Virov, Commander of Depth Headquarters and the Military Academies, expresses the conception whereby existing jointness is insufficient:

> Cooperations between organizations is an old story. The new story requires the courage to get organized from the ground up in a

heterogeneous and multidisciplinary manner, with a multidimensional solution. The basic perception in the military today is that when I have a mission that I am responsible to perform, I will ask myself – how can others help me? On a ground mission, at the end of my to-do list I will check how the Air Force, Intelligence, Cyber and others can help me. I do not analyze the ground from the same angle as the Air Force or Spectrum or UW (Underground Warfare). The premise should be completely different: rather than helping and joining each other, we must create a joint basis. The ground must be analyzed by the pilot and the cybernetics and cyber person, and not only by ourselves. In fact, we have yet to change the basic thought model. Status assessment, situation analysis, decision-making – this is military thinking, which is done separately and not really in unison.

The various disciplines are within their own silos, and so it should be, as you cannot train a pilot and a tank commander and an infantry division commander in the same silo. People develop and train separately, and meet at a very late stage. Fighting demands reorganization. The idea that sleeping next to each other in the training camp for lieutenant colonel will conceal unidimensionality, has absolutely no basis. Work plans should jointly incorporate the question of challenges and goals. When the formation of work plans synchronizes the plans of various arms, then jointness exists. However, this only happens to some degree. There is constant improvement, with large shared and significant projects taking place, but these moves are insufficient in the face of the challenges. We must establish multidimensional organizations. For example, transfer some of the squadrons to field commands or create more heterogeneous battalions while maintaining platoons homogeneous. These procedures are relatively easy to perform in a professional army such as the US military, but due to the nature of the IDF, the process will be much more challenging. It is necessary to create new organizations and not just examine cooperations between old and diverse organizations.

An example of such an experimental capsule is the "Refa'im" (ghosts) unit, set up in 2019 as a multidimensional unit. It is an elite combat unit, integrating diversified capabilities as part of the preparations for fighting in the battlefield of the future. The IDF regards this unit as a significant pilot of the multidimensionality concept.

Whether the definition is "jointness", "multidimensionality" or "fusion", the IDF and the entire defense system have yet to build an orderly model that will properly advance interfaces and collaborations. Along with many successes, there are also discrepancies and difficulties in implementing collaborations. Many leaders recognize its importance while, at the same time, point out contradictions and dilemmas in its application: Is it a question of value? Of operational perception? A worldview? Or maybe just a recommendation for an outline whenever it is relevant and feasible?

Organizations whose relevance largely depends on collaboration should have an explicit interest to advance its existence. Jointness is therefore ostensibly a cornerstone of the operation doctrine. Why only ostensibly? Because there is often a gap and even contradiction between the declared directive and the actual conduct. The main conclusion in a study by two IDF organizational consultants (Brush & Amitai, 2017) refers to the gap between the alleged shared conduct in the General Headquarter Forum, "on the table", the senior management of the organization, and between the hidden plain, where separate "estates" exist and covert processes are carried out. Many years of managing separate strategic processes make it difficult to create a common ground. Thus, it is written in this study, for example, that

> Generals who command over "strong" and well funded units may feel that cooperating within the General Staff Forum reduces their power, so they prefer to advance the interests of the unit they are entrusted with in other ways, or as one of the interviewees called it – in indirect paths.
>
> **(Brush & Amitai, 2017)**

Is it possible that senior officials in various organizations of the defense systems have no real desire to embrace a change and shape a clear joint, committed and assimilated concept systematically? Is that the main barrier of collaboration in this arena? Indeed, it is very possible that this is the case. These organizations emphasize command and leadership in almost every aspect related to organizational culture, power building and operation doctrine but very little in the integrative context. The middle rank commanders and managers in these organizations describe adequate relationships in the junior and middle ranks and, in conjunction, point at significant difficulties in the senior arena.

Additional aspects of this complexity are reflected in remarks of a brigadier general holding a central position:

> The spirit of the commander is perhaps the most influential factor, but if it is not translated into action, into details, then the situation might be even more dangerous. Field ranks work well among

themselves, whereas seniors much less – partly because the senior focuses on resources. Furthermore, the idea of pooling resources is by no means trivial. Senior commanders are prone to "colonialism." If I have achieved something, I will do my best to achieve more in a similar fashion. I gain something from another factor through jointness, but then my attempt to gain five percent more than was agreed upon, will raise objections and impair jointness. At the end of the day, in order to maintain jointness I will have to give up ten percent, and gain a total addition of thirty percent. However, this requires relinquishing in the short term, along with a long-term systemic vision. The difficulty that seniors encounter is also related to the manner in which a task is identified. Not everyone recognizes jointness as a significant parameter. I am aware that there are those from whom I will receive full cooperation and others from whom I will not. Implementing these moves is also related to an explicit cultural encounter between arms and organizations. One has to recognize the differences between the cultures in order to construct something together.

It would seem that a lack of full and structured application of jointness addresses the needs of the commanders. The military maintains a high level of independence for its commanders, partly because personal strength is necessary in this system. The natural narcissism and hubris of commanders, as well as the organizational and cultural legitimacy given to the expression of such tendencies, is another contributing factor. In addition, jointness has a personal price tag: How do I approach the task? Am I the leader, or am I doing my best to make the mission a success? This is a profound issue that is not sufficiently discussed. Some senior commanders and managers hold the perception that jointness is not always the lever that will add to their prestige, prominence and promotion in the system. They do not always have the desire to achieve clear regularization, as they wish to maintain maximum independence.

General Itai Virov adds to this issue:

> In terms of the message, everyone talks about jointness and multi-dimensionality, but in practice, they do not want to change. Once you change you lose grip on a personal level. There is a very big story here, which enfolds identity, history, habits, ego difficulties, fear of change and credit. Logically everyone understands it, but there is a dissonance, requiring a kind of self-scheming. Strategy is what you do and not what you say. A high level of self-awareness and ego management is needed to motivate myself from one place to another.

A long-term organizational phenomenon probably produces more value to the organization than harming it, even if it is perceived as negative or is in conflict with the declared values. Commanders will operate to create collaborations only when they understand that collaborations are beneficial and not only due to the importance of their mission. The value of collaborations for the organization and for them should be higher than the value obtained from a lack of collaboration, which is very advantageous for them.

Command and control constitutes a very convenient and deep anchor as a central organizing idea, educating commanders from a very early stage. Even in relatively senior positions, many experience difficulty resolving what they perceive as contradicting conceptions – command and collaboration.

Beyond the analysis of the collaboration-command dissonance, there are other barriers that have a unique expression in the military arena. There is a long tradition of organizational differentiation, various disciplines and trainings, activities of separate units, differentiated technological aspects, organizational culture and unique identity. Often these differences are accompanied by external expressions, such as the color of berets and other visible characteristics that create in the units feelings of pride and belonging. More elements are a lack of profound familiarity between arms and organizations, territorialism and sectarianism, intra-organizational commitment, excessive fear of losing identity, competition and struggles for prestige, difficulties in trusting others and a reluctance to depend on them, as well as the presence of limited resources. There are also conflicting interests that are not easily mediated. For example, the Air Force strives to maintain a state of isolation for operational efficiency. At the same time, it is essential to create cooperation between the aircraft and the maneuvering battalion to create a closed "fire circle".

At times, real misunderstanding about the need for collaboration and a lack of conviction in this path makes application difficult. Another influencing factor is the tendency of tactical and task-oriented thinking, based on deep codes of warfare and obstruction, and less on systemic and procedural thinking. These are task-oriented, hierarchical and extremely segregated organizations that exert power and are victory oriented. Whenever an operational or tactical need for cooperation arises, it will often be addressed, but that does not mean that long-term strategic collaboration processes are built between entities.

A notable phenomenon that is typical of these entities, especially in the intelligence community, is the tendency for compartmentalization. The mere use of compartmentalization is very important, but sometimes it has an excessive impact on the perception of interfaces. The need for its existence often forms a solid foundation for an argument against collaboration. It is hard to argue about the need for compartmentalization and separation, though in some cases, its use serves completely different interests and is a legitimate excuse for the underlying interests. Due to the inherent competition, managers and commanders in the arena sometimes react cynically to the definition of collaboration. They identify much more with the term "coopetition" than with the term "collaboration".

Brigadier General Baron further clarifies the complexity involved in adopting jointness. First, he describes the reaction of a former senior member in the intelligence department, relating to a process of strengthening jointness that was performed in the organization: "It may take away the pluralism on which the intelligence system was built after 1973 Yom Kippur War. You combine everything, and when that happens no argument will take place." Baron focuses on a number of disadvantages and limitations, as he perceives them:

> Jointness has drawbacks in terms of the ability to argue, because everyone begins to think similarly. When the Americans introduced the idea of jointness, a whole discussion arose whether it would not kill the uniqueness of the different arms. The separate silos have an advantage when it comes to doubt and argument, a highly significant issue, especially in the intelligence community. Over the years, intelligence has really worked in silos with ideology and history. The pendulum has swung to the other side. It is a positive move, but requires caution and balance. These are generational processes that require a lot of time.

In the past, geography solved part of the issue because it created clear and convenient definitions. But today there are far fewer fortified walls between the organizations, as they are now geographically inseparable. It has also become impossible to differentiate between war, terrorism, cyber, homeland security and more. The American intelligence community internalized it the hard way. One of the consequences of the 9/11 attacks was establishing the DNI (Director of National Intelligence), a managing and integrating body of the intelligence community organizations. In 2007 they issued a "500-day plan", which included a defined strategy for strengthening jointness within the American intelligence community, a factor they defined as a "power multiplier". This is a systemic profound and broad plan, creating a cross-organizational collaboration strategy, translated to concrete actions and solutions, emerging from time to time. The plan did not prevent many problems and did not address all challenges, but it is a milestone in perceptual change and in taking responsibility for this issue (DNI, 2007).

Change processes can be implemented more easily when it relates to the same organization with one leader, but even then, collaborative, adaptive and courageous leadership is required. One of the most significant moves took place in IDF, when Major General Aviv Kochavi was head of Intelligence Division and led the "Intelligence Directorate Act" – a process of deep and fascinating change, which began in 2011 and lasted for several years. This is how the essence of the move was defined:

> The Act was born not only by understanding the need to adapt the organization to the present era. The process emerged from a basic philosophy, according to which one must recognize that the circumstances – that is, the strategic, social, military, technological, economic, environment etc. – in which the organization operates are constantly changing. Change is the only constant in life.
>
> **(Kochavi & Bartal, 2014)**

The leading idea of the intelligence commanders was that change itself is an existential need, an organizational thought process and a worldview: "The Intelligence Directorate must be built so that its central feature will include the ability to change quickly, thus ensuring that the organization is relevant, adapted to the reality and capable of leaving an impact on it" (Kochavi & Bartal, 2014). The process of change in the Intelligence Directorate derived from existential needs cutbacks, a disparity between the quality of intelligence knowledge at the senior levels and the knowledge available to the operational ranks in the Second Lebanon War, as well as non-collaborative norms between the intelligence units, defined as "slack confederation". This was written in the document: "It was clear to everyone that differentiation, and sometimes even alienation, between the systems and divisions in the Directorate are more dominant than the cooperation narrative" (Kochavi & Bartal, 2014).

Many in the system thought that change was not necessary, or they did not believe that any significant change could be accomplished by the organization. Frustration and cynicism toward previous processes and internal and external organizational complexity created a challenge in formulating the process. The leadership of the Head of Intelligence, Aviv Kochavi, and the sophisticated structuring of the change process led by the organization management created the appropriate infrastructure. They chose to make decisions, following in-depth analysis, with reference to all relevant dimensions: objectives and strategy, structure and organization, work processes and organizational culture. They identified that "as long as the organization and its senior commanders remain in their 'comfort zone', there is no real incentive for change … therefore, the ability to view ourselves critically and sharply constitutes a condition for any process of real change" (Kochavi & Bartal, 2014).

The systemic learning, incorporated within the process, examined the history, the premises and the relevance gaps and barriers. Alongside the intra-organizational aspect, a parallel observation was made, related to the perspective of the entire military and other intelligence community organizations. Maximum participation of officers at various levels and from as many disciplines as possible took place throughout the entire process, including non-intelligence officials who were integrated into the thinking and planning teams. The deep and courageous examination of the fundamental questions naturally led to the creation of more built-in jointness mechanisms in the organization and its surroundings. One of the most significant applications, defined as "intelligence in colors", included the definition of new and different work interfaces between the organization units, combined with a high level of collaboration and even mutual dependence on knowledge and abilities.

The "Intelligent Directorate Act" has led to significant changes in all aspects, including significant exceptions from traditional intelligence frameworks and development of new types of intelligence that had not been in the arena before. The document states: "The intelligence department is turning into a partner in the IDF's effort of winning the war and in the impact on the environment in the campaign between the wars" (Kochavi & Bartal, 2014).

The implementation and assimilation phase were given high importance as part of the process, based on the understanding that even the best plan may go down the drain in the absence of accurate implementation:

> As serious as the motivation for the process may be, a framework and a viable platform are required to ensure a profound, continual (enduring) and practical process allowing the organization not only to survive, but also to change and retain relevance. Every strategic process entails a double challenge – determine the destination towards which it is advancing (the what) and lay stable rails over which the process will travel (the how).
>
> **(Kochavi & Bartal, 2014)**

The leading principles at this point were high-level managerial attention, alongside flexible adjustment and change along the way, in conjunction with maximum participation of all levels in the organization. The message was "we mean what we agree upon", and that is why it had such a big impact on the doing and organizational culture. Throughout the process, its leaders (the organization management) were open to criticism and feedback. In stark contrast to the recognized official military rules of debate, one of the most important tools in the process, success was the encouragement of free and critical discussion among all ranks. Realizing that each participant, wherever he may be positioned within the organization, may influence the process was given vast importance.

Kochavi and Bartal's document states that "only culture measuring change and renewal may enable organizations to develop adaptability, but culture is not enough – mechanisms, tools and processes that are systematically and constantly activated are required" (Kochavi & Bartal, 2014).

The practice of collaboration and adjustments for the purpose of its assimilation have enabled the IDF, in the last years, to provide a quick and accurate response in complex arenas that are not even distinctly defined as its missions. Thus, for example, a new unit was established to manage cooperation between Israeli and Syrian citizens, in order to aid organizations and various units during the civil war in Syria. This unit, which was given the name "Good Neighborhood", was established as a unique military unit, which sought to address Israeli interests (mainly in stopping the establishment of Islamic extremists near the border) and for the needs of civilians in the Syrian Golan. Colonel (res.) Eyal Dror, who set up and was Commander of this unit, says:

> We had to create something which had never been done before. Without combat theory or an orderly outline. We understood that learning was required and that there was a need for adjustment in the process, following successes and failures. The challenge was forming a partnership with those who were educated to hate us; to start speaking the language of the other side and not what we thought we understood. Trust is built by giving what is needed whenever needed.

The collaboration and multidimensionality in the Israeli defense system are constantly improving; however, these moves are made partially and randomly rather than in the structured and systematic way that is familiar to this system, when it wishes to do so. The future vision – both in the internal aspects of the defense system, which is the largest and most complex body in Israel, and its influence and connections with many organizations – is committed to take clear and systemic responsibility regarding the issue of collaboration. There are many different solutions to choose from and implement, but the leverage for change is in leadership at all levels and, most importantly, in senior leadership. At the same time, systemic language, work methodologies, systematics and practicality must be implemented, as well as new organizational processes and structures.

The defense and intelligence organizations in Israel are a significant learning arena for implementation of collaboration. During a lecture about cooperative leadership held before a group of advisors, a former Mossad senior spoke about the concept and practice of jointness over the past two decades. He said:

At that time we did not understand it. We worked in separate silos both among ourselves and with others. Over the years, we have learned and invested a lot in it, and today it is natural and clear in the organization and in the community.

It has been my privilege to accompany as a consultant these leaders and organizations which have made profound changes in organizational culture, interfaces and work processes. Based on experience rather than blind faith, I am certain that it is possible to create the required change in any organization and in any arena. The investment in creating effective collaboration as a core value translated into a shared language and work processes, both within the organizations and between them and with the security systems of several other countries, was clearly reflected in the ability to successfully manage the challenges created during the war that began with the Hamas attack on October 7, 2024.

Epilogue
A look to the future

Only through the power of collaboration and trust can humanity redeem itself and create a future that values humanity, development and prosperity. Furthermore, in the unfolding global struggle between the values of liberal democracy and the forces of fascism, repression and extremists, the victors will be those who powerfully master the art of collaboration, drawing strength from diversity and unity.

The world as we know it through human history is characterized largely by prominent components of power and control, hierarchy and authority, separate disciplines, competition, confined territories and hubris. The world that many of us strive to create is defined to a large extent by components of freedom and diversity, connection and dialogue, agility and relevance, information sharing and networking, humbleness, caring and solidarity.

Obviously, the reality is more intricate and less dichotomic, but as we gaze into the future of humankind, it is clear that our next evolutionary leap will depend on this transformation and on our ability to forge unprecedented levels of collaboration and trust across organizations, disciplines, cultures and borders.

Both at the global and local levels, collaboration strengthens community ties and builds resilience. When people come together to tackle challenges, they build networks of support that enhance the social fabric and improve the quality of life for everyone involved. Collaboration also instills a sense of hope and feelings of belonging and solidarity. By working together, people feel that they are not alone in facing their challenges and that collective action can lead to meaningful change and impact. Cultural bridging is crucial for creating a more inclusive world where all voices are heard and valued. Collaboration accelerates the pace of innovation by pooling resources, expertise and creativity.

DOI: 10.4324/9781003514992-15

Wherever we look, it is worthwhile asking is there value in transitioning from "ego-system" to "eco-system". In most cases, the value is clear, but change does not always seem possible. Opportunities for collaboration and coopetition are appearing in this era at all places and levels. In order to make the right decisions and create value in partnerships, it is imperative to work in a professional, systematic and structured manner. Effective collaboration cannot be manifested in our complex world in a random, partial and incidental way. It requires elements of leadership, structure, process, relationship and commitment.

This book outlines the architecture of collaborations, in an attempt to create order and structurality in this challenging issue. The first anchor in the new paradigm illustrated in the book is simplicity. Simple tools such as the ECA model and working with interests and needs can generate great changes. Simplicity is a necessity in a complex world. The second anchor is a paradigm, accompanied by an applicable model, of systematic, accurate and structured understanding and managing of collaboration. The third anchor is the insight of collaborative intelligence and the competence of creating a shared language – one that can impact culture as well as organizational culture, and ultimately leadership. It all comes down to leadership.

The decision to write the book – aspiring to impart into it the most precise knowledge, experience and tools for leaders and managers – is a part of fulfilling my leadership mission and purpose. This purpose is defined in the simplest terms:

> Our world can and should be a better place, for us and for our children. It is our responsibility to make it so. The future of human society depends on us. The only way to do this is together, through collaboration and trust.

My calling is focused on assimilating this conception among leaders. This is the purpose of this book, and everything I have been doing in the past 25 years, and the main part of my mission in the next 25 years.

Leadership in an age of complexity is based on the ability to create high relevance and value through effective, structured and capable management of interfaces and partnerships in all organizations and systems. Collaboration is becoming a very significant part of leadership and management. The ability to handle crises and changes, create impact and innovation, relevance and effectivity, survival and growth – all these components depend, now more than ever, on our capacity to contain and lead the transition from the old world to the new by effective collaboration.

A huge enigma regarding leadership and collaboration in the new world lies in the political arena. Can local and global political systems make the transition from ego-systems to eco-systems? Give up the old divisive politics and adopt a new type of politics, promoting connection and creating value and durability? There is no question that for us as citizens, this is the most relevant path, but it is not clear if the same can be said for politicians. Most of them hold fast to the old narrative, according to which it is necessary and legitimate to win at all costs, and partnerships occur solely on the basis of short-term interests, blended with cynicism and an inherent lack of trust. The entire world is affected by a brutish political arena (excluding few leaders) of disconnected and alienated, hooked on honor and ego, creating a sense of separateness, alienation and distrust, and lacking empathy and compassion.

In my view, it is our responsibility to change these arenas too, making them relevant to us and to our future. Collaboration is not merely a tool but the very foundation upon which the edifice of a peaceful, prosperous and just society must be built. Synergy is essential for addressing global challenges such as climate change, poverty, terrorism, health crises and more. The fate of humanity hinges on our ability to unite and collaborate across systems toward common goals. The leaders in our midst are responsible for designing this future. Those among us who fail to understand and implement this lose their relevance. No force can stop a truth whose time has come.

As a father, entrepreneur, commander and social influencer, as a CEO and consultant, and as a local and global citizen, I am committed to bind these concepts and practices to the Israeli society and global humanity. We all have absolute freedom of choice whether we wish to lead the changes necessary in the new era. Each one of us, in his own sphere, according to his values and influence, can affect and implement many of the ideas and tools detailed in this book – provided we understand and define the value. Processes of change require accountability, perseverance, effort and at times going against the flow and the norms.

I would like to thank all my partners and clients, who have been my best teachers on this journey. A special thanks goes to the professional team at Gome-Gevim Group, who have contributed from their experience and wisdom. We are all acting from a sense of moral mission, which constitutes the basis for both our work and this book. My gratitude to anyone who contributed to the writing process. A heartfelt thank you to my insightful partner Effi, to my supportive parents and to my children, Atalya and Nevo, who are and always will be a significant guiding light in everything I do.

References

Arbinger Institute. *The Outward Mindset: Seeing Beyond Ourselves*, Berrett-Koehler Publishers, 2016.

Arsenault Jane. *Forging Nonprofit Alliances*, Jossey Bass Publisher, 1998.

Aveling Emma-Louise and Graham Martin. "Realizing the Transformative Potential of Healthcare Partnerships: Insights from Divergent Literatures and Contrasting Cases in High-and Low-Income Country Contexts", *Social Science & Medicine* 92 2013: 74–82.

Axelrod Robert. *The Evolution of Cooperation*, Basic Books, 1984.

Bardach Eugene. *Getting Agencies to Work Together: The Practice and Theory of Managerial Craftsmanship*, Brookings Institution Press, 1998.

Barringer Bruce and Harrison Jeffrey. "Walking a Tightrope: Creating Value through Interorganizational Relationships", *Journal of Management* 26(3) October 2000: 367–403.

Bass, B. M., and Avolio, B. J. Improving organizational effectiveness through transformational leadership. Thousand Oaks, CA: Sage Publications, 1994.

Baum Joel A. C. and Helaine J. Korn. "Dynamics of Dyadic Competitive Interaction", *Strategic Management Journal* 20(3) March 1999: 251–278.

Beier David and Bronstein Max. "Partnership Offers Hope for COVID Drug Development", *Biocentury*, May 2020, www.biocentury.com.

Boon Susan and Holmes John. "The Dynamics of Interpersonal Trust: Resolving Uncertainty in the Face of Risk". In: Hinde, R. and Gorebel, J. (Eds.), *Cooperation and Prosocial Behavior*, Cambridge University Press, 1990: 190–211.

Brandenburger Adam and Nalebuff Barry. *Co-opetition: A Revolutionary Mindset That Combines Competition and Cooperation*, Currency Doubleday, 1996.

Calabresi Massimo. "Wikipedia for Spies: The CIA Discovers Web 2.0", *Time Magazine*, April 8, 2009.

Camarinha-Matos Luis. "Advances in Collaborative Networked Organizations". In: A. Azevedo International Federation for Information Processing (Ed.), *Innovation in Manufacturing Networks*, Springer, 2008, Vol. 266: 3–16.

Camarinha-Matos Luis and Lima Celson. "A Framework for Cooperation in Virtual Enterprises". In: Mills, J. J. and Kimura, F. (Eds.), *Information Infrastructure Systems for Manufacturing* II. The International Federation for Information Processing, Springer, 1999, Vol. 16.

Chris Huxham. *Creating Collaborative Advantage*, SAGE Publications Ltd, 1996.

Chrislip David and Larson Carl. *Collaborative Leadership: How Citizens and Civic Leaders Can Make a Difference*, Jossey Bass Publishers, 1994.

Cilliers Paul. "Knowing Complex Systems". In: Richardson, Kurt A. (Ed.), *Managing Organizational Complexity: Philosophy, Theory, and Application*, ISCE Book Series: Managing the Complex, 2005, Vol. 1: 7–19.

Collins Jim. *Good to Great: Why Some Companies Make the Leap and Others Don't*, Harper Business, 2001.

Covey Stephen. *The Speed of Trust*, Free Press, Simon and Schuster, 2006.

Craven Matt, Mysore Mihir and Wilson Matt. "COVID-19: Implications for Business", Mckinsey & Company, Executive Briefing, Mckinsey.com, May 13, 2020.

Croker Anne, Higgs Joy and Trede Franziska. "What Do We Mean by 'Collaboration' and When a 'Team' Not a 'Team'", *Qualitative Research Journal* 9 April 2009: 28–42.

Director of National Intelligence. "United States Intelligence Community 500 Day Plan for Integration and Collaboration". Office of the Director of National Intelligence, 2007.

Dovev Lavie. "Alliance portfolios and firm performance: A study of value creation and appropriation in the US software industry". *Strategic Management Journal* 28 (12): 1187–1212, 2007.

Driscoll James W. "Trust and Participation in Organizational Decision Making as Predictors of Satisfaction", *Academy of Management Journal* 21 1978: 44–56.

Freedman David. *Corps Business: The 30 Management Principles of the U.S. Marines*, Harper Business, 2000.

Friedman Thomas. *The World Is Flat: A Brief History of the Twenty-first Century*, Farrar, Straus and Giroux, 2005.

Gazley Beth and Brudney Jeffrey. "The Purpose (and Perils) of Government-Nonprofit Partnership", *Nonprofit and Voluntary Sector Quarterly* 36 September 2007: 389–415.

Gladwell Malcolm. *Outliers: The Story of Success*, Little Brown, 2008.

Goldsmith Marshall, Somerville Iain and Hesselbein Frances. *Leading Beyond the Walls: How High Performing Organizations Collaborate for Shared Success*, Jossey Bass Publishers, 1999.

Gottman, J. M. Why marriages succeed or fail: And how you can make yours last. Simon & Schuster, 1994.

Grant Robert. "Toward a Knowledge-Based Theory of the Firm", *Strategic Management Journal* 17 October 1996: 109–122.

Gray Barbara. *Collaborating — Finding Common Ground for Multiparty Problems*, Jossey-Bass Publishers, 1989.

Grobman Gary. "Complexity Theory: A New Way to Look at Organizational Change", *Public Administration Quarterly*, Fall 2005: 350–382.

Gulati Ranjay. "Silo Busting: How to Execute on the Promise of Customer Focus", *Harvard Business Review* 85 May 2007: 98–108.

Gurman Mark. "Apple, Google Bring Covid-19 Contact-Tracing to 3 Billion People", *Bloomberg*, 10 April 2020.

Hansen Morten. *Collaboration: How Leaders Avoid the Traps, Build Common Ground, and Reap Big Results*, Harvard Business Review Press, 2009.

Hansen Morten and Nitin Nohria. "How to Build Collaborative Advantage", *MIT Sloan Management Review* 46(1) October 2004: 22–30.

Heifetz Ronald, Grashow Alexander and Linsky Marty. *The Practice of Adaptive Leadership: Tools and Tactics for Changing Your Organization and the World*, Harvard Business Review Press, 2009.

Hofstede Geert. *Culture's Consequences: International Differences in Work-Related Values*, Sage Publications, 1984.

Hofstede Geert. *Cultures and Organizations: Software of the Mind*, McGraw-Hill, 1991.

Hofstede Geert. "Dimensionalizing Cultures: The Hofstede Model in Context", *Online Readings in Psychology and Culture* 2(1), Berkeley Electronic Press, 2011.

Jessica Mitford, and Jane Smiley. *Poison Penmanship: The Gentle Art of Muckraking*, New York Review Books Classics, 2010.

Jon Pierre, and B. Guy Peters. *Governance, Politics, and the State*, St. Martin's Press, 2000.

Kahane Adam. *Collaborating with the Enemy*, Berrett-Koehler Publishers, 2017.

Kanter Rosabeth Moss. "Collaborative Advantage: The Art of Alliances", *Harvard Business Review*, July–August 1994: 96–108.

Leat Mike. *Exploring Employee Relations*, Butterworth-Heinneman, 2007.

Leavitt Mike and McKeown Rich. *Finding Allies, Building Alliances: 8 Elements That Bring and Keep People Together*, John Wiley & Sons, 2013.

Linden Russell. *Leading Across Boundaries: Creating Collaborative Agencies in a Networked World*, Jossey-Bass, 2010.

Linden Russell. *Working Across Boundaries: Making Collaboration Work in Government and Nonprofit Organizations*, Jossey-Bass, 2002.

Lipnack and Stamps. *Virtual Teams: Reaching Across Space, Time and Organizations with Technology*, John Wiley & Sons, 1997.

Lorange Peter and Roos Johan. *Strategic Alliances: Formation, Implementation, and Evolution*, Blackwell Publishers, 1992.

Maguire Steve and Hardy Cynthia. "Identity and Collaborative Strategy in the Canadian HIV/AIDS Treatment Domain", *Strategic Organization* 3(1) 2005: 11–45.

Marion Russ and Uhl-Bien Mary. "Leadership in Complex Organizations", *The Leadership Quarterly* 12(4) 2002: 389–418.

Mattessich Paul, Murray-Close Marta and Monsey Barbara. *Collaboration: What Makes It Work*, Amherst H. Wilder Foundation, 1995.

McAllister Daniel J. "Affect-and Cognition-based Trust as Foundations for Interpersonal Cooperation in Organizations", *Academy of Management Journal* 38(1) 1995: 24–59.

McChrystal Stanley. *Team of Teams*, Penguin Random House, 2015.

Meyerson Debra, Weick Karl and Kramer Roderick. "Swift Trust and Temporary Groups", *Trust in Organizations: Frontiers of Theory and Research* 166 1996.

Noam Wasserman. *The Founder's Dilemmas: Anticipating and Avoiding the Pitfalls That Can Sink a Startup*, Princeton University Press, 2012.

Pah Adam, Uzzi Brian and Hinds Rebecca. "A Study of Thousands of Dropbox Projects Reveals How Successful Teams Collaborate", *Harvard Business Review*, July 2018.

Peters Linda M. and Manz C. Charles. "Identifying Antecedents of Virtual Team Collaboration", *Team Performance Management: An International Journal*, March–April 2007: 117–129.

Pisano Gary P. and Verganti Roberto. "Which Kind of Collaboration Is Right for You?", *Harvard Business Review* 86(12) 2008: 78–86.

Prahalad Coimbatore and Venkat Ramaswamy. "Co-creation Experiences: The Next Practice in Value Creation", *Journal of Interactive Marketing* 18(3) 2004: 5–14.

Rashid Faaiza, Edmondson Amy and Leonard Herman. "Leadership Lessons from the Chilean Mine Rescue", *Harvard Business Review*, July–August 2013.

Reay Trish and Hinings Robert. "Managing the Rivalry of Competing Institutional Logics", *Organization Studies* 30(6) 2009: 629–652.

Robertson Brian. *Holocracy, The New Management System for a Rapidly Changing World*, Holt Henry and Co., 2015.

Scott W. Richard. "The Adolescence of Institutional Theory", *Administrative Science Quarterly* 32 1987: 493–511.

Scott W. Richard. *Institutions and Organizations: Ideas, Interests, and Identities*, Sage Publications, 2013.

Seifter Harvey. *Leadership Ensemble: Lessons in Collaborative Leadership from the World's Only Conductorless Orchestra*, Times Books, 2001.

Shellenbarger Sue. "The Best Bosses Are Humble Bosses", *Wall Street Journal*, October 9, 2018.

Silver David. *Strategic Partnering*, McGraw Hill, 1993.

Simmons Annette. *The Story Factor: Inspiration, Influence, and Persuasion through the Art of Storytelling*, Perseus Publishing, 2001.

Sinek Simon. *Start with Why: How Great Leaders Inspire Everyone to Take Action*, Penguin UK, 2011.

Steermann Hank. "A Practical Look at CPFR: The Sears-Michelin Experience", *Supply Chain Management Review* 7(4) July 2003: 46–53.

Stone Douglas, Patton Bruce and Heen Sheila. *Difficult Conversations*, Penguin Books, 2000.

Sujansky Joanne Genova. *Power of Partnering*, Pfeiffer & Co., 1991.

Tapscott Don and Williams Anthony. *Wikinomics: How Mass Collaboration Changes Everything*, Penguin Publishing Group, 2008.

Tennyson Ros. "Institutionalizing Partnerships: Lessons from the Front line", International Business Forum, 1993.

Tennyson Ros. *The Partnering Tool Book*, International Business Leaders Forum, The Partnering Initiative, 2011.

Thomson Anne Marie and Perry James. "Collaboration Processes: Inside the Black Box", *Public Administration Review* 66 2006: 20–32.

Thomson Anne Marie, Perry James and Miller Theodore. "Conceptualizing and Measuring Collaboration", *Journal of Public Administration Research and Theory* 19(1) 2009.

Topol Eric. *The Patient Will See You Now: The Future of Medicine Is in Your Hands*, Basic Books, 2015.

Tsai Wenpin. "Social Structure of 'Coopetition' within a Multiunit Organization: Coordination, Competition, and Intraorganizational Knowledge Sharing", *Organization science* 13(2) 2002: 179–190.

Ury William. *The Power of Positive No,* Bantam, 2007.

Warner Michael and Sullivan Rory. *Putting Partnerships to Work: Strategic Alliances for Development between Government, the Private Sector and Civil Society,* Greenleaf Publishing, 2004.

Wenpin Tsai. "Social Structure of Coopetition – Within a Multiunit Organization: Coordination, Competition, and Intraorganizational Knowledge Sharing", *Organization Science* 13(2) March–April 2002: 179–190.

Willer Rob. "Groups Reward Individual Sacrifice: The Status Solution to the Collective Action Problem", *American Sociological Review* 74(1) 2009: 23–43.

Winer Michael and Ray Karen. *Collaboration Handbook: Creating, Sustaining and Enjoying the Journey,* Amherst H. Wilder Foundation, 1996.

Wittenberg-Cox Avivah. "What Do Countries with the Best Coronavirus Responses Have in Common? Women Leaders", *Forbes,* April 13, 2020.

Wondolleck Julia and Yaffee Steven Lewis. *Making Collaboration Work: Lessons from Innovation in Natural Resource Management,* Island Press, 2000.

Wood Donna J. and Gray Barbara. "Toward a Comprehensive Theory of Collaboration", *The Journal of Applied Behavioral Science* 27(2) 1991: 139–162.

Hebrew

Almog-Bar Michal and Ester Zichlinskey. "The Thorn That Should Annoy the Elephant: Relationships between Philanthropic Foundations and Government in Developing Social Initiatives", The Hebrew University, 2010.

Aviv Kochavi and Bartal Eran. "'Ma'asei Aman': Permanent Change in a Changing Reality", Between the Poles, 2, Dado Center – IDF, July 2014, 9–58.

Barash Tamar and Amittai Yotam. "The Whole Is Smaller Than the Sum of Its Parts?!", Between the Poles, 14, Dado Center – IDF, December 2017, 133–149.

Bohm David. *On Dialogue,* Prague Publishing House, 2018.

Efron Razi and Pinhas Yehezkeli. *Israeli Civil Service at a Turning Point – From Selfishness to Interorganizational Cooperation,* The Center for Strategic and Policy Studies, Institute for National Security Studies, IDF, 2007.

Gefen Omri and Holen Yoav. "The Professionalism Beyond Professionalism: Managing Partnerships in the Social Field and a Concept for a New Role", Et Hasadeh, Israel Joint, September 2012, 6–15.

Harari Noah Yuval. *21 Lessons for the 21st Century,* Kinneret Zmora-Bitan Dvir, 2018.

Katz Hannah. "Promoting Inter-organizational, Inter-disciplinary and Inter-sectoral Connectivity in Social Services", Ministry of Welfare and Social Services – Research Division, August 2006.

Keshet. "Promoting Partnerships between Sectors in the Local Field, a Guide for Managing and Leading Inter-sectoral Partnerships", Knowledge Center, Israel Joint, 2010.

Lanir Zvi. "Who Needs the Concept Jointness," Maarachot 401, June 2005, 20–27.

Michael Kobi, Siman-Tov Dudi and Yoeli Oren. "Jointness in Intelligence Organizations: Theory Put into Practice – Cyber", *Intelligence and Security* 1 January 2017: 5–28.

Nassim Nicholas Taleb. *The Black Swan – The Impact of the Highly Improbable on Economics and Life*, Dvir Publishing House, 2009.

Ram Jaulus. *The Age of Urgency*, Sagol Publishing House, 2018.

Rashuyot. The Israeli Portal for Local Authorities, "Cooperation between Corporations in the Tel Aviv-Jaffa Municipality", September 2019.

Rojkes Dombe Ami. "CEO of Medtronic Releases Patents for the Company's Ventilators", Israeldefence, March 31, 2020, Portal.

Shabtai Shai and Gefen Omri. "How Can Jointness in the Intelligence Community be Promoted with an Interservice Course", Intelligence Research – Methodoligical Intelligence Journal, Institute for Intelligence and Policy Studies, December 2016, 126–134.

Shimoni Baruch. "Business and New Philanthropy in Israel – Ethnography of Mega-Donors", The Hebrew University, The Center for the Study of Philanthropy in Israel, 2017.

Printed in the United States
by Baker & Taylor Publisher Services